# Tickle
# &Bight

**Short stories about life, love
and a whole lot of laughter**

Lucy Fitzpatrick McFarlane

ISBN: 978-1-895109-64-1

Published by
James Lane Publishing
43 James Lane
St. John's, NL, Canada
A1E 3H3
Tel: 1-888-588-6353
Fax: 1-709-726-2135
Website: www.jameslanepublishing.com
Email: mail@jameslanepublishing.com


Printed by Friesens Corporation in Altona, MB, Canada

**Mixed Sources**
Cert no. SW-COC-001271
© 1996 FSC

FSC

## Prologue

# When I Grow Up

Pipe dreams…that's what my mother always said years ago whenever I'd talk about what I wanted to do when I grew up. Being a practical woman, she'd remind me that I'd have my mind changed a hundred times by the time I became an adult. "I wish you wouldn't be talking such nonsense about when you grows up, me chile," she'd say. "You'll BE what you'll BE when the time comes."

I didn't realize it then, but years later my mother confessed that because I was the youngest, she couldn't bear the thought of her "baby" leaving home. Now my father always was a little more whimsical and he'd wink at me behind Mom's back. "Ahh, let her dream, Lottie…let her dream. It won't hurt her none," he'd say.

And dream we did as youngsters. I remember on the long lazy days my friends and I would lie in the grass and gaze at the blue sky. There was something about those fluffy clouds that made us feel that we could ask for anything and our wishes would be granted. Young as we were, we all wanted to BE somebody, and finding a space for ourselves seemed to be the most important thing in our small world. We never tired of asking the same questions of ourselves and of each other. "What do you want to be when you grows up?"

Naturally, the answer changed as often as the weather did, for we could never make up our minds. One day we wanted to be teachers or shop keepers, and the next day we'd decide to be movie stars and marry a handsome, rich man. Mostly though, we went back to wanting to become mothers with lots of children. Given the fact that our choices were limited in a small outport and that our imaginations only stretched as far as the next community, we never tired of planning for the future.

From the time I was four years old, my sisters and I sang and step-danced in concerts, so it wasn't unusual that my childhood dream was to be an entertainer. My father and brothers were all musical and they usually accompanied us on the violin, guitar, button accordion and mouth organ. When I became a little older, someone gave me a jewellery box and I was fascinated by the graceful ballet dancer that popped up when the cover opened. I couldn't take my eyes off her as she twirled to the soft music and I longed to dance like that little girl in the box. The only problem was my half-grown body was not physically ready for such graceful movements. Whenever I tried to dance, my arms and legs flailed and veered off in opposite directions, so I squashed that idea. It's no wonder Mom called my childhood whims pipe dreams, for I went from one idea to the next.

When I was 11 years old, I became an avid reader and I'd go up into our attic or sit on the hill up behind our house to read books. The more I read, the more I thought about my future and I would spend hours trying to decide what I wanted to be when I became an adult. From that vantage point, I could see all around the Cove; I loved watching the sea rolling in on the beach and the ships passing against the horizon. Then I wanted to capture that beauty and become an artist, so I'd take my scribbler and pencil with me and sketch everything in sight. But alas, I was not very good at that either, so I found myself writing down my frustrations and thoughts in my scribbler instead. I began putting together little rhymes and poems, and jotting down things in my diary – but never once did I think of actually becoming a writer.

One day as my father passed me on the hill, he asked what I was doing. I told him I was writing about a dream I had the night before. "You want me to read it for you?" I asked eagerly.

He sat down beside me and rolled a cigarette as I read. When I finished, he was staring at me. "You put all of dem words together yourself?" he asked in amazement.

Pleased at his reaction, I assured him that I did and shoved the scribbler in his hands. "My dear, dat's some wonderful good what you wrote there!" he exclaimed. "What a head you got on your shoulders... what a head!"

He suggested I keep it somewhere safe so I could read it when I grew up. Even though it didn't seem significant to me at the time, I kept it anyway.

Not surprisingly, when I was a teenager my focus changed again. Our Catholic upbringing played a big role in our high school lives and when the Mission Fathers or the nuns visited the church and schools to talk about their work in foreign countries, it had a great impact on us. Being young and impressionable, we wanted some noble purpose in life. What better cause than to do the Lord's work helping the poor and hungry? We all thought that a religious calling was a sure ticket to heaven, and being tucked safely inside a convent was every mother's dream for her daughter. One day I announced to my mother that I was going to become a nun and go to Africa. "Glory be to God, Lucy!" she gasped. "You'd better mind what you're saying or God will strike you blind! Africa indeed...what will you think of next, I wonder?"

I changed my mind a month later when someone told me that nuns had to eat bread and water, sleep alone in a dark room and take a vow of silence. I didn't mind a diet of bread and water or even the vow of silence, but I couldn't imagine sleeping alone. At our house, we usually slept three to a bed; besides, I was afraid of the dark. When I told Mom I had changed my mind again, her bottom lip bivvered. "That settles it then. You'll be staying home a bit longer after all," she said as she wiped at her eyes.

I guess we can't always get what we hope for; that's

unrealistic. Life gets in the way sometimes and often we have to settle for an alternate route, but it shouldn't keep us from trying. I remember asking my father what he wanted to be when he was a lad. His answer was immediate. "I wanted to be a doctor, but I never had the learnin' for it," he said. "I knows I would've been a good one if I had the chance, but I always did what I could to help others anyway."

And that he did. Besides raising nine children, he was a fisherman all his life and, as I recall, nothing daunted him if there was an emergency. My father had a knack for knowing what to do when someone was hurt or sick, for there were no doctors around home. He was usually called upon for the birthing of animals, making up concoctions to relieve ailments and stitching up cuts on both humans and animals. A slight man weighing 125 pounds soaking wet, his huge hands seemed not to belong to the rest of him, yet his deft fingers could stitch a cut before you could blink. It always amazed me how his big fingers could touch the strings of the violin and make such beautiful music. "Do you regret anything about your life?" I asked him.

His blues eyes twinkled. "Naw. I wouldn't take back a minute of it even if you paid me!" he said. "Your mother and me raised a fine crowd, and family is all that's important in life."

Sometimes when I think about that day 45 years ago when I read my first story to my father, I think about the pride I saw in his eyes. Whether or not he knew it, he allowed me to explore my hopes and dreams and it made me believe in myself. Maybe that's why I still hang on to my pipe dream of being an entertainer and a dancer. Even though I'm supposedly all grown up now, I still don't know what I want to BE. Maybe I never will, but one thing I am certain of is the joy and satisfaction I feel when I sit down to write. I wonder if somehow in his wisdom, my father knew that I had already found my niche before I realized it myself?

# 'Tis the Seasons

*The colour of springtime is in the flowers,
the colour of winter is in the imagination.*

– Terri Guillemets –

# Scared Witless

We've all experienced it at some point in our lives, that numbing sensation of fear that sets the pulse racing and the knees knocking... the kind of fear that strips you of all common sense and impairs the thinking process. When you're reared on a hearty dose of superstition like I was in the '50's, you believe every ghostly tale and gruesome story you hear. As I recall, we were afraid of our own shadow and when darkness descended on our small outport, our fears overwhelmed us. We were afraid of everything... darkness itself, thunder and lightning, storms, graveyards, black cats and of course, the imaginary evil spirit that parents used to frighten children into good behaviour.

We had our own, Bessie Boo-Bagger, that lived in the cupboard under the stairs. Between the sting of Mom's broom and the threat of being put under the stairs, we made it through childhood practically unscathed, because Mom and Bessie ruled our house with an iron hand.

I think our greatest fear centred around the cemetery, especially on October 31, All Souls Day, for that's when everyone visited the graveyard to pray for the dead. We didn't celebrate Hallowe'en then like we do today, but we did believe the stories about spirits of dead people roaming around looking for someone to take their places. In Lord's Cove, the graveyard stands on a hill, away from the rest of the Cove, surrounded by the ocean on both sides and the dirt road there is rocky and narrow. There is nothing that can compare to the darkness of an outport in October on an overcast night without a moon or stars to guide you, for there were no street lights then. Usually by the time we got home on the school bus, it was dark, but parents didn't accept that as an excuse not to go to the cemetery... we were more scared of what might happen if we didn't go. We were afraid to venture beyond the gate alone, so we usually went in groups, especially the girls. We'd hold hands, walking so closely that we'd trip on each other's feet and sometimes we prayed aloud or sang hymns to prove how brave we were.

One year a bunch of mischievous boys played a trick on us that gave a new meaning to my cousin's explanation that R.I.P. on the headstones meant "Rise If Possible." The natural setting that particular night was a movie producer's dream, for the sky was so black that it was like walking blindfolded. We were keenly aware of the eerie atmosphere, for the roar of the sea was deafening and the waves were heaving on the beach with such a force that our voices were lost on the wind. Just as we got inside the gate, it slammed shut behind us. Then the whole graveyard seemed to come alive with moaning and groaning as dark shadows rose up all around us with outstretched arms. Hands grasped at our arms and legs and hoarse voices called our names. We were so terrified that we ran in circles until someone found the gate. We literally threw ourselves over the fence. Screeching and bawling, we ran until we collapsed on someone's doorstep, blubbering about dead people chasing us.

One of the men went out to see what the racket was all about and found the culprits still sitting inside the graveyard, howling with laughter. They were laughing so hard that they didn't hear him approach and when he jumped out from behind them, they took to their scrapers, and left the telltale sheets and flashlights behind. We never had any more trouble with the boys after that and we noticed that they never teased us about ghosts again.

I guess it was the isolation of our outport and the abundance of ghost stories that made us believe in superstitions and made us so gullible. My brother Raphael always preyed on those fears, and the first time I saw a movie with ghosts in it, I was convinced that they really did exist. He made me believe that the ghost of the old man who once lived in our house walked through our attic on stormy nights, searching for the money he had hidden. One day when I tattled to Mom that Raphael had stolen a neighbour's bloomers off her clothesline and used them for target practice, he vowed he would get his revenge when I least expected it. The time came about a week later, when we had a terrible thunder and lightning storm. When Mom put the statue of Our Lady of Perpetual Help in the window, we feared something sinister would happen. My sister Kate refused to let me sleep with her and, in desperation, I waited for her to fall asleep and quietly got into her bed. Our house shook and creaked with the wind, and I was convinced I could hear the sound of chains scraping along the floor in the attic. Then I got this terrible feeling that someone was in the room with us for I could hear heavy breathing. Suddenly the bed began to move beneath us, and we were lifted clear off the floor as a flash of lightning lit up the room. I jumped on top of Kate, and when she awakened and found someone holding her down, she nearly killed me with her bare fists. We scared each other so much that our screams brought our parents tearing into the room to find Kate sitting on top of me, and Raphael trapped beneath the bed, moaning in pain. In his haste to escape, he had hit his head on the bedpost and almost knocked himself senseless. When he finally came to and saw Mom standing over him with the broom, his face went three shades of pale and he almost fainted with fright. But it was only a temporary setback, for he tried his pranks many times after that, and yes, this naive child was scared witless every time. But that was long ago, and I've outgrown that part of my life now. Oh, sure, I still hate storms and black cats, I avoid walking under ladders, I still have my rabbit's foot and my four-leaf clover, and I always keep a drop of holy water around the house, but at least I'm not superstitious anymore.

# Do You Believe?

I still remember cringing under the bedclothes when I was a child, afraid that a green monster would come out from under the bed because I didn't eat my bread crusts at suppertime. I believed there was actually a "crust monster." Of course, I know now it was just a ploy by our parents to get us to eat the meals they prepared. "Don't leave the table 'til you're finished every crumb on yer plate!" Mom would warn us.

Back then, I guess a guilty conscience for not doing what we were told made our imagination work overtime.

Did you believe all the stories you heard that scared the living daylights out of you when you were a child, or did you take it with a grain of salt? I was gullible enough to believe everything I was told when I was growing up in Lord's Cove. Believe me, we were a superstitious lot. After all, who didn't believe that bad luck would befall you if a black cat crossed your path or that breaking a mirror would bring seven years of bad luck? I daresay the reason for that is because Newfoundland's history is steeped in folklore, old wives' tales and myths. Many people in small communities back then were religious and superstitious, believers in the unknown. If our parents and grandparents told us these things were so, then we took it as the gospel truth and never questioned what we didn't understand.

As I recall, the greatest fear we had as youngsters was the graveyard, where ghosts and spirits roamed at night. We dared not pass the cemetery without saying a prayer in respect for the dead. "Don't forget to bless yourself or the poor souls in Purgatory will haunt you after dark!" someone would yell. It's amazing really, how we took everything literally. We were always afraid of stepping on a grave, for we thought a bony hand would come up through the ground and try to drag us down.

But it wasn't just the children who had supernatural beliefs. Some of the older people were convinced that if you didn't kneel to pray, your prayers would go no farther than the ceiling. A stye on your eye could be cured if someone crossed your eye with a blessed wedding band. If someone got a wart on the hand, then Mr. Bill Harnett or Mr. Jack Andrew would mark an X on the afflicted spot with a piece of chalk and put another X on the back of the stove. Supposedly, as the chalk mark disappeared on the stove, so did the wart. Of course, we also had the regular good luck charms – a rabbit's foot or a four-leaf clover – but would you believe that mopping the floor under someone's feet would take away that person's good luck? If you had a guilty conscience you'd surely get the hag and wake up screaming from a bad dream.

As I recall, a number of things we believed didn't make any sense. My sisters and I thought eating too much burnt toast would dry up our blood, or making fun of someone's affliction would get us punished. "My dear, if the wind changes when you're making fun of someone, then your face is going to stay screwed up for the rest of your life!"

These days, I'm sure some of the things our elders told us were meant to put the fear of God in us or to keep us from misbehaving. No matter what we did, we always got a warning about something. Mom was terrified of lightening, so she'd put statues and pictures of Our Lady of Perpetual Help in the window to protect us. Many times, after we were all in bed, we'd be wakened by the feel of cold water on our faces. We'd find Mom standing at the foot of the bed splashing holy water over us. "Go back to sleep now," she'd say. "You don't have to worry about getting struck dead while you all sleep 'cause the holy water will protect you."

Sure, like we could go back to sleep with that vision in our heads!

Oh yes, our parents weren't above making up consequences to get the truth out of us. If we got caught telling a fib, we were told we'd go cross-eyed, that our noses would grow longer or that our tongues would turn black. When my sister Kate was very young, she'd run to the looking glass before Mom caught her to see if her tongue was black. If she couldn't get to the mirror, she's clamp her teeth together and cover her mouth. Some stories were told just to keep certain truths from us. As children, my sisters and I thought the stork brought babies or that mothers found them in a cabbage patch. Later, when we began to question those theories, someone told us that airplanes dropped babies. Geez, talk about being naïve…my cousin and I at 10 years old would be screaming and waving at every airplane that passed over Lord's Cove: "Drop me a baby! I wants a baby girl!"

They say that seeing is believing, so I'm not sure what accounted for our beliefs back in my day. Perhaps it was the strong respect for the wisdom of our parents and grandparents, and the history of storytelling through the ages that piqued our vivid imaginations. No matter what the reason, it made life interesting for us. We listened, we learned and we remembered. We believed. Didn't you?

# The Hag

I love scary movies. I'm not talking about the gory stuff like Chain Saw Massacre, Friday the 13th or Halloween, but thrillers that make the hair curl on your legs and have you gnawing your fingernails right smack up to the elbow. I'm not afraid to admit it. I love getting scared out of my skull when I watch a good thriller. The anticipation of the unexpected, the thrill of feeling the adrenalin pump through the veins, the reruns that play in your head long after the movie is over... that's the stuff that keeps people like me watching scary movies.

I suppose growing up in an outport can account for my love of a good spooky tale. And why wouldn't it? Listening to the older folks telling ghost stores was our greatest form of entertainment... and the source of every child's nightmare, or the hag as we called it. Many times I'd sneak out of bed at night and sit at the top of the stairs listening to my father and his friends swap ghost stories. They sparked my imagination and kept me spell-bound. Even though the stories terrified me, I couldn't tear myself away and I hung on every word until I was caught and sent off to bed again. Then when I'd sleep, I'd get the hag, dreaming that the demons were after me and I'd wake up in a sweat, screaming and carrying on something fierce. It's no wonder my sisters banished me from their beds, because they got tired of my sniveling and my pitiful pleas for them to stay awake until I went to sleep.

It was not until the movies came to the Cove that the whole concept of the word "fear" changed for me. Up till then, it was the fear of the unknown that fascinated all the youngsters, for we relied on our imaginations to make the stories we heard come alive. Each of us conjured up our own vision of what the ghosts and spirits looked like, but when we actually saw one up on the screen at the show, suddenly it all seemed so real. We were convinced then that ghosts and demons really did exist and that the folk stories were actually true. Being gullible and impressionable, we had no concept of how a movie was made, so we believed everything we saw. Our imaginations went into overdrive and we'd convince ourselves that once darkness fell upon the Cove, evil forces were at large. We imagined that we saw ghostly figures flitting through the graveyard and heard the chilling sounds of the devil himself dragging chains behind him. All it took was four little words whispered in the dark to make us take to our scrapers in terror.

"What was that noise?"

No, life was never dull in Lord's Cove in my younger days. We amused ourselves by swapping ghost stories to see who could tell the most frightening tale… and we loved every minute of it. Whenever we saw a spooky show in the hall, the boys took full advantage of the situation and played on the insecurities of the girls. They had no mercy for us, sneaking up behind us after the show was over and scaring the bejeepers out of us. We'd huddle together as we walked, afraid to put one foot in front of the other, waiting for someone to jump out from behind a rock. And those foggy nights were the worst, for everybody knew the boys would be lying in wait somewhere along the way. But there was a method in their horseplay. They knew exactly what they were doing. Even if a girl had no interest in the fella, she'd let him walk home with her because it was easier on the nerves to have him close-by and not have to worry about getting a surprise around the next corner. Besides, it gave them something to brag about the next day, for if it was dark and a boy and girl walked on the same side of the road, you were on a date.

Oh, yes, very few of us girls were brave enough to walk home alone after dark. I remember one night in particular when my cousin and I sat on the daybed in her grandmother's kitchen listening to her tell one tale after another. And no one could tell a scary story better than her grandmother, for she acted everything out, right down to making the sound effects. The sky was blacker than tar that night as she stood on the porch to see us off and in a very dramatic voice, she urged us to bless ourselves and recite the Hail Mary when we walked past an old stage on the way home. Fear overwhelmed us as she told about the devil trying to possess the souls of female travellers on moonless nights. She scared us so much that we held hands and ran all the way home, but when we arrived, we were afraid to separate and go the short distance between our houses. We must have made four trips back and forth with each other, for neither of us was brave enough to let the other out of grabbing distance.

Finally we decided to take the shortcut over the fence and talk to each other until we reached the porch door. I guess we were making so much noise shouting back and forth that we awakened her father. The sound of an angry voice in the stillness of night made us screech in terror. "What the devil are you two fools bawling about out there in the middle of the night?" her father bellowed from the upstairs window. "You're making enough racket to wake the dead!"

Well, the words "devil" and "dead" did it. I scravelled over the fence so fast that I didn't even notice I had landed in a patch of prickly stingers and spent the rest of the night scratching welts that formed on my bare legs.

Over the years since, I've outgrown my fears, but there's still a part of me that enjoys the excitement of watching a good thriller. And when I really get involved in a movie, I sometimes get carried away by my emotions and react foolishly by jumping or covering my eyes. But I try not to let it get the better of me because it embarrasses my husband. Now when we're at the theatre, I prepare myself by closing my eyes whenever I think something unexpected will happen. And it worked so well for awhile that I got a little overconfident and I actually felt smug when I saw other people react the way I used to. But I did get caught off-guard once when an old friend from Lord's Cove came to visit me and we went to the theatre to see "Cape Fear."

I had been warned that this movie was a little frightening, but my friend had no idea what the story was about, so I thought I'd have a bit of fun at her expense. And let me tell you, she gives the word skittish a new meaning. She gets totally carried away and even crazy glue couldn't keep her in her seat. She screams out loud at the slightest little thing. I managed to stay in control of my emotions, even though it was hard at times and I laughed at her every time she clamped her hands over her mouth or squirmed in her seat. The last few minutes of the movie were action-packed as the two men struggled and fought in the water. And when the good guy finally succeeded in killing his assailant, I sank back into my seat, closed my eyes momentarily and congratulated myself on getting through another movie without biting my nails to the quick.

Then suddenly, my friend let out a blood-curdling scream. Oh, me nerves! It startled me so much that I automatically covered my face and screeched as loud as she did. But other than the racket we were making, there was not another sound in the theatre. She was anticipating a big surprise ending, but nothing happened. The movie was over... THE END. When the lights came on, there we were, two nitwits clinging to each other with our knees drawn up in fetal position. Some people actually laughed out loud as they filed past us to the exit. We just sat there, too embarrassed to hold our heads up. But as soon as they left, we had a great laugh at our own expense.

Oh, yes, it's not easy trying to deprogram your subconscious mind of childhood fears. I'm not sure I want to do that anyway because that would erase the excitement of it all and a good thriller just wouldn't be the same without that element. For me, that's the whole point of watching a scary movie.

Mind you, I'm not too keen on watching one on TV when I'm home alone. Awhile ago I saw one about a stalker and it sent chills down my spine... not enough to make me change the channel, mind you, but just enough to make me bivver all over. I guess I fell asleep and wouldn't you know it, I got the hag again and dreamed that the stalker was coming through the window. At that point, Murray had just arrived home and, trying not to wake me, he quietly slipped into bed. When I felt the covers moving, I started screaming and kicking like a wild cat. It's amazing the surge of strength that one can muster up when fear takes over.

He never did that again.

# The Joys of Christmas Past

If I was asked what memories I treasure most in my life. I think I'd have to say that it was those of Christmas, for that was always a significant event in my life. It's not surprising either that certain recollections are indelibly etched in my mind, for every Christmas was special back when all our family was together...family that has since departed. And that's what it's all about, isn't it, making memories with people who are important in our lives? Everybody has stories from childhood to pass on to their children at Christmas and each one holds something new and different. As we all know, memories are made of many things, some good, some bad. Even amusing things that happen unexpectedly can leave an impression.

Take last Christmas day at my niece's house, for instance. There were 23 of us there for dinner and after we set the dining room table, Darlene's mother-in-law thought she smelled smoke. The rest of us were too busy gabbing and laughing to notice and when Norma investigated, she found smoke and flames coming from the table where a candle had ignited a paper serviette in the bread basket. By the time she alerted the gang and got the flames under control, the tablecloth and the wicker basket had caught fire. What a commotion that was, for everybody got in each other's way as we scravelled to get things off the table. Thanks to Norma, the Barry Fire Department didn't have to leave their families on Christmas day after all. My niece was so flustered after the smoke had cleared away, that instead of putting corn starch to thicken the gravy, she accidentally used icing sugar. She was going to throw it out, but

Norma would have none of that. "Don't you dare throw it out, Darlene!" she said. "Nobody will ever know the difference unless you tell them."

She was right, nobody even noticed the sweet gravy because we were too busy stuffing our faces with turkey and buns that had been toasted with our own bonfire in the centre of the table.

We had a similar experience another Christmas past at my sister Leona's house. Just after she had put the turkey in the oven, the stove went on the blink, so she put the turkey in the microwave. I'm not sure what she did with the temperature control, but when she took it out that evening, it was still raw in the centre, so she barbecued hamburgers instead. There have been other incidents in the family celebrations, too, where the turkey has accidentally slipped off the platter onto the floor en route to the dinner table or it got burned too badly to be consumed, but it never spoiled our celebrations.

Many years ago when I was a child and all the family was still together, the anticipation of Santa's arrival was the most exciting part of Christmas. After we decorated the tree on Christmas Eve and hung our worsted stockings on the mantle, my father ritually had us write our notes to Santa, reminding us that we shouldn't ask for a lot because Santa had to share with all the other children in the world. Then he'd lift the cover off the old wood stove and let us drop our notes into the fire. After mom had scrubbed us all till our faces shined, my father would come in from outside and casually drop a hint that sent us scampering off to bed in a hurry. "Well, just heard that someone spotted a sleigh and reindeer up in Lamaline, so you youngsters better get to sleep before he gets here!"

My sister Leona and I were talking about gifts we received as youngsters and even though most of ours were homemade, we thought they were very special anyway. The best gift of all for us was colouring books and crayons we found in our stockings. Christmas wouldn't be complete without getting those things in our stocking, for that was the one time of the year we enjoyed such a luxury. The rest of our gifts would be something that our parents made by hand and if we were very lucky, occasionally someone other than our parents might give us a small present. We seldom got what we asked for because money was scarce and we were happy with whatever we got. We were disappointed at times as well, but we got over it.

I remember Mom telling me how my oldest brother, Fred, reacted when he got something he didn't want when he was 10 years old. He had asked for a penknife but instead he got a little plastic boy doll...the first ever in the opposite sex that anyone back then had clapped eyes on. My father saw it in a shop in St. Pierre and, thinking it looked like Fred, he bought it, hoping he'd be thrilled to see the likeness. The doll's face was clearly defined, with a turned-up nose and a couple of freckles on each cheek. He was wearing a red shirt, black pants with patches on the knees and had a cap with the rim turned to one side, the way Fred wore his. Fred was not impressed and when saw it, he hated it immediately. "What do I want an old doll fer!" he grumbled. "Besides, he's ugly and he got a pug nose!"

He was furious when the rest of the family talked about how much the doll looked like him and the more attention that doll got, the madder Fred became. He kicked up such a dido that Daddy finally gave him his own pocket knife to keep him quiet. Then one day during Christmas, Mom discovered that the poor doll had his nose pushed in just enough that nobody could see the face clearly. 'Course Fred never did admit to defacing his "other-self," but Mom kept it anyway. For years after that, the little boy doll had a special place on the tree and after Fred got married, it was passed on to him to put on the tree for his own children.

Gift-giving has always been a big part of Christmas and even though our parents didn't have much money to buy things, that didn't stop us from wishing we could get them. There were very few toys available to us in Lord's Cove back then, but when we got a little older and saw the Eaton's catalogue, we wished for everything in there. The boys looked at the pocket knives, flashlights, cowboy hats, fancy holsters and shiny guns that used real caps that made a popping noise when the trigger was pulled. My sisters and I would spend hours looking at the clothes. "Oh my, I wish I could get that green coat, and that hat...luhh...did you ever see anything so beautiful? I wish... I wish..."

We saw the toys we'd never seen the like of before. We marvelled when we read about the wind-up toys that zipped, bopped, whirred and made noises. We could only imagine how exciting they could be. When my sister Kate saw a picture of a piano in the catalogue, she wished for months that Santa would bring her that red piano. And she got her wish that Christmas. It was red like she asked for, except it was a miniature one in a small box with six tiny keys. Kate had envisioned a full size piano for the parlour where she could sit on a stool and play. But her disappointment was short lived and she managed to play "Jingle Bells" on it anyway.

Often, we received gifts from relatives who lived off the island and when our sister and brothers left home, they sent us wonderful things for Christmas. I remember the gift that impressed me most. It was a doll that my brother Raphael brought home from Vancouver the first year he went away from home. She wore a bridal dress and veil and when you held her hand, her legs moved and her head turned from side to side as she walked. I thought she was the most beautiful thing I'd ever seen.

I recall, too, my sisters getting awesome gifts from our aunt in St. Pierre, like a doll carriage, a high chair and a miniature tea set. One year my sister Helena received a jewelry box that had a pretty ballerina dancer inside. When you lifted the cover, a tune played and the ballerina turned around in a circle on a little mirror platform. Leona got a wonderful toy once that she kept for years. It was a miniature girl pushing a pram with a doll inside and when the wheels turned, the bells on the parasol tinkled. As we got older, over the years we saw other marvelous toys, like a wind-up baby that crawled, a puppy that wagged its tail and barked, and a toy soldier that beat on a drum. My, my...we were so impressed with all the new inventions back then that they left a lasting impression.

To this day, even though I have two grown sons, I still look forward to the blessed celebration as much as I did when I was a child in Lord's Cove. The memory of the excitement I felt on Christmas Eve has always stayed with me. I still like to hang up my stocking and scurry off to bed early so I can wake up at dawn and see what Santa brought me. You see that little girl inside me still likes to harken back to days of Christmas past when I felt happy and secure. I know those memories will always be there when I need them most. The thought of it warms my heart.

# A Different Christmas

I always find it fascinating to learn what makes unique memories for people at Christmas. The usual response brings a nostalgic look at a childhood experience, the recollection of a family gathering or a special event. Sometimes it is a particular gift that leaves a lasting impression, even though it may not be in the traditional way. My sister Kate still talks about a Christmas present she received over 42 years ago, a gift that taught her a valuable lesson in a different kind of way.

She was a teenager then and overjoyed to find a brand new coat under the tree for her. Kate couldn't wait to go to church on Christmas morning to show off her new coat with the imitation fur collar, and she made sure everybody saw her when she made her grand entrance. At communion time she deliberately walked slowly back to her seat and lingered much longer than necessary beside a girlfriend's pew. She dawdled so long that someone behind her gave her a poke in the back and made her fall against the elderly gentleman in front of her... a grumpy old man with a short temper. As he tried to steady himself, the heel of Kate's boot caught in the wide cuff of his trousers. When she tried to yank it free, he tripped and fell to the floor, pulling her down with him. Horrified, Kate scrambled to get up but she couldn't free her foot. Every time one of them managed to stand upright, the other one fell down. The poor man was livid and pushed Kate off his back, sending her heels-up on the floor. There was such a commotion that the service came to a standstill and someone finally managed to get them untangled. The old gentleman glowered at her before he stomped back to his seat and everybody, including the priest, laughed out loud. Kate was so embarrassed that she kept walking straight out the church door and never showed her red face in public until Christmas was over.

Pearl Chaytor Adams, a Newfoundlander now living in St. Catharines, Ontario, remembers a time 66 years ago in St. John's when things didn't go quite smoothly on Christmas Day at her home on Brazil Square. The problem started when her little sister, Maud, tried to return a Christmas present. Eight-year-old Pearl couldn't have been happier with the dainty pair of patent leather shoes Santa left for her. They were exactly what she longed for. Maud, however, was very unhappy that she had received a sturdy pair of lace-up shoes because, more than anything, she wanted a shiny pair like Pearl's. The little girl promptly told her mother that she hated her Christmas gift and that she had given the ugly shoes back to Santa so that he could replace them with a pretty pair like Pearl's. "Where did you put them, dear?" Mrs. Chaytor asked.

"In the fireplace where Santa can find them."

Everybody dashed to the fireplace, but the shoes were nowhere in sight. "I threw them down there," Maud announced, pointing to the door of the flue inside of the fireplace.

Mrs. Chaytor discovered the shoes stuck halfway down the clean-out pipe in the basement. It took a little poking and prodding to get them out, but the shoes were finally retrieved, much to the little girl's disappointment. But all was not lost, for Mrs. Chaytor was able to clean most of the soot and grime from the shoes to make them presentable. Maud grudgingly agreed not to try and return any more Christmas gifts herself and Mrs. Chaytor promised to buy her the shoes she wanted so badly.

My sister Leona likes to recall a time 25 years ago when she and I spent Christmas Eve stranded in a van miles away from home. We were living in St. John's then and our brother Raphael drove from Lord's Cove to bring us home. It was very

late when we got on the road, so we covered ourselves in
blankets and lay down for a long sleep. The moon was bright
and the air crisp and sharp that night, but there was no snow.

Leona and I were very disappointed because we couldn't
imagine having Christmas without snow. Three hours later, the
drive shaft broke on the van and we found ourselves stranded
on a dark road with not another vehicle in sight. There was no
place within miles to get help or even a phone call to our
parents, so we had no choice but to wait until someone came
by. Leona and I were very disturbed because we were going to
miss Christmas, but Raphael insisted that we were going to
celebrate Christmas in the van. He persuaded us to open our
meagre gifts that we had for our parents and we came up with
a fruit cake, a bucket of candy, a bottle of wine, a flask of whisky
and a wool hat. Raphael pulled the hat down over his head,
threw a blanket around his shoulders and played the part of
Santa. Despite our dismal mood, he never stopped trying to
amuse us with his jokes and he had us giggling in no time. We
forgot all about our misfortune and sang carols, clapped our
hands, told jokes and laughed until our sides were sore.
Morning came before we realized it and, thankfully, somebody
stopped to help us. When we finally reached home, it was
almost noon on Christmas Day. And just a few miles outside
Lord's Cove, something wonderful happened. It began to snow.

Huge snowflakes fell from the heavens and by the time we got
to the hill overlooking the Cove, everything was covered in a
blanket of white. It was like one of those scenes captured by the
artist's brush, with children dashing outside with new sleds and
smoke rising from the chimneys as the snow softly gathered on
the rooftops. It was indeed a sight to behold on Christmas Day
as relieved family and friends greeted us. Our gifts were still
under the tree, the turkey dinner was still simmering on the
wood stove and for the first time in her life, Mom didn't say a
word when we confessed to drinking the bottle of wine. It was

indeed, a memorable Christmas in more ways than one.

So you see, sometimes it is the unexpected things that bring back memories of a Christmas gone by. Let's hope that this Yuletide season will bring each of us happy memories of something new and exciting to add to our repertoire of nostalgia for a future Christmas.

# The Unforgettable Gift

Christmas throughout the world has always been steeped in old traditions and customs that have been passed on to many generations. While everybody may have their personal customs, the one thing that has stayed the same is the practice of gift-giving.

Every year without fail, when the holiday season comes around, I find myself reminiscing about my Newfoundland childhood when the nine of us were together with our parents. Those memories in themselves are the greatest gift I could ever want, for they will last me my entire lifetime.

Although it was many years ago, I've never forgotten the excitement in our house on Christmas Eve when we hung our worsted stockings over the mantle in the parlour. My sisters and I couldn't wait for Santa to make his yearly visit. Helena, Leona and I always crawled into bed with our sister Kate, for Santa usually left our stockings hanging on each of the bedposts for us. I was always the first one awake in the morning. I'd throw back the heavy quilts and holler for the others to get up: "Wake up...wake up! Santa Claus brought us presents!"

Then I'd scramble to the bottom of the bed and empty the contents of my stocking. We usually got peppermint knobs, an apple, an orange and one small store-bought gift, for most of the things under the tree were handmade by my mother. How my eyes lit up when I saw a colouring book and crayons. Though it was small compared to the elaborate gifts children get nowadays, I felt I had received the most wonderful gift of all. I'd thumb through every page before deciding which picture to colour first, taking in every image of Santa, his reindeer and the Christmas tree decorations. I chose each crayon with great deliberation and carefully put them back into the box, for I wanted to make my gift last for the whole 12 days of Christmas. To this day, I still believe that it just wouldn't be Christmas without a colouring book and crayons.

As we got older, my father often went to St. Pierre and Miquelon for our Christmas stuff. Money was scarce, but still he managed to bring back fabric, shoes, clothes and one gift for each of us. He seemed to have the knack for picking exactly what we wanted. My eldest sister, Marceline, who usually helped Mom look after the rest of us, remembers a gift that my father picked for her when she was 16 years old. It was a beautiful gift box that contained French perfume, scented powder and rouge for the cheeks. "I had never seen anything so beautiful in my whole life and it made me feel so grown-up. I couldn't believe that Daddy picked that for me...especially when Mom gave him her disapproving look," she recalled with a laugh.

But Mom need not have been concerned because Marceline thought her gift was so special that she kept the box intact for years and even took it with her when she left home.

I remember Daddy sneaking in the things he brought back from the French islands when he thought we weren't around. As soon as our parents went out, my sisters and I would search in every nook and corner, for that was part of the excitement for us. When I was nine years old I mustered up the nerve to peek under the stairs in the hallway. When I spied a box with a picture of a doll wearing a bridal fit-out, I was elated, but I dared not tell my secret in case old Bessie Boo-bagger (the scary woman Mom warned was watching us when we got into mischief) found out. For three weeks, I dreamed about that doll and I rehearsed being surprised so nobody would know I had discovered it.

Come Christmas morning when I saw the box wrapped under

the tree, I could hardly wait for Daddy to pass out the presents. When he finally picked up the box, I was so excited that I almost knocked over the tree. "That's my present!" I squealed.

But instead, Daddy handed it to my sister Leona. My heart dropped right down in my wool socks as I watched her pull out that beautiful doll. However, I managed to coax Leona into exchanging the doll for the xylophone Santa brought me – and you can bet that old Bessie never caught me snooping again.

Oh yes, sometimes the most unexpected choice of gifts can be a pleasant surprise. Just last year I met a woman who thought that her husband had given her the ultimate Christmas gift. During the holidays, friends of ours brought their mother to Niagara to see a distant relative whom they had never met before. The middle-age Italian woman was thrilled to meet her relatives and she kept feeding us delicious food. Sonea and her husband insisted on showing us everything in the house, including the gifts under the tree. When she ushered us upstairs, we had no idea why...until she flung open the door to the bathroom. "Come in...come in and see whatta my Gino give me for Christmas! It's sooo beautiful, no?" she said as she pointed to the new bidet next to the toilet.

She literally shoved all five of us into the small bathroom and, beaming with pride, she pulled the handle so we could watch the water swirl. We tried to make a hasty exit, but she insisted that we all try out her brand new bidet. I was first on her list and she kept talking at me through the closed door: "Go on...sit...sit and flush! The warm water feel so good, no? Keep flushing..."

Just the idea of having people on the other side of the door was enough to make me blush, so I pretended to use the bidet and flushed several times for good measure. When I came out, the others looked amused – but not for long, for Sonea insisted they take their turn in the bathroom. I'll never forget that satisfied look on her face, for it was evident to all of us that her gift was unforgettable. I know it was for the rest of us.

Sometimes, though, gifts are not always appreciated. Last year a neighbour told me that her teenage son was very hard to buy for, so she devised a plan to ensure that Cliff got exactly what he wanted. She asked him to go shopping on the pretense of buying gifts for his cousin Brian. He never told his mother that he and Brian had a disagreement, but he went shopping anyway. Just to get back at his cousin, he deliberately chose gifts that he knew Brian would hate. Come Christmas morning, no one was more surprised than Cliff was when he opened the gifts from his mom and found the very things he had chosen for Brian.

On the other hand, there are those who appreciate everything they receive. Recently when my cousin, May Doyle (Gutierrez), was visiting from Montreal, she talked about her first Christmas away from Newfoundland. An only child, May was 12 years old when her mother passed away. When her uncle found a job on a boat for her father, they moved to Halifax in 1945. There she went to boarding school at Mount St. Vincent Academy, and during holidays she stayed with her Aunt Gertie who had a daughter the same age as May. As Christmas approached, May was feeling sad and lonely, so when her aunt asked her to go shopping and help her choose a coat for her daughter Kay, May happily agreed and promised to keep it a secret. "I took a lot of time choosing and finally I picked a pink coat that had a hood and shiny buttons," she said. "I felt so envious of my cousin!"

For several weeks May dreamed about owning a coat like Kay's, but in her heart she knew it would never be. It got to the point where she didn't even care if Christmas came that year. When Christmas morning dawned and Kay proudly strutted around in her new coat, May tried not to cry. "I was trying to hold back the tears, so I didn't even notice that Aunt Gertie had put a present beside me," May said. "When I opened the box, I found a turquoise coat...the most beautiful one I'd ever seen!"

What the girls didn't know was that May's aunt had planned the perfect surprise by asking each of the girls to choose a coat for the other. "I never forgot that Christmas present...not just because Aunt Gertie gave me the lovely coat, but because of her kindness to me," May told me. "She was my lifeline that first Christmas without my mother and I'll never forget her for that."

Unforgettable gifts that bring joy to others...those are the kind that money can't buy, for they come straight from the heart. That's what Christmas is all about, isn't it?

# Listen to the Music

The word Christmas always conjures up a childhood memory of my father sitting in the rocking chair playing his violin. On the night before Christmas Eve, he'd take his violin down from the kitchen wall, resin up the bow and tighten the strings.

"Are the mummers coming to our house d'night, Daddy?" I'd ask hopefully. "Can I stay up late and listen to the music?"

He'd just smile without looking up. "Now you knows that the mummers don't come out 'til after Santa Claus comes, remember?" he'd say patiently. "But if you're good, I'll play a few songs for you."

Then he'd sit for a spell in the rocking chair, fiddling through his tunes and ditties that set our feet tapping on the floor. When he launched into "Christmas in Kilarney" and "Jingle Bells," we knew that the fun and excitement was about to begin. The sound of holiday music resounding all through the house set the tone for the 12 days of Christmas.

Throughout the ages, music has been linked with Christmas celebrations around the world. That tradition lives on today in homes, in churches and in public forums through dancing and the singing of carols and hymns. Even though the Christmas story has been retold in different languages in many countries, the celebration of the Christ Child's birth is as alive today as it was centuries ago when the angels announced the news to the shepherds in the field. Many new traditions, customs and legends have since evolved, but the message of joy and wonderment remains. In some countries, bagpipers and bell ringers go house to house playing tunes and singing carols while others dance around the Christmas tree.

I know music and song was always a big part of our Yuletide celebrations in most outports in Newfoundland, for that's when family and friends came together as a community. For weeks before Christmas, folks rehearsed skits and plays so they could show off their talent by singing, dancing, telling stories and playing various instruments. Each performance was followed by a dance where everybody socialized and kicked up their heels. Even to this day, the traditional concerts are still the highlight of the holidays, and my sister Kate and her friends in the Cove still prepare for the festivities like we always did.

No Newfoundland Christmas back then would have been complete without the age-old custom of mummering or jannying, where people dressed in funny costumes and went knocking on doors. "Any mummers allowed in d'night?" they'd ask in a disguised voice.

Once inside, the mummers entertained by dancing, whistling, singing or playing an instrument while the host tried to guess their identities. Every night until Old Christmas Day on January 6, the mummers went from one house to another and as more people joined in, the night usually ended with a house party.

Oh my, yes…everybody looked forward to house parties. Folks always came to our house at Christmas to hear my father and my four brothers play. Two of my brothers played the violin and guitar, and the other two the button accordion and mouth organ. We darn near had our own band, for the five of us girls loved to sing and step-dance as well. Other people brought their instruments with them, be it the jews harp, flute, spoons, washboard or whatever they could find to make music. My parents never seemed to mind how many people came to our house and often there was barely standing room. They welcomed everybody. "Come on in and find a spot to sit down wherever you can," my father would say.

There was always a boiler of soup simmering on the back of the stove and cakes, pies, sweet bread and molasses buns for visitors.

Sometimes when the menfolk would partake of the liquid spirits that came from St. Pierre and Miquelon, we were sent off to bed to let the adults celebrate. I remember one Christmas party years ago when Leona and I wanted to listen to the music and singing, so we sneaked downstairs and hid under the daybed in the kitchen. The pipes on the wood stove literally shook in the ceiling from the weight of the step-dancers, and the house was filled with laughter. When Mr. Robbie Walsh stood up to sing, you could hear a pin drop as everybody gathered around to listen to his wonderful rendition of the song "Leaf of a Rose." I couldn't resist the temptation to stick my head out from under the daybed to see him and when Leona started humming, I found myself singing along, too. We got so caught up in his song, we didn't notice that Mr. Robbie had suddenly stopped singing and we continued to belt out the chorus…at least, until he yanked both of us out by the ankles. There we lay, red-cheeked and dressed in our flannelette night dresses with our curls tied up in rags on the tops of our heads. When everybody stopped laughing, we scravelled up the stairs before Mom could reach us.

"You little rascals! You git into bed right now or you'll feel my hand on yer backsides!" she warned.

The violin has always played an important role in our family. The legacy of music was passed on from my grandfather FitzPatrick, who taught six of his sons to play. Over the years, Dad and his brothers were always willing to provide the music for weddings, concerts and dances. My Uncle Jim, in particular, loved to play for the square dances and often he would play all night without stopping. Sometimes he even fell asleep as he played and toppled off his chair, only to pick himself up and start again.

Although my father and his brothers have since passed on, their music has not been forgotten. Eighty-three-year-old

Dolph McCarthy, who grew up in Lamaline, recently told me the FitzPatrick brothers definitely influenced him.

"We lived in the lighthouse on Allan's Island back then and I wanted to play the violin, so my dad bought me a cheap one from the catalogue," he said. He remembered getting discouraged to the point of distraction, but eventually he learned how to play with help from others, including the FitzPatrick brothers.

"I learned a lot from some of the great fiddlers like your dad and his brother Jim," he told me. "I was lucky to be able to able to play with the best."

Dolph, who lives in Brampton, Ontario, still plays his violin and belongs to a fiddle club. His love of music takes him to several senior citizen homes every Sunday where he and his son Kevin entertain the residents.

The violin has always been my favourite instrument, especially at Christmas time. Many years ago, when Daddy would tell us the story of the birth of Jesus, he'd bring it to life by pointing out that it happened in a stable like ours. 'Course, every household had animals and a stable, so I could almost visualize what it must've been like in Bethlehem. The animals were very important, he told us, for they kept the baby Jesus warm with their breath and, in return, the animals were given the gift of speech.

"Every year since then, on the stroke of midnight, every animal in the world faces east and they fall to their knees and speak in tongues," he'd say. "I've heard it said that if you listens hard enough, you can hear the roosters crowing, birds singing and the cows, sheep and horses making sounds, but only the other animals can understand what they're saying."

Then he'd pause a minute as he laid his violin against his shoulder and played. Perhaps it was my childish imagination back then, but as I listened to his bow quivering against the strings while he played "Silent Night," I thought it was the most beautiful sound I'd ever heard.

Call it nostalgia if you will, but even now, many years later, I can still feel the awe and wonder of that moment. When I close my eyes, I can visualize the animals in the stable and I can still hear the sweet strains of my father's violin in the background.

Christmas just wouldn't be the same for me without the sound of his music to reflect on.

# Winter Delights

Lately, whenever I have to drive on icy roads or scrape the snow off the windshield in frigid temperatures, I have to keep telling myself that I didn't always dislike winter. When I was a child in Newfoundland, I loved everything about the season, from the moment the first white flakes fell upon the frozen earth, until nature released its icy grip in spring thaw. I realize, of course, that time has changed the circumstances drastically over the years, for winter in a small outport is very unlike anything one sees in a city. Besides, we see things differently when we're children. I know we certainly did when we were youngsters in Lord's Cove; for to us, it meant months of enjoying winter delights on the snow-clad hills and ponds. Nothing could compare to the wrath of a raging storm with wind sweeping off the sea across the rocky terrain, leaving in its wake snow drifts as high as the rooftops.

As I recall, the first storm of the season was always the most exciting one, especially if it started early in the morning while we were still in bed. Our old house would creak and tremble at the mercy of the howling wind and we'd burrow farther beneath the heavy quilts, dreading the thought of my father's voice urging us to get up for school. Usually, his words fell on deaf ears and he'd have to come upstairs and literally make us get out of bed. And then would come the day when he said the magic words we'd been waiting to hear. "Don't bother getting up this morning, 'cause there'll be no school today," he'd say, sticking his head inside the door. "It's storming so bad that you can't see a hand in front of you, so the bus won't be going nowhere in this weather!"

We nearly ran him over before he finished talking, for the house came alive with the thunder of bare feet running down the stairs to look out the kitchen window where the heat from the stove had melted the frost off the panes. At last our fun could begin, for we could find lots of things to do from morning till night – snowball fights, making snowmen, building snow forts, sliding down the hills on a homemade sleigh, lying on our backs and making snow angels in the fresh snow and skating on the ponds. That was our favourite pastime. Parents knew where we could be found at any time of day or night and if they didn't, there was one person in particular whom they trusted to keep an eye on us.

Bess Harnett was housekeeper for the Lambe family who lived across the road from the skating pond and although she never married, she loved children and made it her business to watch over us. All winter long she was vigilant, yelling warnings at us to stay away from the black ice, chastising boys for jumping clampers or fighting amongst themselves. We certainly didn't need a telephone because she knew everything and everybody, so whenever we heard her raspy voice calling, we stopped whatever we were doing. Not even the bravest teenage boys dared to disobey her, for they knew she wouldn't hesitate to tell their parents. She seemed to know by instinct who was supposed to go home when and for what reason and she called everybody by name, sometimes all in one sentence. "Roy, you go on home and cut up some wood and Jim, your mother got supper on the table and Johnny, it's time for you to go home to milk the cows and tell Freeman his father is looking fer him!"

Her kind heart belied her gruff exterior, for she was always around to comfort us or tend to scrapes and bruises. I doubt that we appreciated her good intentions back then, but I'm certain that the rest of the folks considered her a guardian angel.

No matter how bad the weather or how cold it was outside, it never daunted us. Mothers made sure we were well dressed, for there was no getting away from wearing long johns, snow pants, toques, hoods, mitts and extra wool vamps in our boots. "You are not setting a foot outside that porch door unless you wears a hood," Mom would say to us girls, "and be sure to keep your scarf over your face so you don't get frostbite!"

There were things that had to be done on those stormy days. The menfolk dug out doorways and paths for the elderly and those who lived alone. The boys willingly gathered up wood for the fire, brought in buckets of water from the well and made sure the animals were fed and safe inside the stables. As long as they didn't have to go to school, they'd do anything. 'Course, for mothers, that meant extra work in the kitchen making soup, loaves of bread, molasses buns and whatever else they could think of to feed a bunch of hungry youngsters traipsing in and out all day long. Naturally, everybody had their kerosene lamps ready for stormy days in case the lights went out, which used to happen frequently. In those days, other than the radio and the lights, nothing else was affected by the loss of electricity. We were equipped with everything we needed without it. The clothes were washed in the wooden tub, dried on the outside clothesline in good weather or hung up over the stove and on the banister of the stairs on bad days. The wood stove took care of all the cooking and baking as well as heating the house, the water was always ice cold in the barrel in the back porch and the vegetables, jams and fish were preserved in the root cellars. By today's standards, that might sound like a hardship, but not to us, because we never knew any other way of life.

If we were really lucky, a storm would last several days and by then, our parents would be looking for an excuse to get away from us, so they'd go somewhere to play cards at night. And as soon as they were out of sight, we'd start cooking or baking. The boys would pile extra wood in the fire to make it hot enough to roast slices of raw potato directly on the stovetop. My sisters and I knew that Mom would cuff our ears if she caught us doing that instead of using a frying pan. My brothers often made cabbage stews, fried up onions with pork fat or made soup. One Saturday night when Harve was about 16, he decided to make soup with the salt-water duck that my father had brought home for Sunday dinner. Only problem was that the duck was still wearing his coat of feathers and although he had never de-feathered one before, Harve was confident he could do it as he'd seen my father do many times. It took him almost two hours trying to get the knack of plucking feathers, for he was yanking them off one by one. He even tried to cut some off with the scissors and by the time he finished, he was full of blood and the poor thing looked like it had been mauled to death. The next step was to singe off the remaining down with a hot poker and when he got a whiff of burnt skin, he started to gag. We didn't know it then, but uncle Har from next door, had noticed the sparks and smoke funneling out of our chimney and came to investigate. When he opened the door, a gust of wind sent the feathers airborne and by the time the flurry had settled, Harve looked like a bird himself as most of it was stuck to his hair, which was slicked down with brylcream. Anyway, uncle Har rescued my brother and finished the job for him. It wasn't too hard to figure out why Harve passed on his serving of salt water duck at Sunday dinner the next day.

From the time we started the seventh grade and on through high school, we had to travel by bus from the Cove to the school in Lamaline, so it wasn't unusual during the winter to get stuck on the narrow, dirt roads. I remember one stormy day in particular when I was 13 and the bus got stuck after school. Since darkness was upon us and it was unsafe to stay in the cold bus, we had no choice but to walk to nearby Point au Gaul. Even that was thrilling for us, for our bus driver, Mr. Sam Lambe, had to find a place for each of us to stay and the good people there willingly took us in for the night. The next day, the roads were still impassable, so a dozen men from the Cove came by horse and sleigh to bring us home. The bus driver rounded us up for the meeting point and we were so excited as we stood awaiting their arrival. What a sight that was when we finally saw the black line of moving spots emerge through the white drifts and blowing snow. My father had wrapped brin bags around the four posts of the sled to shut out the wind, while inside there were blankets and a big salt-water rock, still hot from the wood stove, to keep our hands warm. It was a bitterly cold day and a slow ride home, for the horses had to contend with the wind and making their way through deep snow banks. But we didn't mind at all, for we were too caught up in the drama of being rescued and treated like we were precious cargo. It was an experience I never forgot.

It's a strange thing to say, I know, but there was something about Newfoundland winters that was different, memorable even. Maybe it was the sights and sounds of winter delights that can only be appreciated by those who are lucky enough to live in an outport. For me, it might have been the incredible beauty of the Cove after a fresh coat of snow, the starry skies on a clear night or the scent of wood burning in the stove. It might even have been the sound of wind whistling through the stove pipes, the smell of bread baking in the oven or the sight of smoke from the chimneys on a frosty morning. Chances are, it is all of the memories I cherish from my childhood and the feeling of peace and quiet that I felt when I was home. I know now that in my heart it was the simplicity of it all that stayed with me.

# Cold Comforts

With fall coming to a close, my mind is already turning to the beginning of winter and things that have to be done, such as bringing the dreaded heavy coats and boots out of storage and putting winter tires on the car. Years ago, though, when we were kids, winter was all about fun.

I can still picture it in my mind's eye. It is the early 1960s on a frosty winter's night and the full moon casts a silver shimmer on the hill behind Mrs. Kate Harriet's house. Excited voices resound across the meadow where ice has formed over patches of swamp area. The night is alive with the sound of boots slapping and skidding on the hardened snow and somewhere in the distance a young man's voice is heard above the others: "Alright girls...brace yourselves 'cause we're ready to push off!"

Shrieking with giddy laughter, adolescent girls cling to each other as strapping males on the verge of manhood push the wooden slide down the hill. Sparks fly as metal runners grate against rocks that jut out of the frozen ground. Jumping on and off the runners to slow down or speed up, the daring rascals, bent on scaring and impressing the girls, bring the slide to a jarring halt just inches away from the picket fence. Then they push the slide back up the hill again to begin another joyride on the starry winter night.

That was a typical scene in the Cove back in my teenage years, for we took advantage of every moonlit night to go sliding and skating on the ponds. We enjoyed every minute of the long, cold winters. On weekends, we'd be up bright and early and the only time we went indoors was to eat and sleep. Our sleighs were usually handmade, but we also used cardboard from Carnation milk boxes or a piece of linoleum, for that made for a wicked ride down the hills. Sometimes we'd sneak in and tear off a piece of canvas from the porch floor, for there were never enough sleds for everybody. One winter our back porch was down to the floorboards from all of us ripping off a piece to ride on. "You mark my words…if I finds out which one of you tore the canvas off the floor again, you'll be getting the broom across yer backside!" Mom warned us.

It was always more fun when the boys borrowed the larger slides that were used to haul wood and kelp. You could pile six to eight people on one of those at a time. My, how we loved stormy days. Our parents never had to drag us out of bed on those mornings, for once we heard the howling wind and saw snowbanks as high as the rooftops, we knew there'd be no school for us. Sometimes it would take a week for the one snowplow to get to the five communities and clear the roads. The bigger the storm, the better we liked it, for we'd dig our way through the snowdrifts and jump into the snowbanks. We must've driven Mom right foolish because we'd be traipsing in and out all day, covered in snow and looking for food to warm our bellies. Mom always had a big boiler full of soup or a pot of stew bubbling on the wood stove and there was always fresh bread and molasses buns for a quick mug-up.

I liked the frosty days best of all, especially after the ponds froze over. I never did learn to skate well, mainly because there was only one pair of skates that I had to share with my three sisters. I had the biggest feet, but I squeezed into them anyway and because there wasn't room to wear extra wool socks, my toes would literally freeze in the skates. Trust me, there's nothing like the pain from chilblains on your feet. I'd come home crying and my father would have to remove my skates because my toes would be frostbitten and swollen. Sometimes I'd be limping for days, but when my turn came to wear the skates, I'd endure the pain without complaining.

One of our favourite sledding spots was on the hill on Mrs. Lambe's property. Once the snow was high enough to cover the picket fence, you could coast down the hill, cross the road and continue riding onto the pond. Naturally there were always injuries, but it never stopped us. We'd bump into other sleighs at the bottom and plow down the skaters on the pond. Seemed like every outing someone came home with teeth missing, bruises, sprained ankles or bloody noses. There were many times when the centre of the pond wasn't frozen solid and the sleigh and rider went through the ice. Lord knows that Mrs. Lambe reminded them often enough to be careful: "If I catches ye scoundrels going near the middle of the pond again, I'll be telling yer father and you won't be coming back again!"

My 78-year-old friend, Teresa Anderson Davey, once told me how much she loved winters in Newfoundland when she was growing up. She was wishing that she could go ice sailing again like she used to do as a child in Burgeo, and she related a story of one of her escapades when she was 12 years old. It was a bright, windy day and Teresa wanted desperately to go ice sailing. Her father was too busy to take her, so she decided to go without his permission and took her younger brother Jack with her. The rough-hewn contraption resembled a sailboat with one sharpened runner along the bottom to cut into the ice. She didn't have a sail or a pole to use as a mast, so she took one of her granny's flannelette sheets and the pole from the clothesline.

"It was early morning, so I knew Mom wouldn't have the day's wash ready for several hours," Teresa said, "so I borrowed the pole, figuring that I'd have it back before they knew it was missing."

Once Teresa and Jack got the mast up and working, they were having so much fun gliding up and down the pond that they lost track of time...and failed to notice that the wind had picked up considerably. No matter how much she tried, she couldn't stop the sailboat and Jack began to cry. Like the resourceful girl she was, Teresa quickly came up with a solution.

"Don't be scared, Jack...I'll get us stopped!" she told him. "You just help me steer toward that big snowbank on the other side, okay?"

Jack was screaming in terror when they hit land and they were both thrown into the air, landing face down in a 10-foot snowbank. Teresa scravelled to find her little brother beneath the snow. He was sputtering and crying, "We're dead...we're dead, Teresa, and Mom is gonna kill us!"

Once she convinced him that they were still alive, she saw her mother and granny running toward them and she knew she was in big trouble. "Don't move, Jack...stay quiet and maybe they won't see us!"

That was wishful thinking on her part, for her granny literally yanked her out of the snowbank. "Mom grabbed poor Jack by the arse of his pants and I was grounded for a fortnight," Teresa laughed at the memory. "That was the end of my ice sailing career!"

Every time I think about Newfoundland, I'm reminded of when I was a youngster and sleeping in the bed between my two sisters. I'd climb out from under the cozy, down-filled comforter where a big saltwater rock kept our feet warm, for the upstairs was not heated. Trembling from the cold, I'd run downstairs before my sisters were awake so I could sit in the rocking chair beside the wood stove. I'll always remember the warm feelings I experienced on those cold mornings when I'd smell bread toasting on top of the stove and hear the porridge gurgling in the iron pot. Mom was always in the kitchen making bread and I knew I could coax her into making toutons for me. "Now don't tell the others or I'll never get the bread done," she'd say with a smile. Then she'd pinch off little pieces of dough and let me drop them into the frying pan. My mouth would water watching her stir the hot molasses and I couldn't wait to sink my teeth into them.

I'm not sure what it was exactly that made me feel so warm inside when the weather was so cold outside. Maybe it was the memories of the fun we had with our friends, or perhaps it was our youth that made us feel carefree and contented. Looking back now, I can still visualize the familiar scenes...watching smoke make pencil lines in the night sky, blowing a hole in the frost on the inside of the window to look outside, sliding on the hills and skating on the ponds. While they may sound like cold comforts to some, for me they hold warm memories of a time gone by. I think I'll always miss that part of my life. Winter recollections...they're priceless.

# Straight from the Heart

Valentine's Day. Some people feel it is just a diversion to chase away winter blahs, and others think it is just an excuse to rekindle the romantic ambiance for the fanciful and the young at heart. But not me. I always thought the whole idea was so romantic.

In my younger days, that was the one time of the year that bashful youths and hopeful damsels dared to reveal their secret crushes and infatuations. At least that's the way my friend Helen and I recall it.

Helen and I got to talking about how we improvised and made our own valentines before we got store-bought ones. Oh, yes, for a whole week before St. Valentine's Day arrived, we'd start drawing hearts, cupids and arrows on scribbler paper and cutting out hearts from pieces of leftover wall paper. Then we'd colour them with crayons, decorate them and write little verses on the back to give out to our friends at school. But the best part of all was the interchange of valentines between the boys and girls. We literally wore our hearts on our sleeves in hopes that romance would blossom, for each valentine we handmade was very special because it came straight from the heart.

When we looked back at the excitement of that day, Helen and I laughed, for we were remembering how silly we acted as adolescents. Of course, 12 is a lot older now than it was back then because we led very sheltered lives. To us, if you walked down the road with a boy and it was dark, then you were practically "going steady." We were all too shy to pursue boys openly, but it was quite acceptable on Valentine's Day. We'd never deliver our valentines to the boys face to face, for the playful banter of being flirtatious was a big part of the excitement. And we didn't restrict our fancies to one boy... oh, no, we teasingly gave valentines to all of them without signing our names so they'd have to guess who the sender was. And if there was someone in particular that you liked, then you'd sign your name and sneak it into his desk or give it to a classmate to deliver it for you. 'Course you didn't expect anything to come from it at that age, but it was a thrill if the one you chose to be your valentine singled you out. If a boy teased you, pulled your hair or threw snowballs at you during recess, then you knew he was your secret admirer.

As we got older, however, we were ready for a little romance and Cupid's arrow was aimed at specific people, especially on Valentine's night. In Lord's Cove, we had a custom that we called DROPPING VALENTINES, but as I understand, not everybody did this. At least Helen didn't and she lived only 10 miles away in Lamaline, but my sister Leona and I remember it well. It was like a game of SECRET ADMIRER. The object was to make a special valentine with two hearts on it, address it to a boy or girl that you had a big-time crush on and leave it unsigned. If you wanted it to be a bit more daring, you might write one initial as a clue, but usually the sender remained anonymous and simply wrote GUESS WHO? Then, under the cloak of darkness, you'd go "dropping valentines." You'd creep up to a house, throw the valentine into the porch, knock on the door and run away before anyone saw you. Usually you hid behind the wood pile or a big rock to make sure your message got into the right hands. There were times, too, when over-protective fathers took chase after the boys or perhaps a mischievous brother would set a trap, dousing them with a bucket of icy water when they opened the porch door. Still, the smitten boys took their chances every year.

Now, all of this was very exciting for the girls and if you were lucky enough to get a "secret admirer" valentine with Cupid's arrow through the heart, then that was as good as getting a love letter. Naturally we couldn't wait to show them off to our friends the next day at school and we'd try to figure out who our Casanova was. On that day, too, the boys would be a little bolder in their pursuit of the girls while they had the chance to flirt. They came to school with their hair slicked back and collars turned up, reeking of their father's aftershave. The girls dressed in their best attire, looking the part of a damsel awaiting her suitor to sweep her off her feet. Now Cupid's aim was off course sometimes and when the arrow landed in the wrong place, some bashful boy would suddenly become the target of a girl's whimsical smile and batting eyelids.

"I remember watching every boy to see if he was looking my way or acting different," Leona said. "Sometimes you'd find out your secret admirer was someone you had no interest in and it was so disappointing when the guy you gave your valentines to was making eyes at someone else!"

Oh yes, we all have our memories. I've never admitted it to anyone, but I had a crush on a boy when I was in the seventh grade, but he thought the valentine I hid in his bookbag came from someone else. I was heartbroken when I saw him roll up the silver paper from inside the wrapper of a stick of gum, cinch it into a circle and slip it on her finger... for every girl knew a ring was serious business. But I cheered up when another boy who thought I sent him a valentine approached me in the school yard. For his sake, I won't reveal his name, of course, but I think it was the most romantic thing that ever happened to me in my adolescent years. I still get choked up when I recall how he sneaked up behind me, yanked my hand behind my back and drew a ring on my finger with his ball point pen. I never knew what his intentions were that day and I never did find out, because both of us were too shy to look at each other after that. All I know is that I was so proud that I never washed my hand for a week.

Strange, isn't it, how everybody has their own idea of what romance is? People express their admiration and love for each other in different ways and even though they may not always say the actual words, February 14th allows them the perfect opportunity to say "I love you" in their own way. Men, in particular, say it with flowers, chocolates and cards with beautiful verses that symbolize what they're feeling in their hearts. Oh yes, males are very romantic when it comes to love and they buy gifts that clearly indicate how they feel. I see it every year at Mappins Jewellers when young and old alike flock to our store to make a purchase. They take a great deal of time deciding on what to choose for their sweethearts, for they want to make the occasion a memorable one. They usually buy diamonds and gold, all in a heart motif, be it a ring, locket, necklace or earrings. Often there's a story behind each choice piece of jewellery... to commemorate a first kiss, a first date or to celebrate an engagement or a wedding.

The one thing that is evident here is that Valentine's Day is a significant event and it proves that there's a romantic side to all of us. Maybe we all need to set aside a time to take a sentimental journey and remember those in our lives who make us happy. And when love is in the air, wonderful things can happen when that feeling of amour comes straight from the heart.

# Blowing in the Wind

There's nothing more wonderful than the sight of sheets on a clothesline billowing in the wind, is there? Every time I go back to Newfoundland and see women hanging out the day's wash, it gives me an overwhelming feeling of contentment. Without fail, someone will comment on the weather, and if it is a good drying day for clothes, then that's definitely a plus. "Some nice day on clothes d'day, isn't it? Hope the weather keeps up."

The familiar, welcoming sight conjures up all kinds of delightful memories, for the sweet smell of fresh air and the feeling of wide open spaces are all I need to make me feel like I'm home again. Ever since I can remember, the clothesline has been an integral part of every community back home, and it is so comforting to see that this enduring tradition has stood the test of time, not because of necessity, but simply because of preference. As a child, I loved the smell of clothes that had been dried and bleached in the sun, for the salty air mixed with the outdoor scent of summer is very distinct and can never be experienced in a city. No clothes dryer or scented Fleecy sheet could ever come close to duplicating nature's fragrance, and no other colourful public display could add more character and personality to an outport community.

You remember Wash Day Monday in Newfoundland, don't you? That's how we referred to the first day of the week when I was younger, for that was the day set aside for washing clothes. For the women, it was an all-day affair that started early in the morning. By the time the first rooster crowed a throaty cock-a-doodle-doo, they were already up stoking the fire and getting buckets of water heated up on top of the stove. Trust me, scrubbing clothes on a washboard in a wooden tub was no easy task, and before the women sat down for breakfast, they had hung out the first load of clothes. By noon, almost every house around had a line of clothes blowing in the wind. Most families had more than one clothesline, depending on how large the family was, and before the advent of the pulley line, they were made of heavy twine attached to a long pole in the centre that could be adjusted higher or lower to accommodate the direction of the breeze. On occasion, the clothesline got knocked over by the animals that roamed freely around, and if the clothes got trampled on, the poor women would have to do the washing all over again. It wasn't unusual to hear a woman yelling at a sheep that stopped to nibble on a pair of trousers or see another swatting the rear end of a stubborn cow that was getting a good scratch against the rough surface of the pole.

The clothesline – now there was something that reflected the personality and individuality of the matriarch of the family. Women took great pride in their wash, for a lot could be gleaned from the items that were hung on the line and the manner in which they were displayed. Heaven forbid that they hang out any article of clothing that looked dingy or grey, for that might indicate laziness. If things were strung haphazardly on the line, that would certainly be a reflection of the way a woman's house was kept inside, and Lord knows nobody wanted to risk tongues wagging in a small community. They made sure everything was properly washed, sometimes using Sunlight soap or homemade lye soap for stubborn stains and Rinso to make coloured garments brighter.

As I recall, Mom always used some kind of caked cube of clothes bluing on the white shirts and sheets to make them whiter. Like everybody else, she had her own method of hanging out the wash, taking care to separate the dark clothes from the light in case the colours ran. She always put larger items on the

highest point of the line and smaller items at the end, making
sure that the sheets and blankets were pinned in the centre and
on both corners so the wind could circulate properly. Then came
the towels, dresses, shirts, and then smaller items like pillowcases,
tea towels and socks that were hung in pairs. Undergarments, of
course, were always hung in an inconspicuous spot at the end of
the line farthest away from the road.

Now everyone knows that the clothesline was the central
starting point for gossip, because women did their socializing
across the fence as they tended to the day's wash. How else
would they know what was going on in the Cove back then? As
in every small community, people tended to talk about each
other, mostly out of concern for each other or just out of
curiosity, but often, things could get a little personal. You might
see a bunch of ladies carrying on a conversation over the fence,
and the topics could touch on everybody and everything in a
matter of ten minutes. Perhaps there was some credence to the
saying "Don't air your dirty linen in public", for often idle
gossip led to speculation, just from looking at the neighbour's
clothesline. There could be four or five women talking about
what was going on inside someone's house without ever setting
foot inside the door. The conversation might even be totally
disjointed, yet they all heard what the other was saying. "They
must've had company over the road there 'cause she got her
good sheets and towels out on the line. Now who do you
suppose that was this time?"

"Did you see that poor dear lugging in water from the well
herself and she with the bad leg and all! That big slouch of hers
is probably stretched out on the daybed having 'is nap."

"Well now, no diapers on the line d'day. It's about time she
got that big youngster trained to sit on the chamber pot!"

"Herself down the road there must've slept in because there
wasn't a stitch of clothes on the line this morning. Wonder if
she's sick or something?"

Oh, yes, nothing escaped the watchful eyes at the clothesline on Mondays. If it got overcast or started to rain, then it was brought to everybody's attention so that the clothes could be taken indoors. Damp clothes usually got hung up over the stove, on the backs of chairs or stretched along the railing of the stairs. However, on a sunny day when all the nippers, bees and horse stingers were about, we had to shake out the clothes before we brought them inside. There was nothing worse than getting dressed and then feeling something crawling around inside your clothes or getting stung in a place you can't reach. Even in the winter, the clothes were hung outside and by the time they got taken in at night, they'd be frozen stiff. Sometimes on a blustery day, items would get tangled on the line and then they'd freeze together in odd shapes. A shirt sleeve wrapped around the leg of a pair of overalls looked like a shuffle had been interrupted, while a pair of long johns twisted around a flannelette nightdress might give the illusion of an intimate moment.

At a distance against a darkening sky, they looked like real people caught in action and frozen in time. It was almost a shame to separate the ice sculptures when they were brought into the warm kitchen, but oh how I loved the freshness that filled the house when the clothes thawed out. It was a breath of fresh air that promised an end to the long winter months.

Often when I'm hanging out clothes now, I think of the times I used to do this when I was a teenager. Everybody knew when you got a new garment once they saw it on the clothesline and it wasn't surprising if your friends asked where you got it or if they could borrow it. I remember once when I got a new dress for St. Patrick's Day and I was dying for my friends to see it, so I hung it out on the clothesline nearest the road, hoping that Mom's sharp eyes wouldn't see it. But she saw it and made me take it off the line.

"You should be ashamed of yerself trying to show off to your friends, my dear!" she said. "I got a good mind to send that dress right back to Eatons where you got it!"

I finally convinced her otherwise, and after ironing all the clothes and doing the dishes for a week, she let me keep the dress.

Thinking back now, I'd have to say that Mondays were always special for my sisters and me, especially after school was out for the summer. In between washing clothes, Mom usually made tea buns for us as they were our favourite. Once we were filled up, we never minded having to take the clothes off the line, fold them and put them away. Usually the ironing was left to do on Tuesdays, but the sheets and pillowcases were done on the same day, since they were scarce in those days and they had to be put back on before bedtime. The only thing I objected to was ironing the men's white shirts. Mom used to starch them, and they'd get so stiff that you had to sprinkle water on them to get the wrinkles out. It's no wonder the boys hated wearing them because those rigid shirt collars must have been unbearably scratchy on the Adam's apple. I suspect that men are grateful for the wrinkle-free shirts that are available today. I know that women are grateful for clothes dryers.

Since time is a major factor for working people, the clothesline has virtually become obsolete and in cities it is sometimes believed to detract from a neighbourhood. But nothing could be farther from the truth as far as I'm concerned. I think it is an indispensable luxury, a thing of beauty. While the clothesline still remains in many parts of the world, the spirit may be lost from days of yore when the clothesline united families in the communities. I can't imagine going home to Newfoundland and not seeing women putting out their clothes and letting it all hang out for everyone to see. Somehow the absence of the sound of sheets and blankets blowing in the wind would change everything, for they tell a story and speak a colourful language all their own.

# April Showers

Rain has always held a fascination for me and while some may find it dreary, I enjoy it. I suppose it was my vivid imagination, but as a child I always fancied that rain had a cheerful, musical sound. When I'd go to bed at night, I liked to listen to the rain thundering on the rooftop and I'd try to make up songs to go along with the tempo.

If you listen carefully, you can hear music in the falling rain, for it does have a distinct rhythm when it pounds, pours, spatters and drips. Haven't you ever closed your eyes and just listened to the soft pitter-patter of rain against the window or stood in the pouring rain just to feel it on your skin? Or maybe you've sat on the porch and listened to the raindrops dripping into a puddle of water.

When I was a child in Lord's Cove, we were used to wet weather and children, in particular, loved the summer rain. It held a special kind of excitement for us. "Oh, luh...it's raining again! Come on, let's put on our rubbers and go jumpin' in the potholes over on the back road."

Most people in Lord's Cove had large families back then, so having all the youngsters underfoot during summer holidays must've driven our poor mothers foolish. Sometimes when it rained, my sisters and I liked to play dress-up and hide-and-go-seek in our attic, but most of the time we opted for the outdoors, for it was the perfect excuse to get wet and dirty. I realize that kids today probably don't find playing in the rain exciting, but when you lived in an outport where cars were scarce and dirt roads and meadows were natural playing grounds, it was lots of fun.

Free from any restrictions, we waded into the overflowing brooks in our rubber boots to catch prickly backs. Once our buckets were full, we'd set them free again. Then off came our rubbers so we could roll up our trousers and run barefoot through the mud and jump into the puddles. After the rain subsided and the fog enshrouded the Cove, we'd go scavenger hunting to see what treasures the tide deposited on the landwash. Finally, gut-foundered and dirty, we'd traipse home, knowing full well that we'd be spared the sharp tongues of our mothers on those glorious days.

As I recall, the weather was usually the topic of everyday conversation because so much activity depended on it: hanging laundry on the clothesline, going fishing, spreading hay to be dried in the meadow or even going into the country to cut firewood.

"What's the weather doing out there d'day?" people would ask. "Any sign of rain yet?"

"Naw b'y, not a drop…maybe tomorrow," came the reply.

Curiously enough, a number of the older folks believed that the behaviour of certain animals indicated a change in the weather. They used to say that rain was on the way if they saw cats licking their paws and washing behind their ears or when pigs wallowed about and squealed. Others believed that if cows huddled together in a meadow and horses twitched nervously, or birds chirped more loudly, it would rain the next day. My father always said that bad weather was on the way whenever he saw a halo or a circle around the moon, and my mother insisted that if you killed a spider it would rain for seven days.

For a long time in my younger days, I actually thought that our neighbour, Mrs. Lambe, had some kind of magical power because she always knew when it was going to rain. It could be a lovely sunny day and suddenly she would run outside and take her laundry off the clothesline. Then she'd alert my mother.

"Lottie, you'd better get the clothes off the line before it rains 'cause the hens are firking again!" she would say.

Strangely enough, not 15 minutes later, the sky would darken and we'd get a rain shower. It wasn't until I got older that I finally asked Mrs. Lambe what the hens had to do with rain. She explained that when the hens start clucking and scratching the ground in a frenzy, it was because worms always came to the surface just before a rainfall. She called this odd behaviour "firking."

Sometimes it didn't rain for weeks on end and the wells would run dry, but when the skies finally opened up, it could rain for days. We used the terms "raining buckets" or "raining cats and dogs" in heavier showers and on those days, my sisters and I would stand under the eaves trough and wash our hair. We used rainwater for our baths as well and after supper, my father would lug in buckets of water from the rain barrel. We didn't have running water back then, so water was heated in boilers and pans atop the wood stove and then poured into a big aluminum or wooden tub for bathing.

Sometimes in the spring, when we'd get a sudden squall of rain that lasted only a few minutes, my sister Leona would peer up into the sky and make the oddest comment. "It's cleaning day up in heaven and it looks like Holy Mary spilled her bucket of water while she was washing the floors!" For whatever reason, we never questioned her.

As I recall, when I first came to Ontario many years ago, I was struck by the fact that whenever it rained, people were reluctant to engage in outside activity. If they did go out, they wore raincoats and carried umbrellas, even in the summer. The first time we'd ever seen an umbrella in Lord's Cove was when my father bought Leona a three-piece outfit from St. Pierre when she was eight years old. There was a reversible raincoat with a matching hat and umbrella. The "umbreller," as Leona called it, was her pride and joy. Despite the fact that it was a hot August month and it hadn't rained for three weeks, she was determined to show off her new fitout. Like the cock of the north, she strutted up and down the roads, stopping everybody to demonstrate how the umbrella could go up and down. She wanted desperately to have rain and every morning she'd run to the top of the stairs and ask Daddy the same question: "Is it raining yet, Daddy? Can I use me umbreller d'day?"

By the time it finally did rain, though, all Leona had left was her raincoat, for her hat had blown away one windy day when she was berrypicking and her umbrella was broken. (Apparently our cousin Glenzon was so intrigued by the mechanism that he dismantled it to see how it worked and nobody could get it back together again.) Poor Leona was heartbroken, but she wore her raincoat anyway and stayed outside all day with her broken umbrella hung on her arm.

I still love watching the rain and hearing it on the rooftop at night. It brings me comfort, it lifts my spirits and it makes me smile. When I close my eyes, I can still hear music in the raindrops, see myself running barefoot in the wet grass or sitting on the hill behind our house watching the beautiful rainbows appear after the sun peeps through the fog.

# The Holy Month of May

I've always thought that May month is such an uplifting time of year, for there is so much to look forward to once the winter freeze loosens its grip. The very word "May" conjures up interesting things for me. No matter how long I'm away from home, memories of days gone by come rolling back like a warm fog on a mauzy Newfoundland day. Everybody welcomed the familiar sight of fishermen preparing for a busy season, the smell of tarred nets drying in the sun, the sound of bleating lambs and the smell of kelp on freshly overturned earth. It's no wonder that the older people used to call it the holy month of May, for it was a time of rebirth when people and animals alike shared a closeness with nature.

As I recall, there was an elderly lady in Lord's Cove whom I'm convinced had a special connection with God's creatures. Mrs. Kate Harriet lived alone in a small house across from us, and whenever she went outside, just the sight of her drew the animals from all around. Although none of them belonged to her, she named them, talked to them and fed them. Nobody would be surprised to see the rear end of a horse or a cow sticking out of her kitchen window, because at mealtime she fed them her table scraps. She reminded me of the Pied Piper when she walked down the road because there was usually an entourage of cattle, sheep, hens, dogs and cats hot on her heels. Often we'd hear her cuss at them when she wanted them to go away. She'd stand in the middle of the road heaving rocks in their direction and flailing her arms. "Stop torturing me, ye measly bunch of scavengers...go on, get away from me before I gets upsot! You're as ugly as sin, the whole lot of you, now go home where you belongs!"

Kindhearted woman that she was, she couldn't stay vexed for long and a few minutes later you'd see her patting their heads and calling them her little dears.

There are many things that remind me of May in Newfoundland, especially the colour blue. The whole month was dedicated to the mother of God and we wore a blue ribbon and a holy medal on our lapels in honour of the Blessed Virgin. As well, blue was the colour of the flowers that grew wild in the graveyard and we often picked the bluebells for Mom on Mother's Day.

It was indeed a holy month because there was a lot of praying going on everywhere. At school, the teachers prepared a special altar in honour of Mary and we'd sing hymns and pray to her for special intentions for others. At home, we made our own altar using a statue and pictures of the Blessed Virgin, a drop of holy water and a bouquet of bluebells arranged on a small table. If we walked by the altar, we had to kneel and pray a few Hail Mary's or at least bless ourselves and genuflect in reverence. Not every family had what we called a "Mary Altar," but we did and we took pride in decorating it. Besides, it was a topic of conversation between friends. Bear in mind here that we were merely youngsters, so the religious aspect was not always on our minds, especially when one was trying to outdo the other. My sisters and I were consistently moving the display from one room to another and that caused many arguments. I'd put Mary's statue at the top of the stairs, then Leona would move it to the parlour and Kate or Helena would set it up in one of their bedrooms. We literally came to blows at times and at least one of us came away with a fist full of hair once the dido settled down.

Mom would get so annoyed when she went looking for the altar and couldn't find it. "Now where in the name of God did the Blessed Virgin go now? I wish you'd leave that poor woman in one place long enough for me to say my prayers!"

We'd heard so much about the power of prayer that we expected miracles to happen when we prayed to God's mother. We didn't always understand that the miracles were of a spiritual nature, so we'd look for some physical manifestation. Often when a few of us would be together, we'd recount stories we'd heard about the Blessed Virgin appearing to a group of children somewhere in the world, and we'd make ourselves believe that it could happen in Lord's Cove. Many times we sat staring at her statue, hoping that she would speak to us or give us some kind of a sign. But as much as we wanted it to happen, we were still terrified that it might. There were a couple of times that we made ourselves believe that something was about to happen. "What was that? Did you hear a woman's voice?"

"Nah, b'y...that was Mom calling the dog out in the yard!"

One of our friends insisted that she saw a tear in the corner of Mary's eye, but upon investigation, we discovered it was just a spatter of rain from a leak in the ceiling. Mind you, there was another time at my cousin's house when we were convinced we saw a cross emblazoned in the sky outside the window behind Mary's statue. Our excitement was short-lived though, for it turned out to be lights from a car that shone momentarily on the hydro lines outside.

No, we never witnessed any miracles, but it was not for lack of trying. There was a lot of daily praying going on in Mary's name at school and at the church. Every Sunday the holy Rosary was recited in the church, and it was done in the homes with family on a daily basis. The Rosary beads hung on a hook in readiness at all times and as you might imagine, this ritual was not always a welcomed one for the youngsters. It could last for half an hour or more, depending on how many other prayers someone chose to add. I remember well how we had to kneel up straight on the hard kitchen floor and pray out loud. Nothing stopped the recital of the Rosary in our house once it began. If someone came to our house during prayers, it didn't matter if they were Catholic, for my father would keep on praying and indicate that they had to kneel as well. I hated kneeling because my knees were so bony and when Mom wasn't looking, I'd lean on a chair or sneak a pillow off the daybed until she took a swing at me with her prayer beads. She could be in the middle of saying a prayer and throw in a warning all in the same breath. "Holy Mary mother of God, pray for us sinners...Lucy, put that pillow back and kneel up straight...now and at the hour of our death, Amen."

Most of the time, we'd be trying to rush through the prayers so we could go outside to play before dark. To be truthful, I didn't always pay attention and simply repeated the prayers out of habit. I was so used to hearing the mass being said in Latin that often I got it all confused and mixed up, sometimes throwing in Latin with English words. I liked it when my father's turn came to lead us in the Rosary because even though he added a litany of extra prayers, he said them so fast that we couldn't keep up with him. I had no inkling what he was saying and I never questioned him, so I'd improvise and mumble along with him. It wasn't until recent years that I was asking my brother Raphael about a response to a particular prayer my dad used to say. "It was in Latin, remember? I don't know how to spell the words, but it sounded something like this," I said, repeating the words as best I could. "Delard shallopen mollips, datong shanounces preys."

Once Raphael recovered from laughing, he translated for me. "The Lord shall open my lips, thy tongue shall announce his praise."

Turns out my father was speaking English after all.

Ah, yes, those sure were interesting times back then in Newfoundland. That's why I decided to make this month a little different here in Niagara Falls this year. Since hubby was still in Bosnia, I thought I'd surprise him and do the lawn before he came back. I had never in my life done any kind of lawn care but wanting to do a good deed for him, I went out and bought fertilizer, top soil, weed killer and grass seed. By the time Murray came home, I had everything finished. But since he arrived in the middle of the night, I decided to keep it a surprise till morning. I made sure he was up early the next day and I sent him outside on the pretense of getting something out of the car. Proud as a rooster in a henhouse, I stood at the window so I could see his reaction. I saw his mouth drop open as he walked slowly across the lawn and I knew by his expression that he was overcome with emotion. Finally I went outside to where he was kneeling on the grass with his hands covering his face. He was all choked up when he spoke. "Where did you put the fertilizer?" he asked in a quiet voice.

"On the dandelions, silly...where did you think I put it... on the grass?"

I heard him say something under his breath and as I leaned forward, I caught the tail end of his words. "...holy mother of God."

I can't tell you how moved I was, for that was the first time I'd heard him pray aloud. And considering the fact that he's not even Catholic, I'd say I witnessed my first miracle.

# Prelude to Summer

The countdown began as soon as we saw the mist hovering above the thawing earth. As soon as the June sun chased away the nip of the night air and shone warmly through the school windows, we longed for classes to be over. I can still conjure up the image of our old elementary school in Lord's Cove – the sound of pencils scratching on scribbler paper and restless feet scraping against wood floors, while eager faces gazed out the window.

We couldn't wait to shed our warm jackets, wool sweaters and socks. Oh what a relief it was for us girls to get rid of our argyle stockings and garters. The sunshine beckoned us to expose our lily-white legs and we gleefully rolled down our bobby socks and stockings during recess and lunch break. To us, this was the prelude to summer and we looked forward to every minute of it.

Once the last day of school was out, the Cove came alive with the sound of excited youngsters celebrating their freedom. Two elderly neighbours used to lean on the picket fence waiting for the last clang of the old school bell so they could catch the moment when the teachers opened the door. "Watch them now, going their wincy like a herd of wild horses let loose from the stables," Mrs. Lambe would say with a chuckle.

Mrs. Kate Harriett always added a few colourful words of her own. "Look at the little scalawags, full of vim and vigour and up to no good," she'd laugh. "God love 'em. The Cove will never be the same again!"

I remember how, once vacation started, my sisters and I would tumble out of bed and race downstairs for breakfast. "What in heaven's name are ye youngsters doing up so early?"

Mom would ask. "I just started making bread and the kettle is not even boiled for tea yet!"

"Mom...it's summer holidays and we don't want to miss anything!" we'd tell her.

I imagine that with the large families in the Cove back then, mothers were kept on their toes. Kids would be up bright and early and out all day long, darting into the house only to gobble down dinner. Mom used to bake a dozen loaves of bread every day just to keep up with our appetites. She would cut thick slices from oven-fresh loaves and we'd smear on Good Luck butter and molasses. "You got yer gobs full now, so go on out of the kitchen and let me git my work done!" she'd say.

What stirred the blood in our veins and piqued our curiosity, you might ask? Well, everything seemed exciting to us. It seemed like we didn't have a worry in the world. "Come day, go day, God send Sunday," is what the elders would say. But we didn't care what day it was.

We loved berry-picking, trouting in the ponds, walking to Pump Cove and Sandy Cove to swim in the gut, catching prickly backs and laying in the sun making plans for our futures. There was nothing more beautiful than those Newfoundland summers.

Goodness, how we loved it when Mom sent us off to pick berries for pies and tarts. We'd take our sweet time dabbling in the brooks and skipping flat rocks across the ponds. Sometimes though, we'd be so hungry that we'd eat the berries and come back empty-handed. "You mean to tell me that the three of you ate ALL of the berries?" Mom would say, planting her hands on her hips. "Now how did that happen?"

We always had a good explanation. I usually stuck to the story that I sat down in a hill of pissmores (ants) and dropped my berries. Helena maintained that Leona and I picked all the berries and she couldn't find any. And Leona...well, she told the truth. Instead of putting berries in her jug, she ate them all.

There were so many summer delights in our younger years.

We'd go up behind Grandfather's hill to get blasty boughs for kindling and we'd walk the cows to the marsh every morning to graze. I was particularly fond of Maize, one of our cows. She always lagged behind the others and I usually had to fetch her or else she'd never come home for milking. Maize was a good listener and often I'd confide my dreams and secrets to her as she munched on her cud. It sounds crazy, but whenever she mooed softly, I felt she understood my ramblings.

I always enjoyed spreading the hay to dry and then stacking it into "pooks," as we called it. Whenever my friends and I played hide-and-go-seek in the stable hayloft, we'd throw the hay all over until Daddy scolded us and made us fix it. Finally, tired, happy and dusty, we'd head for home with our hair looking like mops and brooms.

When I became a teenager my life changed in a sense, for then I loved everything about Lord's Cove. I could sit for hours on the hill behind our home watching the fog steal around the houses, or enjoy the quietness of a mauzy day and marvel at a rainbow reaching clear across the sky. The fishermen would take their dories and skiffs out early every morning, long before I rose, and return at noon with the day's catch of cod. The pungent smell of salt water, kelp and seaweed mixed with the sound of sea rushing to shore was enough to make you feel lucky to be alive.

Romance was certainly a part of outport summers. On moonlit nights we'd sneak out for a walk with a boy we fancied. Our favourite thing was sitting on the wharf in the moonlight and wandering into Mr. Anthony Lambe's meadow so we could sit against the stacks of hay and have a little smooch…until, of course, we'd hear one of our mothers calling us to come home. "Git home here right now before I comes looking for you!"

Sometimes we'd have moonlight parties in Sandy Cove, where we'd sit around a fire on the beach. There was always someone with a guitar or a mouth organ and lots of singing and laughing going on.

Of course, we all had chores to do, though we'd try to evade them. My job was to clean the little metal spouts of the dreaded Separator so Mom could make butter. I'd almost gag at the smell of sour cream. "Mom, can't I do something else instead? The sour smell makes me stomach turn upside down!" I'd complain.

But Mom paid me no heed. The five of us girls helped Mom with the household chores, while the boys worked with my father outside. On Saturdays, my sister Leona's job was to wash and starch the menfolk's white shirts and press their trousers for Sunday church. Thinking it was an easier job, I persuaded her to trade with me. Not wanting Mom to know what I was doing, I didn't ask how to do laundry and I threw the whole box of starch into the hot water along with the two blocks of blue cubes. I figured, the more the better.

When I took out the white shirts, they were very blue and so hard they could stand up by themselves. Afraid of what I'd done, I never told anybody...until it was too late. Come Sunday morning, Mom made the boys keep on what they were wearing. They sat stiffly in church with white collars dabbled in blue and pants that looked as wide as the shadow of a bus.

I wouldn't trade the way I grew up for anything in the world. When I go home to Newfoundland now, I still miss the sound of children's voices and the games we played. Pity, really, that all those outport delights are almost nonexistent now. Kids today sit in front of the television or a computer, chat and text on their cell phones and surf the Internet.

As I recall, when summer holidays neared their end we even looked forward to returning to school. Once we got off the school bus, we all talked at the same time, trying to catch up on each other's news. "Tell me what you did all summer! Oh...wait till I tells you about the cute boy I saw in St. Lawrence this summer..."

Yes, summer indeed was over, but that mattered not to us, for we had so much to look forward to as we began another school year.

# A Newfoundland Summer

Summer is here again and as always, memories of days gone by come rolling back to me like a warm fog on a hazy Newfoundland day. Nothing can compare to waking up the first days of summer in an outport… the scent of kelp on steamy earth freshly overturned, tarred nets drying on the beach, the putter of dory engines, the bleating of baby lambs and caplin rolling in on the sand. Every youngster knew when summer had officially arrived by the sight of clotheslines laden with longjohns and heavy quilts and by the chatter of elderly women talking across the fence. "My, my what a day we got! Now everyone knows I never poked me nose outside the door since I caught that dose last winter, but it was so warm dis morning that I went down to the shop with not a stitch of clothes on me and that's the God's troot!"

No youngster was ever stuck for something to do once school was out. The first thing we did was make a new hoop and guider, for nobody went without one of those homemade contraptions. A metal stave from a porkbarrel served as a rolling hoop and the guider that steered it was fashioned from a piece of wire bent into a semicircle to fit around the hoop. It took skill and coordination to run with the hoop and keep it rolling in a straight line and getting around the rocks and potholes on the dirt road was quite a challenge. We usually practiced outside the post office at Bernadette Lundrigan's house where we indulged in our favourite pastime… waiting for the mail truck to come. We spent hours gathering bluebells and then we'd stretch out amongst the buttercups on the hill overlooking the ocean to listen to the seagulls and the waves heaving upon the beach in Job's Cove. The only thing that would disturb our rest was the screech of a mother's voice on the wind, urging us home for supper.

We seldom had time to be bored back then, for we always had chores to do, but that was part of everyday life for us. There were always animals to be fed, butter to be churned, clothes to be washed in the wooden tub, barrels to be replenished with drinking water and cows to be milked. Off and on during the summer, we had to make a few trips to the landwash and lug beach rocks in buckets and wheelbarrows to spread around the house to keep the grass from growing up. After that, the animals kept it cropped.

Rain and fog didn't hinder us none back then, for we found things to do. Everyone knows how stunned cows are about directions, for they can never find their way home, especially on a foggy day, so it was a full-time job looking for them at sunset and driving them home for milking. We always took someone with us because it gave us a chance to socialize and do a bit of trouting in the brook or make little boats out of the tall bulrushes that grow in the ponds. Sometimes we'd take our slingshots and shoot at the clumps of red crackerjack berries in the woods, wade in the brook to catch prickly-backs or walk a few miles to Sandy Cove Beach to spend the afternoon swimming or catching eels. We made many all-day excursions to pick bakeapples, blueberries or partridgeberries and it gave us a good excuse to have a mug-up in the great outdoors. The aroma of tea boiling over an open fire kindled with blasty boughs was enough to whet any appetite for a feed of dried rounders and thick slices of bread smothered in molasses. Usually, by the time we got home before nightfall, we'd eaten most of the berries, but we always managed to save a jug full to be made into pies and tarts.

We didn't travel too far from home back then, mostly because transportation was scarce and any place outside Lord's Cove was like a different world to us. Going on a holiday could mean staying overnight in Taylor's Bay three miles away, but it was still a big event for children. I had never been away from my family until I was nine and when Uncle Dave Benteau persuaded Mom to let me spend a weekend at his house in Point May, just 15 miles away, I was elated.

I bragged about "going on me holidays" to everybody and I had my grip packed for days before I left. We got a ride with a shoe salesman who passed through the Cove every Friday and by the time he stopped in every place on the way, it was bedtime when we arrived in Point May. I was doing fine until Uncle Dave pointed out the lights from the French Islands of St. Pierre and Miquelon across the way. Suddenly, I wanted to go home to familiar surroundings. I got homesick and started bawling my head off to see Mom and Daddy. Nothing or nobody could calm me down and I refused to take off my clothes or go to bed. Poor Uncle Dave sat up all night holding me in the rocking chair so that his family could sleep. Early next morning he hired someone to take me back home and I arrived sobbing and hiccupping. I was so tired that I crawled into bed between my two sisters fully clothed and slept though the rest of the day.

Despite my traumatic experience, I still bragged to everyone the next day, elaborating about my long journey in the salesman's truck and telling about the bright lights of St. Pierre. It seemed unimportant to tell them the part about getting homesick or the fact that I had spent a mere ten hours in Point May without even opening my grip. The important thing was that I had actually gone on a holiday and that was enough excitement for any outport youngster. What I wouldn't give to relive one of those Newfoundland summers... but the difference in then and now is as wide as air!

# A Charming
# Way of Life

*To succeed in life, you need three things:*
*a wishbone, a backbone and a funnybone.*

– Reba McEntire –

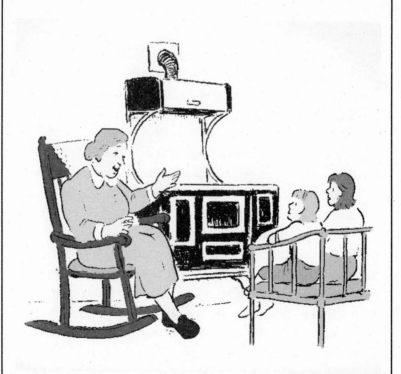

# We've Got Personality

I realize you've heard me say this many times before, but I'm going to say it one more time. Newfoundland is the most wonderful place in the world. You guessed it… I've been back home again to rejuvenate my spirits and to gather a few yarns to keep my pen in motion for another year.

Eager as a sailor on a two-hour pass, I set out for home and after a two-week stay, I returned to Niagara Falls strung out like a sheet on a clothesline. You know what it's like… up gabbing till the wee hours of the morning, on the go all the time and getting more than my share of good food and belly laughs.

Each time I visit, I come away from the island with a few more laugh lines than when I got there. And it's all because of the people, for every time I go back, I'm reminded of what I'm missing… that Newfoundland sense of humour that makes life so interesting. Newfoundlanders have a unique way of expressing themselves, not only in their own dialect, but in the amusing way they say things. It is seldom contrived or intended for a laugh, but rather a droll, witty repartee that rolls easily off the tongue. Oh, yes, there's no doubt about it, that's what gives our province and our people personality.

You have to admit that there's some validity in what I've said. Take this friend of mine from Lord's Cove whom I've known all my life. Ten minutes of listening to Fred Hennebury can cure what ails you, for he can make the cats laugh. Not only does he have a way with words, but he literally dramatizes everything as he speaks and the expressions on his face are priceless. The last time I talked with him, I inquired about the head injury he had received in an accident a few years ago. "If I felt any better, dear, I couldn't stand mesself," he said, nodding his head empathetically.

Then he elaborated on his check-up with the doctor and said that his last brain scan showed that everything was fine. "The doctor told me that my brain looked perfect," he said, taking off his cap and rubbing his head, "…and why wouldn't me brain be perfect, Lucy, m'dear. After all, it's never been used before."

Fred is unmarried and in his early 60s, and like many Newfoundlanders who fished all their lives, he had little time for school in his younger years, for he helped support their large family after his father died.

"Sometimes we didn't even have enough grub to eat and there were mornings when the only thing we had on the table wuz our elbows," he said with a twinkle in his eye. "I 'members one time when we sat down for supper and me poor mudder had a piece of paper on each plate with BALONEY written on it… now that's what I calls poor."

Fred related many stories and yarns and each in turn always had a little anecdote. When I asked about his brother who had a retina transplant a few years ago, he said Earl was doing well. "Oh, Earl's the best kind now that he's got his new eye. My dear, his eyesight is so keen now he can see the wind."

"Well that's good," I said.

"No, that's bad. You see, Earl got one blue eye and one brown eye now and he's gone all cross-eyed 'cause his new eye keeps trying to see what the other one is looking at," Fred replied quickly. "Now when the poor bugger cries, the tears run down his back."

'Course he knew perfectly well that I didn't believe that Earl was cross-eyed, but Fred prattled on about it anyway. "Earl bumped into me in the kitchen d'other day and he sez to me, 'Why don't you look where you're going, Fred?' And I sez to him, 'my son, why don't you go where you're looking.'"

Ah, yes, the world would be so much better off if everybody had a sense of humour like Fred's and they could laugh at themselves, wouldn't it? Just recently when George and Babe White of Niagara Falls showed me a video of their first trip to Newfoundland, I realized that the things I take for granted were the very things that impressed them most about our province. As they showed me photographs and talked excitedly about their experience, it occurred to me the whole essence of Newfoundland and our people. George said it beautifully. "We can't wait to go back again! It was incredible how friendly and helpful the people were," he said. "Wherever we went, everybody had a smile for us and made us feel at home. The people were so wonderful and so interesting, too. No matter what their personal situation was, they all seemed to have such a great outlook on life and a terrific sense of humour."

Now what better endorsement do you need to promote Newfoundland than that, eh? Babe, George's wife, said they got their first sample of what she calls "the down east humour" when they stopped in Twillingate. A man came up to them and asked where they came from and where they were headed. When they told him they were going to St. John's to see the icebergs they'd heard so much about, he smiled. "Don't need to go all that ways to see icebergs, 'cause they all have to come here first before they get to St. John's."

The Whites thoroughly enjoyed their boat trip from Bay Bulls, where they stopped alongside huge iceberg sculptures that had been around for thousands of years. They were in awe at the sight of two whales so close that they could reach out and grab their mighty tails. Babe proudly showed me her certificate that proved she had been "Screeched-in" and laughingly showed a picture of herself in oilskins kissing the butt end of a stuffed puffin instead of the traditional cod. "Hard to believe, isn't it… to be in Newfoundland and not have a fish!"

According to them, the scenery was spectacular. They were

intrigued by the sight of the wood-framed houses perched precariously on the side of the cliffs overlooking the ocean as they drove along the coast and marvelled at the way the weather changed from sunshine, to fog, to rain, to wind storms all in one day. As a result, The Whites soon learned the secret of being able to stay on their feet on windy days because they learned what they called the "Newfie Stance"... feet planted wide apart as you lean into the wind. They couldn't believe how everybody seemed to trust each other and related a tale of how the owners of a bed and breakfast in Rocky Harbour went off for the day and left them in the house to help themselves to whatever they wanted. "It was amazing! They knew nothing about us, but still they trusted us. 'Just lock the door behind you if you go out'... that's what they told us," Babe said. "They were wonderful people."

The Whites took turns telling about the interesting people they had the pleasure of meeting along the way. They especially enjoyed Maude, a lady they met in Summerville, who did odd jobs for the owners at Janes' Bed and Breakfast. When they arrived they were surprised to find eighty-year-old Maude standing on a chair in the kitchen hanging wallpaper. She informed them she had just finished painting the other walls. Babe commented on how agile she was for her age when Maude told her all the things she did, like house cleaning and baking bread every morning for a local bakery. "I could do a lot more you know, but I'm almost blind now from the cataracts on my eyes," Maude sighed. "They're so bad now it's like looking through dirty windows."

After Maude finished her cup of tea, she said she had to hurry home because she had to go up on the roof of her house to fix some shingles. Astounded that a woman her age would even consider such a thing, George asked her why she didn't get somebody to do the work for her, but she just waved his suggestion aside. "Humph! I've been on me own for a long time now and I'm used to doin' things meself," she grumbled good-naturedly. "Besides if I hired someone to do it, I'd have to go up there and show them what to do, so I may as well do the work meself."

They chuckled at the time they were sitting in a restaurant having lunch when an elderly man walked past their table and greeted George. "Hello, Garge… how's you gettin' on, b'y?"

George was taken a back to be called by his first name, but the man continued walking and sat at a table across from them. Perplexed that this stranger should know his name, George finally asked if they knew each other. "Sure I knows you, Garge… I've see you around here lots of times before."

No matter what George said, the man kept insisting that he knew him. But the mystery was finally solved when they discovered that the friendly gentleman had simply mistaken him for somebody who looked like him and who, coincidentally, just happened to be named George.

Judging by all the good things I've heard from visitors to our province, one thing is perfectly clear. It is the people who make them all want to go back a second time… people like Maude, Fred and all the many warm-hearted folks who leave them with a smile on their face, a spring in their step and a glow in their hearts. And in my mind, that says a lot about Newfoundlanders. We've got personality.

# Odd Expressions

Ever since I've lived in Ontario I've been asked about the expressions and words that sometimes roll off my tongue. Naturally, I tell people that Newfoundland speech is brim full of colloquialisms and colourful words that span four centuries of use.

Our lively dialects and accents date back to the early settlers from England, Ireland and Scotland and are something we like to boast about – although spirited Newfoundland language can sometimes baffle unsuspecting newcomers.

Chock full of odd words and terminology, our speech patterns might not make any sense unless you were born and raised in Newfoundland. Sometimes we even drop a letter at the beginning of a word and stick it on t'other end.

The older folks had a plethora of odd sayings and peculiar phrases that boggled the mind. It's hard for outsiders to decipher these peculiar words and expressions that describe everything from using the bathroom to having babies and courting. Nor is it uncommon for visitors to the province to ask a Newfoundlander to repeat something, for often we're quicker than quick when we speak.

Nonetheless, Newfoundlanders have an endearing way with words. In most of the province's communities, people you don't even know will smile and say hello – often with a cheery "How are ye doing today, m'duckie?" thrown in for emphasis.

Some age-old expressions may raise an eyebrow or two, so be warned if you're planning a Newfoundland visit. The first time my husband visited Lord's Cove he got an unexpected greeting from my uncle. "How ya getting' on, me ole cock?" he said, grasping Murray's hand firmly.

Seeing the look on Murray's face, I explained quickly that "cocks and hens" are freshwater clams that fishermen used for bait.

"Nice to meet you, sir...how are you?" Murray hesitantly replied.

"The finest kind m'son...if I was any better I couldn't stand meself!" my uncle grinned.

My father used some unique expressions. Whenever he was photographed, he'd say he "got his likeness taken" or his "snap took." If he was hungry, he'd say he was "gut-foundered" and he referred to his food as "grub" or "prog." When he finished eating, he'd say he was "chock full to the bung."

Whenever Dad forgot the name of something, he'd use filler words like chummy-dinger, do-jigger, ting-a-bob or a do-flicky. We actually became accustomed to those names and whenever he'd ask us for one of his chummy-dingers, we knew exactly what he was talking about.

My mother always used a few choice words as well, such as bivver, quat and nishy. Bivver meant the same as shiver, quat was to sit or crouch, and nishy meant delicate. She always warned us to "quat down" on a chair when we washed her china cups. "Be careful and make sure you don't let your hands bivver because the cups are right nishy!"

When I was a child, some of the expressions people used would baffle me. I think I asked so many questions because people would say things that left me wondering. My Uncle Dave Joe, for example, struck me as being confused all the time. He had a knack of using the negative to make the affirmative more positive. He'd walk through the doorway and rub his hands together. "Now don't say it's not some ugly cold out there this mornin'!"

If we had a thunder storm, he'd make yet another comment: "That was some wonderful bad storm we had last night, wuz'nt it?"

What perplexed me most was when he'd say that "the missus

over the road enjoyed poor health."

For the life of me I couldn't understand how anyone could like being sick.

My mother often told me that I was a curious, gullible child who was forever asking questions. She claimed that I had a fertile imagination and I suppose I did. Since I was the youngest, I think my siblings often had a chuckle at my expense, for I believed whatever they told me.

Nobody corrected me. I'd conjure up mental pictures of things I heard but didn't know what they meant. One day I overheard someone tell my father that an elderly man in the Cove had passed on. "It was just a matter of time," he said. "That poor old fella had one foot in the grave anyway."

I was horrified to think that some poor soul had buried one foot in the graveyard with the other one sticking out of the ground. As usual, I asked my sister Leona about it. "As true as God might strike me dead... that really happened!" she said, reverently thumping her fist against her chest.

I believed her.

The older people in our community usually referred to idle chitchat as prattle or prate. Mom always called me a "prate box," but I had no idea what it meant. Every time someone said it, I'd stick out my chest in pride. One day when I was at my aunt's house, I heard an older woman talking about the unusual warm weather they were getting in May. "It was so hot d'day that I went to the shop with not a stitch of clothes on me!"

I could hardly believe my ears, so I ran home to tell Mom the news. All the way home, I visualized that dear old lady going into Rob Lambe's Shop – stark naked! I was in such shock that every time I opened my gob the words got tangled up. Finally, Mom figured out I had misunderstood the expression.

"'Pon me soul to God, Lucy. You got my brain addled from listening to you!" she said, fanning herself with the *Farmer's Almanac*.

When everybody laughed at me, I got my nose out of joint and went to bed screeching and bawling. It was a lesson well learned and, after that, I kept things to myself.

Mrs. Lambe, our elderly neighbour, was an interesting woman and I loved going to her house. She always said I was as perky as a starling and curious as a cat. She patiently answered my endless questions, but if other youngsters came with me and acted silly or made noise, she'd put them in their place. "Who knit you and dropped a stitch, my dear?" she'd ask.

If she thought somebody was shooting the blarney she'd let them know they couldn't pull the wool over her eyes. "Go on with you, b'y…you got enough mouth for two faces!"

She had expressions for everything. If she believed someone wasn't being truthful, she'd say, "You tells more lies than a horse can haul."

Mrs. Lambe also had a knack of knowing how to tell somebody they were gabbing too much, but she always said it with humour. One day when a chatty woman dropped in for tea, she prattled so much that Mrs. Lambe couldn't get a word in edgeways. Finally, she interrupted.

"Yer tongue must be getting right tired now, m'dearie." she quipped. "Why don't you put it in the prate box and give it a rest?"

My father also had a sense of humour. At night if friends dropped in for a chat and he wanted to go to bed, he'd drop a subtle hint. He'd casually wind the alarm clock, set it on the table and put the cat out. Then he'd stand up and yawn. "Well, we'd better go to bed, Lottie, in case these good people might want to go home."

Mom would be mortified as everybody reached for their hats and coats.

I have fond memories of my parents and their friends having a game of cards at our house. The men usually played against the women and Mom and her best friend, Sis, were always partners. My, how they argued and bantered over the cards.

"For heaven's sake, Sis...why didn't you trump that play when you know dem sleeveens are winning?"

"Lottie, look at the rotten cards I picked up, me chile! I wouldn't feed dat hand to a starving nun!"

"It's your fault we lost that game, Sis!" Mom would say.

"Oh...kiss me jigger, Lottie!"

"You're as saucy as a crackie dog, you are, Sis!"

"Oh grow up, Lottie ...grow up!"

Then they'd both crack up laughing. My mother was 80 years old at the time and Sis was 83.

As a youngster it seemed that everybody talked about the weather. My father would look up at the sky and shake his head. "Going to be a mauzy ole day d'morrow... breeze comin' in from the suddur," he'd say. Or, "Some hot d'day... sun's splittin' the rocks." "Some day on clothes," the women commented to each other whenever it was sunny and breezy.

Mom could be in the middle of a conversation with the priest and, looking out the window, exclaim: "My Lord, the hens are firkin' again! We're in for a squall of rain." (For the record, "firkin" is a quaint word used to describe hens scratching in the dirt looking for worms just before a rainfall.)

So be prepared for an auditory experience like no other when you come to Newfoundland. Once you get past saying "Pardon?" a dozen times or more, you'll get used to us. Like we say in Newfoundland: "Don't stay where you're to, b'y...come where we're at!"

# Making Perfect Scents

When I was a child, my mother used to say that if I ever got lost I could find my way home by using my nose. My sensitive nostrils could detect certain scents a mile away, especially when it came to food. "Mom, I smell cherry cake... can I have a piece?" I'd ask, even though it was nowhere in sight.

She'd just look at me and shake her head. "My dear, what kind of a sniffer have you got on your face, at all? That turned-up nose of yours never misses a thing!"

In retrospect, I'm inclined to agree with my mother's observation because my nose has never failed me yet. For me, scent is the strongest tie to memory, a way of preserving familiar things that kindle emotions and keep memories alive. I have a tendency to associate things and people with certain smells; often when I get a whiff of something on a passing breeze, it will remind me of something or someone. Recently at work when someone came into the jewellery store, I knew by the familiar smell of mothballs that it was an elderly person before I looked up. As the little blue-haired lady in the ancient tweed coat asked the price of re-stringing her pearls, I had a flashback of my mother taking our winter coats out of the attic. Those mothballs were so strong they permeated the whole house and the musty bouquet stayed on our clothes from one season to the next.

It has been said that Newfoundland has a unique culture as well as expressions and colloquialisms, but I think it also has distinct scents. What Newfoundlander can get a whiff of salt water, kelp and seaweed and not be reminded of home? There

are many things I love about the island and often when
nostalgia overwhelms me, I start thinking about the little things
I miss most. It's not just the sights and sounds, but the scents of
home…the aroma of homemade bread toasting on top of the
wood stove, cocoa simmering in a big aluminum dipper and
turpentine melting on the splits in the oven. Just the thought of
it makes me homesick.

Oh, yes, you could tell a lot about people from their homes
and the scents around them, especially in Newfoundland. If you
went into someone's house where there were lots of youngsters,
it was safe to say that someone had a cold or flu if the air reeked
of Vicks VapoRub or Buckley's Mixture. If it was an elderly
person's home, you knew by the telltale sharpness of ginger
wine that they had an upset stomach, or that their limbs were
ailing when you caught a whiff of Wintergreen Oil and Minards
Liniment. "The old arthritis acting up again, is it Missus? Must
be all the rain we've had this week."

"Oh, yes, me chile…the arthritis is serving me some bad! Sure
I couldn't wash the loft with me leg yesterday."

On weekdays in every home, you could usually smell Sunlight
soap, Rinso detergent and the cleanliness of homemade lye soap
made outdoors in an iron kettle. I liked Sundays best because at
our house there was always the fragrance of shaving soap in a
mug and the wholesomeness of Old Spice aftershave that my
father and four brothers used. If you visited somebody, you could
smell sweets for afternoon tea and Sail tobacco from the old
men's pipes. Those were common in every household and to this
day, I still associate them with lazy Sunday afternoons when the
menfolk got all dickied up in their best clothes.

While most scents from my childhood were pleasant ones,
there were a few that reawakened bad memories. Whenever any
of us got sick, Mom tucked us under a blanket on the kitchen
daybed beside the stove and let us listen to the radio. That was a
treat for us as my parents only turned it on in the evenings to save

electricity. Mom always knew what to do to make us feel better. Remember the little balls of lemon crystals for colds and sore throat? I loved that lemon flavour when the crystals dissolved in hot water and the way the drink snapped the taste buds awake. At dinner she made beef broth; just smelling the vapours as it simmered on the stove helped chase away our misery.

On the other hand, there were certain scents that made me queasy – especially the foul odour of cod liver oil. I'd hide under the daybed or in the closet under the stairs until someone hauled me out by the feet and poured the sticky stuff down my throat. I had the same reaction to the sickly sweet tea my father forced us to drink to make sure we didn't get worms from all the pork we ate. The smell of that putrid stuff made me bivver all over.

I think it was summertime in particular that held the most interesting assortment of aromas. Nothing can compare to pure, fresh air on a clear day. Mom never had to tell me twice to take the laundry off the clothesline, for I loved to bury my face in the clothes and smell nature's sweet freshness. Oh how my sister and I enjoyed it when we went berrypicking with our father and he'd boil the kettle over an open fire of blasty boughs. There was nothing like the taste of strong tea and raisin bread to whet the appetite on a sunny summer day, and we always went home tired but happy. During the fishing season, it seemed that there was a perpetual odour of Jay's Fluid, which my father and brothers used to soothe the sores on their hands from hauling handlines.

There were certain smells that lingered in everybody's kitchen… some good ones and others not so inviting. You never had to ask what was cooking for dinner because it wasn't hard for the olfactory senses to identify salmon or even fresh cod fried up with pork scrunchions. That fishy smell hovered in the air like a wet blanket and you could live off the odour for a week.

In the winter, I always enjoyed the outdoorsy scent of frost and smoke from the chimneys. On stormy nights when the electricity went out, the sharpness of oil from the kerosene lamps in the kitchen made everything feel cozy and warm. Every home was filled with the same smells of pickled cabbage, salt beef, pease pudding, rabbit, moose, partridge or salt water ducks. I remember my dad plucking feathers and using a hot poker to singe the down off the bird. That usually made Mom gag and she'd cover her nose with her handkerchief. "Merciful Lord, can't you do that outside, John?" she would say. "I can hardly glutch with that stink of burning flesh up m' nostrils!"

There's no doubt about it, our sense of smell does evoke many images and sensations and it's only in retrospect that we become aware of it. All I know is that the different smells that I associate with Newfoundland are just as vivid now as they were when I was a child. Whenever I think of them I can visualize sitting in somebody's kitchen with those comforting smells all around me.

But alas, the scent of fish and Jay's Fluid that reflected the lifestyle of many outport fishing families no longer exists. Times have changed to make way for progress and we've become accustomed to more sophisticated things. Now we have scents and perfumes for men and women that come in a bottle, in the form of aromatherapy. And they're not restricted to the kitchen anymore; they're in bedrooms, bathrooms and spas – to stimulate, relax, or even be used as an aphrodisiac. Mind you, this concept is not necessarily new: long ago many a woman would rub vanilla behind the ears and on the neck to attract a suitor.

Come to think of it, maybe there is something to the idea of kitchen smells being alluring to our mates because I've noticed that lately Murray hangs around a lot whenever I'm cooking. Hummmm...perhaps if I daub white wine behind my ears and rub a bit of garlic and onion on my wrist, it will incite hubby to do something wild and wonderful...like loading the dishwasher. Who knows, if it worked for other women, it just might get me out of the kitchen and into the bedroom more often. I don't know about him, but it makes perfect scents to me.

# The Spinner of Yarns

I've always been a pushover for someone who can spin a good yarn, so it wasn't unusual for me to go where I knew I could find one whenever I went home to Lord's Cove. One of the best storytellers was a man named Richard Hennebury who could spin a yarn that could turn a skeptic into a believer. His wit and incredible sense of humour were matched only by his twinkling blue eyes and the way he could turn a phrase. After he'd talk about each of his 13 children and his cat, he'd roll himself a cigarette and then that old familiar glint of mischief would come to his eye and I knew I was going to hear another story. "Did I ever tell you about the time I met the ghost on the road to Taylor's Bay when I was walking to Lamaline? No? Well, I s'pose you wouldn't want to hear that one..."

And then he'd have you baited and hooked before you even knew it! By the time he finished telling his story you didn't know whether it was true or not, but it didn't matter, because he made you believe every word of it and that has to be the greatest gift a storyteller can possess. He could spin a tale and leave you hanging on every word, every gesture, every wink of his eye and you were a captive audience. Richard, fondly known as "Rich," was one of the most interesting people I knew. After he died, I felt that we had lost not just a friend, but a master in the traditional craft of storytelling. I feel rich indeed to have been a part of recording his legacy.

A favourite story of mine concerns the first time Richard left home to go to war when he was 21 years old. He and many more young men from the area said goodbye to their families and off they went with a few belongings in a cardboard box.

"I had nothing but the clothes on me back, hip rubbers and worsted longjohns me mother knit," he said. "I had a change of socks in the box, a few bottles of partridgeberry jam and a bottle of Dodd's Kidney pills for whatever ails ya!"

It was August month and when they arrived in Montreal they had to stop overnight at a barracks. Much to the amusement of the other Frenchmen already there, the Newfoundlanders began to shed their heavy clothes because of the intense hear. "You should've heard them Frenchmen hooting and laughing when they saw everybody wearing long drawers!" said Richard. "I mean, there wuz the Frenchmen parading around in their boxer shorts and singlets and we were dressed like polar bears! And they began jeering us... ohhh, boy, did they laugh and I was spitting mad because me buddies never said a word! I had no intention of every letting them see my drawers because, you see, mom dyed 'em red and I was red all over from sweating! No siree... I vowed I wouldn't give 'em the chance to laugh at me, so I ignored 'em and kept my clothes on!"

One young man kept bugging him to show everybody his longjohns and Richard became so angry that he told him he was wearing fancy shorts that came from the French islands of St. Pierre and Miquelon. Naturally, the Frenchman taunted him even more then and insisted that Richard show them to everyone. Richard realized he had to save face, for his pride wouldn't let him back down. Fully clothed and almost dead with heat, he lay awake wondering how to get out of the lie he told. They had to leave early next morning and it galled him to go without getting back at that Frenchman who called his bluff. During the night he got up to make himself a cup of tea and have a bit of his mom's partridgeberry jam. He spilled the jam on his shirt and try as he might, the stain wouldn't come out. And that's when the bright idea hit Richard!

"Quiet as I could, I crawled under the Frenchman's bunk,

opened his suitcase and stole two pairs of his white shorts and cut the tags off. Then I boiled the kettle, put some jam in water with one pair of shorts and a few Dodd's Kidney pills in with the other and let 'em soak for awhile!" Richard chuckled. "My sonny boy… they was a sight to behold when I took 'em out! One was dyed a dark red from the berry juice and the other was a pale green from the stuff in the pills. Now we're talking fancy drawers!"

So, up through the hatch onto the roof he went and hung them out to dry. Peeling off his itchy long johns in the darkness, Richard laughed silently as he stuffed his drawers down into the chimney. All he could think of was what would happen when the Frenchmen lit the fire for breakfast in the morning. As planned, Richard was awake before the others and he made sure everybody saw him, wearing his red shorts. His buddies were astounded, but Richard silenced them with a wink. "When the young fella woke up, his eyes nearly popped out of his head when he saw me shorts. He sat bolt upright in his bunk and right on cue, I pulls out the green shorts and throws 'em at him." Richard laughed.

"Look… just to show there's no hard feelings, you can have a pair of me shorts from St. Pierre… but just don't go around bragging where you got 'em, okay buddy?" I says.

Richard never forgot that feeling of satisfaction when the Frenchman, not recognizing his own shorts, thanked him and shook his hand. As one last magnanimous gesture, Rich offered to light the fire and just before the smoke screen started, he and his Newfoundland buddies made their escape. That is, of course, according to Richard… the spinner of yarns!

# Fair Game

I've always maintained that anytime there are more than two Newfoundlanders in one room you're bound to hear an interesting conversation. Add a few more friends who are living away from the island and you are definitely in for a grand old time of reminiscing and storytelling.

Like most of us who have moved away from our native surroundings, when we get together we tend to talk affectionately about "home," for family and friends are always on our minds. Recently I found some notes I'd made for a storyline back in 1989 when my husband was working on a hydro project in Wawa, Ontario. There were at least 100 Newfoundlanders on the site as well and, naturally, we got to know all of them. As I read through my notes, I couldn't help but chuckle at some of the stories I'd heard from them. So I've decided to tell you about one particular night when we went to dinner with a few people from Head of Bay d'Espoir.

As it was an evening get-together for a big scoff of rabbit stew, the conversation naturally centred around hunting and snaring rabbits. As usual, the menfolk got to bragging about their hunting skills and before long the conversation became very lively as they tried to top each other's stories about the "moose that got away" or "you should have seen the size of it."

One young man who was trying to get a word in edgewise to tell his story cleared his throat loudly. "I rescued a rabbit from a snare one time that had his leg severed, so I made a wooden leg for 'im and then I let 'im go," Howard said smugly.

With all eyes finally on Howard, he told in great detail how several years later he spotted that same rabbit running through the woods and it was still wearing the wooden leg. "Matter of fact," Howard ventured, "a couple of years later, that same rabbit got caught in my snares again and he freed hisself by chewing off his wooden leg and leaving only a piece of wood in the trap!"

That drew a round of laughter until someone asked how he knew it was the same rabbit. "There was no mistake, m'son, 'cause I had carved me initials in the wooden leg that I made fer 'im years ago."

Nobody could get Howard to admit that somewhere in Bay d'Espoir there is not a three-legged rabbit, faster and smarter than any four-legged one, still roaming through the woods just daring any hunter to catch him.

Well, that story called for a rebuttal, so another Newfoundlander, Doug, told us how he and his friends got even with another hunter who, in their opinion, needed to be taught a lesson in sportsmanship. These men usually went rabbit hunting together and they shared whatever they snared, for rabbits were plentiful that year. Then quite suddenly their luck changed and for several weeks they saw neither hide nor tail of a hare. Discouraged, the men would go back empty-handed and discuss it over a drink at the local bar.

There was one chap, whom everybody called Tricky, who came to the club for the sole purpose of boasting about all the rabbits he was getting and to scrounge a free beer. "Ole Tricky bragged so much that people started placing bets on who caught the most rabbits in a week...and every time he won, we had to fork over our money to that sleeveen!" Doug told us.

What angered Doug and his buddies even more was that he didn't even offer to buy anybody a beer, despite the fact that his wallet was full of money from the bets. According to Doug, the man was so smooth that the bartender had to think twice about it before taking Tricky's cash.

When Tricky started selling rabbits on the run, folks actually paid him for the rabbits he hadn't even caught yet. But every day the other guys would check their snares and not one rabbit would be found. Finally it dawned on them that something was amiss, especially when their snares were empty, yet Tricky's full traps were barely a hundred yards from theirs. That's when they realized that Tricky was stealing their rabbits and lining his pockets with their money...so they decided to turn the table on him.

Carefully they made their plans and enlisted the help of a local policeman. Before the sun came up, they checked their snares. Sure enough, their snares were full like they used to be, so they left one rabbit for bait. One of the guys had brought along his wife's ear piercing gun and they put a stud in the rabbit's ear. Quietly they made their way back home and waited to see if Tricky would show himself for the thief that he was.

By this time, we were all captivated by Doug's story and there was not a sound in the room as he told us how Tricky came into the bar with a sack over his shoulder and his eyes popping out on his cheeks. They pretended they never saw him and instead they crowded around a poster on the wall. "Boys, you'll never believe what I got to show you!" Tricky said breathlessly. "Because dis is the queerest ting I ever saw in all me born days."

The boys deliberately ignored him as Doug read aloud what was on the poster. "Imagine that...a reward for a stupid rabbit!" he said, making sure Tricky could hear him.

Sure enough, Tricky's ears perked up. "Reward? What kind of reward are ye talking about?" he asked.

"Well, some fella from the States brought a special breed of rabbit to Newfoundland to see if it could survive here...as an experiment, you know," he said casually. "There's a marker in its ear and he's offering a big reward for whoever finds it...dead or alive!"

Tricky's jaw dropped open like an oven door. "Holy Geez...I

caught 'im boys! I got 'im right here in me sack!" he squealed. "And as God is me judge, the bugger's got a gold stud in 'is ear!"

Tricky was beside himself with excitement as he grappled to untie the sack. In keeping with the charade, the guys scoffed and laughed. "Go on with ya m'son," they said. "Nobody will ever find that rabbit!"

When he pulled out the rabbit and pointed to the stud in the ear, everybody feigned surprise and quite naturally urged him to go to the police station to collect the reward. Just before Tricky left, he gleefully threw money on the bar.

"Drinks are on me, ye unlucky devils," he said, "and when I gets me reward money, I'll buy ye all another round!"

Well, the guys could only imagine the look on Tricky's face when he found he had been set up, especially since their friend, the Mountie, was on duty. Not only did Tricky not have a licence, but he brought in the evidence to convict himself of stealing. 'Course the men had no intention of laying charges against Tricky, for they only wanted to give him a taste of his own medicine. That in itself was reward enough for them...that and the free beer.

I never really knew for sure if they were telling tall tales that night or not, so I chalked it up to the sense of humour that sustains us homesick Newfoundlanders. Either way, we had a wonderful evening and a good belly laugh.

"After all, Lucy, it was open season," Doug declared with a playful glint in his eye, "and that's what I call fair game."

# Voices of the Past

Every time I hear those familiar words sung on the eve of a new year, I always get misty-eyed. All I can think about is that another year has flown by and I haven't done any of the things I'd planned on doing. This year in particular, I started thinking about all the wonderful people I have known in my life and it made me feel happy and sad at the same time. That's why, when the calendar flipped over at midnight and ushered in the year 2001, I already knew what my New Year's resolution would be.

Usually I don't bother, for whenever I make promises to myself, I seldom ever follow through on them. Most of the time it is because my heart's not in it, but this year, I solemnly resolved to keep in touch with all of my friends, old and new. After I returned from my trip to Newfoundland in November where I saw many of my friends I hadn't seen in a long time, I realized just what I was missing in my life. It was that connection we formed as children, the bond that ties people together for life. Although miles and years had separated us in the past, when we talked and reminisced about our younger days, the thought of all that I'd missed by not being around them made me sit up and take notice. From now on, I want to remember all the friends and acquaintances who have touched my life. That's my New Year's resolution.

Auld Lang Syne. Old friends, good old days, times remembered with fondness, long time ago. All of these expressions reflect the meaning of those three little words, and to me, they speak volumes. Lifetime relationships teach lifetime lessons, and those are the ones that always remain with us.

Whenever I go home to Newfoundland now and look around Lord's Cove, it saddens me to know that so many of the people I knew and loved have long since passed on.

In any small community where everybody knows each other, the absence of even one person affects everybody, for a link of the chain has been broken and it cannot be replaced. Out of sight is certainly not out of mind in our communities. Oh, no, the memory of every person is always kept in the form of stories and tales related. And that is the greatest tribute to life that I can imagine.

Each time I go back home, it seems there is always another person missing from that chain, and this year was no exception. One of my mom's best friends had recently passed on, and since she was always the one I visited first, it was strange not having her there anymore. Aunt Sis, as we called her, was Mom's card partner and for as long as I remember, they always played Rook, their favourite game. Even when Mom was almost 80 years old and Aunt Sis was 83, when it came to a Rook game, they could play till the wee hours of the morning – if they were winning, that is. They hated to lose to the men. Even now, I chuckle when I think about how they'd bicker at each other.

"Ahh, Sis, you makes me some mad, not going slam when you had the first bid!" Mom would say. "Sure you knows they're gonna win now...you're not paying attention at all d'night!"

Then Aunt Sis would throw her cards on the table. "You want me to go slam on the cards I got here? I wouldn't serve the like of dat to a starving nun, my dear!"

"Humph! I've seen you go slam with only one trump in your hand, Sis, so don't give me that excuse."

"Ahh, grow up will you, Lottie, grow up!" Aunt Sis would snap back and then, as always, they'd look at each other and start laughing.

I've always thought that we were blessed growing up in a close-knit community, for we had the opportunity of having some wonderful storytellers to amuse us. Whether or not they realized it at the time, those people passed on a legacy to us, for the art of storytelling is a great gift. It was such a treat to listen to the stories the older folks would tell, especially if they acted it out. It was like we had a live theatre group right in our midst; their tone of voice, their energy and body language gave each story a whole new dimension.

My father told me about a man he knew in Lamaline who'd get so excitable when he was telling a story that he often got into trouble. Once, when he was telling about the moose that got away, he demonstrated in the neighbour's kitchen and showed them how he crawled on his belly, hid behind a tree and then surprised the moose. Using a broom as a prop for his rifle and the wood stove as a tree, he re-enacted every small detail; and when he suddenly jumped up and aimed his gun at the startled animal, the broom hit the chair behind him, knocked it over and he fell backwards under the table. He almost overturned the table with the dishes on it trying to get to his feet, and the hostess, not at all impressed by his theatrics, grabbed the broom from him and chased him out the door. Who knows, had his raw talent not been nipped in the bud, he might have been our first movie star.

Storytelling was the most common way of amusing and entertaining each other. Often, stories were told in the form of a ballad, a song or in recitation; but no matter what, the delivery was always spellbinding. Much to our delight, some told tales that were purely fabricated, others spun yarns that they heard from their forefathers, and others still related true-life stories for the simple purpose of amusing others. And their sense of humour was very heartwarming, for getting a good laugh was the ultimate compliment. Nobody needed a stage to perform on. Most of the time these stories were told during normal conversation sitting around in each other's kitchens or at an impromptu get-together.

There were two women in particular that I loved to listen to when I was a teenager, and they always took the time to sit and talk no matter when you visited. Mrs. Josephine Lambe and Mrs. Kate Harriett could tell ghostly tales that would make your hair stand on end one minute and the next, they'd have you laughing until your sides hurt.

There were far too many great storytellers to mention, most of whom are now deceased, but I used to hang on every word uttered when Esau King from Lamaline or Mick Slaney from Point May came to visit. Both of these men could make the cats laugh once they started, and it wasn't as much that they told funny stories, but it was the way they expressed themselves. Other people, like Robbie Walsh from the Cove and Ches Maddigan from Lamaline, could belt out wonderful songs, while others entertained by reciting ballads and long verses passed on from their parents. They were wonderful entertainers, and although they may not have known it then, they were giving us a gift that would not soon be forgotten.

Even now when I go home, I see the evidence of that wonderful way that people can amuse and delight without even realizing it. I always used to go visit Richard Hennebury because I knew he was one of the greatest storytellers I've ever known and his sense of humour was uncomparable. My, how that man could make me laugh with his constant quips and colourful language! I always came away from his house feeling on top of the world, but he, too, is gone now and I still miss him. However, Richard's sense of humour was not restricted to him alone, for his brother Fred has the same gift. I like to visit him now and his knack for turning a phrase or making a statement is chock full of natural comedic wit. When I inquired about his health, he told me he was doing well. "The old legs are giving out on me, my dear, but like I told you before, the brain is still in excellent shape 'cause it's never been used yet."

While we talked, Fred's little dog came over and wagged his

tail in delight. "He loves the women, you know, Lucy," he grinned. "Every morning he puts on his tie and aftershave, slicks back his hair in the looking glass and off he goes. He's a real good boy, aren't you, me son?" he said, patting the mutt on the head.

A few minutes later, he found the dog pulling the stuffing out of the bottom of the couch where he was trying to retrieve a rubber ball. Fred stamped his foot and the dog's ears flattened. "That's it, I'm sending you off to reform school for being a bad boy," he scolded. "Now you get in there and pack your grip while I calls a taxi."

Only Fred Hennebury can deliver a statement like that with a straight face, and that's why he makes me laugh so much. Just being around people like him with a sense of humour is like comfort food for me, and there's no doubt in my mind that we all need that kind of nourishment.

Call me sentimental if you will, but I like remembering everything about the past, and I enjoy making new friends and spending time with old ones. I want to make sure that even though those times we knew cannot come again, at least we can keep the memories alive. We owe it to the people who have gone before us to let them know that their lives made a difference to all of us, that their voices of the past will remain a part of our future. I know I want to remember, just for old times' sake.

# Tell Me a Story

Storytelling is a wonderful art form, isn't it? I can't imagine how dull life would be without stories and tall tales to entertain us. For young children, listening to parents or grandparents tell a story or read to them can be a memorable experience. Not only does it form a strong bond between them, but it also stimulates their imagination and teaches them valuable listening skills.

The more I think about it, the more I realize how powerful storytelling can be. Just the sheer pleasure of hearing someone relate a tale that makes the listener experience emotion is a gift in itself.

As a parent, I discovered that there was nothing more satisfying than sitting in my rocking chair and having my young sons curl up in my lap while I read to them. Just seeing the delight on their faces was reward enough for me, for it was evident that not only were they listening to every word I read, but they were enthralled with the tales of things they had yet to discover.

Just the other day I came across a little story my oldest son had written when he was very young. Most of his spelling was incorrect, but he had actually remembered things I'd told him about my childhood in Newfoundland. I smiled to myself when I read the beginning line, for it sounded very familiar. "Once 'pon a time there was a little girl who lived by the sea in Lord's cove. Her name wuz Lucy but now it's Mommie."

Goodness, how my sons loved stories that started with "Once upon a time." Every time I sat down for a cup of tea, one of them would be there begging for a story. No matter what mood they were in, I could always rely on reading to them or telling them a story to help them sleep, to soothe a scratch or a bruise, or just to comfort them. It was amazing how retelling an old story or inventing a new one just for them made my children forget what it was that ailed them.

Like my sons, I was intrigued whenever someone told me a story, for the art of storytelling was very much alive when I was a child in Newfoundland. We didn't have books of fairy tales or television to entertain us. We had something better. We had a whole community of natural storytellers in our midst, and with it came a heritage of traditions and folklore to be passed on to their children and grandchildren. Not only were their tales entertaining, but they chronicled the lives of their ancestors by way of the spoken word in songs, recitations, poetry and drama. They didn't just tell a story – they re-enacted the events to make it all the more interesting. They had a flare for drama and could bring even the most mundane event to life.

Oh yes, Newfoundlanders are known for their flamboyant style of storytelling. They can bring a tear to your eye with a sad tale one minute, and the next they'll have you writhing in laughter with their comical sayings. And that was an added gift, for theirs were stories of real people who had real life experiences. Elderly people were always interesting, for they had a wealth of information to impart to the younger generation. They told of hardship in raising large families, of midwives delivering babies and husbands and sons getting lost at sea. They talked of disasters on the ocean, of being snowed in for weeks at a time, and about how they depended solely on the land and the sea to keep their families fed. When they told their stories, we listened and we remembered.

I suppose that's why I liked being around adults, for I was always eager to hear them spin yarns. Every time a different person retold a story, it changed – some tales got bigger and others were embellished to please the listeners. I remember how I'd sit quietly, just waiting for the one-liner that promised a good story. "Do you mind the time when that strange looking box from a German submarine washed up in Job's Cove? Now that was the queerest 'ting I ever saw."

Now who wouldn't be intrigued with that introduction? From there on, others would contribute and the storytelling could go on all evening. "I s'pose I told you about the time me and me grandfather nearly drowned when the horse and slide fell through the ice, did I? No? Well sit down 'til I tells ya."

Most of the older people were superstitious and it rubbed off on us as well. How I loved a good ghost story! What better setting for an eerie story than on a pitch-black night with the wind howling and rattling the shingles and windows in an old house? My sisters and I loved listening to tales of the unknown even though they scared the bejeepers out of us. We always dreaded All Souls Day, for we believed on that night the souls in Purgatory came back to Earth to ask for prayers so they could get into heaven.

One night a neighbour dropped in and he related a story I will never forget. It was late at night when he decided to go to the church to pray for the deceased. When he started to cross the bridge below the church, he suddenly felt the hair rise on the back of his neck. He swore that he saw a ghostly figure following him and when he tried to run, he felt something pulling him back, rooting him to the spot. Hard as he tried, his feet wouldn't move and when a sudden cold wind swept around him, he started to pray for the lost souls. "In the name of the Father, the Son and the Holy Ghost," he prayed.

As soon as he made the sign of the cross, he heard a terrible shriek that made him fall to his knees and cover his ears. "I knows it was the devil himself, trying to stop me from getting to the church and saving some poor soul," he told us.

My brother Raphael remembers a real incident from when he was a teenager that jangled his nerves a little. One evening as he walked past the graveyard, he noticed a thin line of smoke coming up from one of the graves. Despite being a little afraid, he crept up to where the smoke was coming from and peered into a half-dug grave. To his surprise, he discovered Mr. Walsh, an elderly gentleman stretched out full length in the dirt, smoking his pipe. Thinking he had fallen in, Raphael asked if he was hurt. "No, m'son. I'm alright," he replied calmly. "I was just trying 'er out for size."

Apparently Mr. Walsh wanted to dig his own grave to make sure that his coffin would fit properly when his time came. As I recall, though, it took years before he actually was laid to rest in his personalized grave.

I wish I could remember all the wonderful yarns I'd heard over the years of growing up in Newfoundland. It's only now when I'm older that I fully realize how important storytelling is to our heritage, for it helps us define who we are as individuals. Nobody wants to be forgotten, so it's only natural that we reminisce about loved ones and days gone by. Sometimes, I think back to those days when Mom would be sitting at the spinning wheel telling us stories just like I did with my own sons and it all makes sense. That's what gives meaning to our lives. Now whenever I hear the words "tell me a story" it carries a lifetime of memories for me and, in my heart, I know they will be repeated again and again. I hope those wonderful words will last a lifetime.

# Animal House

During a recent visit with my friend Teresa here in Niagara Falls, our conversation kept getting interrupted by her chatty parrot, Rocky, who repeats everything she says. This is a bird that likes attention. "Can you sing something for Lucy this morning?" Teresa asked her feathered friend.

Right on cue, Rocky belted out his favourite song, "I'se The B'y." When I thanked him, he repeated my exact words: "Oh, Rocky…you're a real charmer, you are!"

Teresa chuckled at him. "You're not supposed to thank yourself!"

At 78 years old, Teresa Davey (nee Anderson) loves her pets: three dogs and eight birds, including her beloved parrot. Teresa grew up in Burgeo, Newfoundland, and her family had all kinds of domestic animals just as we did in Lord's Cove. Horses, sheep, cows, hens and pigs were an integral part of every community. Some were work animals, others a food source; all were treated with the greatest respect, as each and every one was a precious commodity.

In the summertime, it seemed like we were the ones who lived amongst them, for our livestock roamed freely all over the Cove. It wasn't unusual to see a horse with his head stuck in an open kitchen window looking for treats, or to see hens and lambs following someone into their house. I remember my sisters and I walking the cows to the marsh in the morning to graze and then going to fetch them again for the evening milking. "Why can't we just wait for the cows to come home themselves?" I'd whine to Mom.

"Because cows are right stunned and they got no sense of

direction!" she'd say. "They'll stay in the same place all day long chewing on their cud unless someone heads them back home again."

Now horses had a mind of their own, galloping off wherever they wanted and returning home themselves. Our horse, Dick, used to let himself into the yard by nudging the rope off the gatepost with his nose. Come morning, our front yard would be filled with everybody else's animals that came to eat the scraps Mom left out for the hens, cats and dogs. Sometimes they'd knock down the clothesline and trample on the laundry she left out overnight. That got Mom's dander up and she would chase them away with a broom.

Did I ever tell you about the embarrassing encounter I had with a cow when I was a teenager? Well, one night at our Garden Party dance, I sneaked out of the hall with a boy who was visiting from the Mainland. It was a foggy night and pitch black outside, and just as I puckered up for a kiss, we were startled by a loud MOOO….and an unmistakable plop on the ground behind us. Startled, he jumped back and when he got a whiff of the stench beside us, he nearly gagged. Grabbing my hand, he started to run in the wrong direction and stepped right smack into another foul pile. I couldn't even look him in the eye when we got back inside, so I hid in the crowd until he left. So much for romance.

When it came to newborn animals, it was easy for my sisters and me to get attached to some of them, even naming the calves, lambs, piglets and chicks. By slaughter time, we'd all be screeching and begging my father to spare their lives. Goodness, how guilty we must've made him feel. "You can't kill Flossy…she's got such big, sad eyes! I promise I'll look after her, Daddy!"

Teresa, however, recalled a different side to their animals, when they weren't so charming. One day when her mother went to get vegetables from the root cellar, a weasel darted out between her feet, causing her to trip and fall in the mud. Their rooster was nearby and when he saw her mother on the ground, he pounced on her and began pecking at her with his claws. "Mom was screaming for help so I grabbed the clothesline pole and swung at the rooster, sending him flying. But he just got up, shook himself off and then came after me," Teresa said.

When her grandmother heard everybody screaming, she came running outside and the saucy rooster took chase after her. Teresa grabbed the pole again and swung at the rooster. The poor rooster never got back up again. "I felt really sad when Granny cooked him for supper and I just didn't have the heart to eat him," she said.

I remember when our hens got broody, they could get downright nasty and peck the eyes out of your head if you got near their eggs. Sometimes my father would put the broody hen in a burlap bag and hang it on the clothesline until she settled down.

The worst animal of all was probably Mr. Tom Hodge's bull. He could be cranky at the best of times. Every adult and child dreaded to see that bull and we were constantly on the lookout for him. When we saw him coming with his head down, snorting as he ran full tilt in our direction, we headed for the nearest fence and threw ourselves over it.

Often, we had other unwanted intruders like foxes and chicken hawks that preyed on the hens in their coops. That was unnerving, being awakened in the middle of the night by hens squawking in terror. Teresa told me about a time, during her early childhood, when her parents took her and her brother on a trip to the Barachois in Burgeo. They were staying in a cabin and one night they were awakened by loud noises like something or someone thrashing about. "Me and Mom were terrified, so Dad got up and fired off several shots into the darkness…and then the noise stopped," Teresa said.

Next morning when her mother went outside to get her husband's long johns that she'd hung on the bushes to dry overnight, they were gone. Her father was very annoyed that they were missing, for the weather was still chilly in early June. They concluded that someone had stolen his drawers or that they had blown away.

Months later when a man named Josh Harvey from Burgeo returned from a hunting trip near Barachois, Teresa's father asked if he had any luck finding a caribou. "No, me son...never got near a caribou, but you wouldn't believe the moose I saw up near your cabin!" Josh said.

Josh described how he came upon a huge bull moose drinking from a pond and stopped short of pulling the trigger. "You might think I'm crazy or that I drank too much Screech, but I couldn't shoot him...not after what I saw!"

Intrigued, Teresa's father prodded Josh to continue. "I've never breathed a word of this to anybody else before, but as God is my witness, when that moose raised his head he was wearing a pair of long johns on over a full set of antlers!"

In retrospect, I think that the very presence of animals living among us gave us a sense of belonging and taught us to live in harmony with nature. There was nothing more comforting than waking up in the morning to the throaty call of a rooster and hearing hens clucking, lambs bleating and the old familiar clang of a cow bell. Although those creatures of God sometimes tested our patience, we had our moments when the antics of those charmers made us chuckle. I can't help but feel that we were blessed.

# The Fitzpatricks
# of Lord's Cove

*"Home is a place you grow up wanting to leave,
and grow old wanting to get back to."*

– John Ed Pearce –

# John & Lottie's Crowd

Whenever my father talked about our family, he proudly referred to us as "our crowd." All nine of us looked alike, so everybody recognized us as being "John and Lottie's youngsters."

There was a vast difference in our ages. I'm the "baby" of the family and my eldest sister is 16 years older. Mom always maintained that the four boys were easier to raise. "Glory be to God, you girls nearly drove me foolish with your argin and fighting!" I once heard her say. "But not the boys, there was never a contrary word out of them...never!"

Like most siblings, one minute my sisters and I acted like we hated each other and the next, we were ready to take on the world together. Sure we competed for attention, but we've always remained the best of friends. Our brothers were literally our keepers back then, for they were all older. Helena, Leona and I were the three youngest and no matter how much we nagged them, they were always so kind and patient with us. 'Course we thought they were extra special, for each of them had endearing ways. From the eldest brother to the youngest, they each assumed the role of our protectors after one of them left home. They made sure we got to school on time, and that we wore our hats and mitts. When the power went out on stormy nights, one of them would patiently bring the kerosene lamp and wait outside the bathroom door till we'd finished our business.

After Marceline and Fred, the two oldest, left home, Raphael was our babysitter whenever our parents went out. Mom would brag that Raphael had a knack of getting us into bed early, but she didn't know that he had conspired with us to pretend to sleep, with a promise that we could get up after they left. Naturally, his plan also included his friends coming over to play cards. After the card game, the guys would give us piggyback rides and tell us stories. Raphael would cook up a big scoff for everybody, then he'd play the fiddle and the mouth organ for us. We'd be so tuckered out by then, that we'd crawl into bed and fall asleep without any fuss.

Whenever Fred came home from Vancouver, it was always a big event. I remember the year he came home with his new car. We were prouder than peacocks when he drove us around the Cove in his 1959 Morris Oxford. Fred also liked to entertain us with the button accordion and he could make a wicked pot of soup.

Then, there were our two other brothers, Harve and Louis. Harve usually entertained us with the violin and guitar. He taught me to sing all the songs he heard on the radio and we'd perform together in concerts. Whenever he went trouting or berrypicking, he could never say no to us when we begged him to take us along. 'Course sometimes we had to pretend we weren't with him if he saw girls coming our way because he wanted them to know he was no sissy.

Now Louis, the youngest of the boys, was a natural caregiver. Without any prompting, he helped us with our homework and nursed our scratched elbows and knees. Leona remembers a time when she was in third grade and Louis came to her rescue. Back then there were no bathroom facilities in the one-room school and although she needed to go badly, she was too shy to tell the teacher. To Leona's surprise, Louis stood up and informed the teacher that his sister needed to leave the room. Then he took her hand and ran all the way home with her, just in time to avoid an embarrassing accident. Years later Leona asked him how he could possibly have known her dilemma. "Didn't take much to figure it out," he drawled. "Your face was screwed up like a can of worms and you were crossing your legs and squirming in your seat."

As I recall, both Harve and Louis became very protective of us when we became teenagers and discovered boys. Sometimes they chased boys away and if that failed, they uttered the dreaded words that sent us running away with our heels hitting our backsides. "If you don't go home right now, I'm telling MOM on ya!"

Sometimes I marvel at the work our parents did before modern conveniences. My mother baked 12 loaves of bread every day, except for Sunday. They carried buckets of water from a well, did the laundry by hand and cooked on wood stoves.

I shudder when I think what Mom went through when the nine of us hit puberty. I had no clue how to help my sons through adolescence, so at the time I asked for her advice. She gave me an odd look and clicked her tongue. "Puberty! Tut...tut...sure my dear, there was none of that stuff going around when our crowd was growing up," she said. "People makes too much fuss over everything nowadays. Just leave 'em alone and they'll grow out of it, my dear."

I can't help but smile when I think about prayer time in our house. We were all on our knees on the floor of the kitchen, with rosary beads in hand, as we recited the holy rosary after supper. My father's eyes were always closed as he led us through prayer, while our cat dashed around, flicking all the beads as she went. Mom didn't realize we deliberately planted the cat there for our entertainment, but my father knew. Sometimes my sisters and I would giggle out loud, and suddenly, without changing her tone of voice, Mom would throw a warning into her prayer: "Hail Mary, full of grace...(Kate, stop laughing)...the Lord is with thee...(you, too, Helena. Stop it!)... blessed art thou amongst women..."

If that didn't work, she'd continue praying as she reached back to sock us upside the head.

My parents often lamented that they only had two photographs of the family in our younger years. When my sister got a camera, none of us wanted to pose for her. "Can't ye crowd just stand still for two minutes and get your snap took?" Mom would say in exasperation.

In one picture, some of us had our faces screwed up while others had sweaters or jackets buttoned up wrong or a petticoat showing. On the second photo, Fred and Raphael had sneaked off somewhere and my sister Marceline was taking the snap so our parents could be in it. We were standing outside our house and everybody was dressed in our Sunday best. Our parents were proudly smiling into the camera, but not us. Kate was chawing on a wad of bubblegum, Helena had her arm over her face to block out the sun, Leona had an old cap pulled down over her head and yours truly had my bottom lip puckered up from crying. Harve's face was all swollen on one side from the mumps, while Louis was busy examining his feet because he was wearing somebody else's shoes that were two times too big on him. Oh, yes...and the girl with the big smile standing beside my sister Kate was her friend. In the confusion of trying to get everybody in place, Mom apparently thought she was one of our crowd and pulled her into the line-up.

We still have that black-and-white photo. Our parents and our brother Harve have since passed away, so it is one of our most cherished possessions. And if you look at the back of that snap, written in my mother's handwriting are the words that sum up our family; endearing words that we'd heard all of our lives: "John and Lottie's crowd."

# You Knows Me...Don't You?

I wasn't always named Lucy, you know. When I was baptized almost 46 years ago, my godmother named me Nora. You see, the priest looked after three parishes and never scheduled times for christenings. Often he'd show up unexpectedly to baptize new babies. So one day when Mrs. Rita Walsh came to tell Mom that the priest was waiting in the sacristy, Mom didn't have time to find assigned godparents, so Mrs. Rita offered to be my godmother. Mom was too sick to go to the church and my father was out fishing so by the time a sponsor was found, my godmother had to scravel to get me to the church on time. It wasn't until the ceremony started and the priest asked for my name that Mrs. Rita realized that she forgot to ask Mom. So she said the first name that popped into her head... Nora. Half an hour later, unbeknownst to Mom, I was back in my crib with a new identity. It took my godmother an hour to muster up the nerve to tell Mom about my name, especially after she found out that I was to have been named after my aunt who had recently died. On the very next Sunday, Mom went to the priest and told him about the mistake. A new birth certificate was drawn up and I was renamed Lucy Marie.

Unlike today, choosing godparents back then wasn't a big deal. Everybody in the Cove was related to each other, so practically everybody was suitable to be godparents. Every adult made it their business to reprimand the youngsters if they got into mischief anyways, and it wasn't at all unusual to see some poor soul being marched home to their parents by the scruff of the neck. We didn't have a prayer in hell of getting away with anything. Sometimes when parents ran out of aunts, uncles and godparents, a guardian was chosen at random. The womenfolk were always at home, but when a godfather was needed, one could usually be found out mowing hay, splitting fish or mending nets. It didn't matter what they were doing when called upon – they'd drop everything and go to the church.

Looking back now, I pity the people who had been godparents a dozen times over, for they always had trouble remembering who they stood to. But the youngsters were always there to remind them, especially on birthdays or at Christmas. That's when a social visit was in order, despite the fact that they never set foot inside the godparents' house all year long. 'Course the object of the visit was to get a little special attention or maybe even a token gift. And even if you didn't get something, you knew you'd at least be invited in for a piece of fresh bread and molasses or a pork bun. And no youngster would dare let on to their mother about the visit, for if she found out, you'd risk getting into trouble for being so brazen. The godmother was first on the list because they seemed to have better memories than the menfolk about their godchildren. It was imperative, of course, to bring along a friend for moral support and to keep an eye out for your mother. Naturally you'd want to look your best, so you'd pause a minute to dip your hand in the barrel of water in the porch, slick back the front of your hair and give the nose a quick wipe on your sleeve before stepping into the kitchen. Often as not, the godmother wouldn't remember your birthday or even that she's your godmother. And nothing could be more devastating than to have your godmother peer at you and ask that dreaded question: "Who owns you, my dear?"

And if that happened, you'd very subtly remind her. "You knows me, don't you… sure you're my godmudder."

After that, it was on to find the godfather. They were always generous in a different way. Your friend played a crucial role here, for the menfolk always had to be reminded of your birthday. The old nudge in the ribs prompted your accomplice to drop a hint and chances were that your godfather would dig into his pocket and give you 10 cents or at least a few coppers. And we all knew what that could buy back then. Off you went to the shop to buy bubblegum or candy, making sure that the shopkeeper put them in a bag so you could show everybody what your godfather gave you.

Maybe it was because of the mix-up in my name at birth, but my godmother never forgot my birthday. And yes, I, too, was guilty of making an annual trip to Mrs. Rita's house, because she usually had something tucked away for me. Even though she had eight youngsters of her own, she made sure there was a gift under her tree for me at Christmas as well, and she always picked the biggest red apple from the barrel and polished it on her apron before she gave it to me.

But not everyone was as lucky as I was. Take my friend, Helen, who lived down behind the hill from me. Neither of her godparents lived in the Cove, so she never got any presents. To top it all, her birthday fell on Christmas Day, so the occasion went unnoticed. The closest time she came to getting something on her birthday was when she was eight years old and even that was a mistake. A man who had been away in Halifax for a few years came to their house one Christmas Day to see his godchild. Assuming the man knew who his godchild was, Helen's mother directed him into the parlour where Helen and her younger sister, Yvonne, were playing. He went up to Helen and said he was her godfather. Right away, she knew he had made a mistake. She was about to tell him when he handed her a beautifully wrapped box, and she was so overwhelmed by the size of it she couldn't speak. When he insisted that she open it, she did. As she shamefacedly recalls now, she knew exactly what she was doing. "I figured that if he didn't remember who his godchild was, then maybe nobody else would. And I desperately wanted to see what was inside that box, so I tore open the box and found the most beautiful doll I had ever seen." But alas, her mother came into the parlour and took the doll from her. What a dido she kicked up when her mother gave it to Yvonne! The poor man felt so guilty that he gave Helen 25 cents to make her stop crying. And she didn't even mind the stings of her mother's hands on her backside, for she was thinking about what she could buy with her money.

But she learned her lesson and even in later years, she made sure that the incident of the mistaken identity never recurred. Who could blame her, what with having 14 brothers and sisters? She'd walk into somebody's house and before they had a chance to ask her who she belonged to, she'd stick out her chin, give them the hairy eyeball and say her usual words: "You knows me... don't you?"

# The Old Rocking Chair

Almost every house in outport Newfoundland had one. Ours sat in the most prestigious spot in the kitchen near the wood stove and never stood still from morning 'till night, as one person after another sat and rocked for a spell. Even after everybody retired for the night, it was never vacant, for one of our cats was usually waiting to curl up on the cushion for a snooze.

There's no doubt about it, our old rocking chair has personality all its own. The faded varnish on the arm rests, the worn canvas beneath the rockers and the hooked floor mat with the foot imprints on it, told the story of a chair that weathered the ups and downs of three generations of our family. My, how I loved that chair. It was roomy and comfortable enough to accommodate any size person. The high back was ideal for resting your head on and the arms wide enough for an adult to cradle a sleeping child. The rockers were perfectly curved to withstand the endless rocking motion of boisterous children climbing in and out of it all day long, but safe enough to keep it from tipping when two children sat double-decker in it for the thrill of a fast ride. Over the years of constant use by our parents, the nine of us youngsters and every other person who came into our kitchen, that rocker was the most sought-after chair in the house. It became a very important part of our family.

As far as I can gather, I became addicted to the comforting motion of being rocked even before I was born, for Mom herself often took refuge in the rocking chair to ease her aching back. As an infant, I slept in a cradle that swung back and forth and when I wasn't in there, somebody was usually rocking me in the chair. Since I was the baby of the family, I suspect it was safer and more convenient for someone to hold me because there was always a crowd in our kitchen and they had to keep me from being trampled on. It's no wonder I was never content to sit on an ordinary chair, because I loved the feeling of movement. "You couldn't sit still for more than a minute," Mom used to tell me. "You were like a worm…always squirming around and fidgeting. And as you got older, you wanted to be rocking all the time and you'd be mad as a broody hen if somebody else got to it before you."

It was just recently in a telephone conversation with my brother in Vancouver, that Raphael inadvertently admitted that he was the one who actually got me "hooked," as he called it, on the rocking chair before I was even two years old. He was barely 13 then and he kept offering to babysit me on almost every Saturday night to get my parents out of the house so he could have his friends in to play cards and have a bit of fun. He chose me because he knew that they could make all the racket they wanted; if I happened to wake up, he knew exactly what to do to keep me quiet. As soon as I'd start fussing or crying, he'd tie me safely in the rocker with mom's apron, pull me beside the table and keep the rocker moving with his foot until the game was over. He had just started playing the guitar and the fiddle, then too, so they'd sit around singing and making a lot of noise, which, according to Raphael, seemed to amuse me immensely. His friends even took turns moving the rocker when my brother's foot got tired.

"All I had to do was stick the soother in your mouth, lace it with a bit of molasses once in a while and keep the rocker moving. You'd sit there all night and never make a sound," he said. "And by the time Mom and Daddy got home, I'd have you tucked in bed and sound asleep."

And to think that all those years I've been bragging to my sisters that Raphael sang and played just for me because he thought I was special. I suppose, though, I should be grateful to him, because I still love sitting in my rocking chair and it has always been my greatest source of comfort.

Goodness, if our old rocking chair could talk, what tales and secrets it would have to tell! It travelled more miles than a spaceship and never left the corner of the kitchen, except when one of us rocked it so hard that it moved across the floor to the opposite wall. No matter which family member was sitting in it, we had to get up and offer the chair to every visitor because that was the best seat in the house. That particular chair holds many memories, for it was passed on from my grandmother to my mother. Over the years, my grandparents and my parents rocked away the hurts, pains and fears of children and it got all of us through many good times and bad times. Not only did it offer comfort, but it was a worry chair and a griping chair as well, for neighbours and friends sat there to talk about their joys and sorrows, to express their opinions or to unburden their troubles.

Through our teenage years, Mom rocked anxiously many a night as she waited for one of us to come home after a dance. Like many women in the Cove, she had her share of uneasy moments where she alternately paced the floor and rocked as she waited to hear the putter of a dory's engine when my father and brothers got caught in a storm at sea.

Old men smoking pipes told stories of the sea from there as we children sat spellbound by every word. Elderly ladies who were simply passing time rocked gently and reminisced about days gone by. That rocking chair heard many different voices crooning a lullaby or belting out an Irish ditty in its day. From that chair, my father played the fiddle for us, took his little power naps in between work or after supper and made splits to light the fire before he retired for the night. I spent many hours as a little girl, sitting in my father's arms while he rocked me and sang to me. It was only when my legs grew longer than his, that I reluctantly left the security of his arms and went solo. Every chance I got, I'd be quat up in that chair, rocking to my heart's content. At times I practically came to blows with anybody who tried to get me out of there. Call it "squatters' rights" if you will, but I claimed that chair as my own. I remember sitting Indian style with my legs tucked beneath me and prodding the arms with my elbows to keep the chair moving while I listened to the radio, read comic books and studied for a school test. When we first got a television when I was in high school, it went in the kitchen during the winter because the parlour was too cold. I'd sit rocking and biting my nails if there was a scary show on. I'd rock faster as the excitement grew until Mom would holler at me and scare the be-jeepers out of me. "Yer getting on me nerves, Lucy! Now stop rocking so hard before you breaks the chair."

But alas, it wasn't I who eventually broke that rocking chair. Raphael was the culprit… and I didn't help matters either. I was 15 when it happened and he had come home for a visit from Vancouver that winter. When the two of us got together, we always laughed a lot but after he'd had a drink or two, he giggled at everything. One night when he came home after a party, Mom was furious with him because he was supposed to have been home earlier in the evening to drive her to Lamaline and, of course, he was having so much fun, he forgot. The madder she got at him for laughing, the more he giggled and when he tried to sit in the rocking chair, he tipped it over and both went crashing to the floor. Perhaps it was the age of it or because it had so many miles on it, but the chair fell apart like match sticks beneath his weight. I managed to haul him upright, but he went flying ass-over-kettle again and we both took to laughing so hard that when I tried to pull him up again, I fell on top of him and flattened what was left of our rocker. It was beyond repair. Let me tell you, Mom didn't take kindly to our snickering at the situation and we both felt the broom handle across our backsides as we scravelled to our feet. We regretted the whole incident, but it happened and we couldn't change that. Still and all, Daddy immediately bought another chair somewhere and as much as I missed the old one, I had the new one broken in within the same day.

It's true that none could replace the sentimental value of that first rocking chair, but it did, however, lay the foundation for another generation as each of us married and brought a new child home to be rocked into contentment by their grandparents. I carried on the tradition of rocking my own boys when they were little and I hope they will do the same when one day they have children of their own. And that second chair that my father bought... well, it is still in Newfoundland where it belongs, for my sister, Helena, still uses it. It sits in her family room right next to her wood stove and every time I go home and sit in it, I can still feel the presence of my parents and it makes me feel warm inside.

The rocking chair. To me it is the most regal of them all.

# My Father's Legacy

Just recently I came across an old cassette tape of my father playing his violin. It was made before he died 14 years ago and as I sat listening to him, I felt like it was the first time I had heard him play. It wasn't, of course, for I had heard his music all my life, but I think it was the first time I had actually listened with my heart and not with my ears. His "fiddle," as he called it, was his most prized possession and his music gave him great joy. I closed my eyes and visualized him sitting in the rocking chair, with his old fiddle tucked beneath his chin and his square-tipped fingers coaxing soft melancholy sounds from the fine strings.

My father was a fisherman and it always amazed me how his huge, calloused hands could make such wonderful sounds from four small strings. I remember asking him once how he made it look so easy. "It's all in the fingers and the bow and the way you tunes 'er up," he said as he put the violin in my hands. "The trick is to press on the strings hard enough to get just the right pitch, but you got to make sure the touch of the bow is light enough to bring out the tone and sound. You got to make it all work together, you see."

I didn't understand what he meant back then, for I never learned to play that amazing instrument, but after I listened to his tape that day, I felt that I had finally grasped the concept of the fiddle and bow working together to make beautiful music. It occurred to me that my father lived his life centred around making things work for his family, for just as his violin was his pride and joy, he cherished and loved each of us in his own unique way. We admired our father for may things, not just because he found a way to spread his attention and affection between the nine of us, but because he made each of us feel like we were the most important people on earth. He had the ability to look on the positive side of life and he always found time to do things with us, no matter how busy or tired he was. My Father loved Sunday afternoons when we were kids because he would take us trouting or berry-picking. Oh, my, I can still smell the aroma of the tea brewing in the kettle on the open fire and waiting for him to cut up thick slices of Mom's homemade bread. It didn't matter to us if we did anything at all, because we were quite content just to hang around him or listen to the stories he told about the olden days.

My father was an easy man to get along with and, more importantly, he was kind and pleasant, yet he knew when to be firm if we crossed the line. His most admirable quality was his patience and, trust me, when all of us kicked up a di-do about something or argued amongst ourselves, he was the one who sorted things out without taking sides with any one of us. He never cared how many of our friends we brought home and on most weekends, every bed was filled from top to bottom. On Sunday morning, he had his own method of getting everybody out of bed in a hurry. He'd stand at the foot of the stairs and call out each of our names and if he had to do it a second time, he expected to hear our feet hitting the floor. "Everybody up for church now before I sends yer mother up there with the broom!" he'd say.

Then he'd pause a minute. "...And if there's anybody else up there that's not one of my crowd, you'd better get down here, too, because you're going to church with us!"

Oh, yes, family always came first with my father and no matter what, he supported each of us in everything we did. He tried to give us advice and guide us the best way he knew how and even if we chose to do things our own way, he let us make our own mistakes. That takes a very strong, wise person to step back from a situation when it involves someone you love.

Recently, I saw someone in the news who reminded me of my father. It was Wayne Gretzky's father, Walter. As I watched Wayne announcing his retirement, I was struck by the fact that the word DAD rolled off his tongue whenever the media asked about his accomplishments as a sports figure. And when THE GREAT ONE was not on the screen, his father was there expressing his admiration and esteem for his son. Walter made sure that his son knew he supported him in what was probably the most important decision of Wayne's life. I've never been interested in any kind of sports, nor have I ever followed the career of any celebrity, but as I listened to father and son interact, I felt that there was a special bond between them that stretched far beyond the game of hockey. I sensed it was something even deeper than friendship. It was a mutual love and respect for each other that could only be cultivated through years of happiness, sadness and sharing a lifetime of hopes and dreams ... dreams that now have changed directions for both Wayne and his father. Wayne proudly talked about the positive influence his parents had in his life and I think his admiration for his father, in particular, was evident to everybody. When talking to his teammates and the media, he summed up that closeness in a brief sentence that spoke volumes. "There's no relationship like father and son."

# No Cure for Curiosity

"Curiosity killed the cat." I can't tell you how often that phrase was applied to me when I was growing up. I was an inquisitive child, always asking questions about everything. My curiosity nearly drove everybody right foolish. "Mom, how did the lead get inside the pencil?" I remember asking her. "Did it just grow in there?"

My father had more patience than my mother did, so he'd try to answer my queries as best he could. "Daddy, why don't the rainbows come out at night?"

"How come hens don't have teeth to chew their food?"

Sometimes he'd just look at me and grin. "What a head you got on yer shoulders, my dear...what a head! That mind of yours never stops a minute, eh?"

Now Mom had a breaking point and I learned to recognize that quick enough. When I'd see her face go all red, I knew she was vexed, so I'd take three steps backwards – Mom could whip the tea towel across your backside before you could blink an eye.

"The Lord save us...what a question box you are, Lucy! You got me nerves rubbed right raw!" she'd sometimes scold.

I've always believed that it's only natural to ask questions – the secret of our existence is to keep our intellectual curiosity sharp. After all, if you don't ask why or why not, then you'll never know the answer. Think of the excitement, the wisdom, the humour and the joy we get from pondering the little oddities of people and life in general.

Does curiosity make you smarter? I believe it does....but only after you've had the experience of doing something stupid, like sticking your finger into a mouse trap to see how it works.

I remember my sister and I wanting to find out what smoking a cigarette tasted like, so we sneaked one of Daddy's cigarettes and hid behind the stable. When I lit the match for Leona, I accidentally singed off one of her eyebrows with the flame and she landed a snock upside my head with her knuckles. When she finally let me have a turn, I inhaled the smoke so quickly that I started to gag and choke and by the time I recovered, I was a putrid green colour.

Needless to say, I never did take up smoking after that incident – nor did my sister. Although she still blames me for the one eyebrow that looks more sparse than the other.

Even now as I think about things, I realize it wasn't just idle curiosity or boredom that made me want to know the ins and outs of everything. When I was nine, I was intrigued by everything around me. I asked questions so I could marvel at all the new things I'd learn.

Mind you, other than Mom, nobody else brought it to my attention – except for Mrs. Lambe from next door. She used to make a visit every evening after supper to chat with Mom. Being the interesting woman that she was, I'd always ask her questions...and most of the time, she'd just glare at me or ignore me totally.

Sometimes Mom would chase me out of the kitchen when there was a private matter to discuss with Mrs. Lambe – especially when it came to someone having a baby. And goodness knows, the words "pregnant" and "sex" never passed anybody's lips. Pure as the driven snow we were back then. Trying to find out where babies came from was impossible, for it was the best-kept secret around.

Personally, I believed that a stork brought babies and left them in a Carnation milk box up behind our house. My brother Raphael, on the other hand, used to think that the midwife brought them to people in her black medical bag. Some even believed that mothers found babies in the garden under a cabbage leaf. It was such a hush-hush affair that siblings in the family didn't know they were getting a new brother or a sister until they were packed off to a neighbour's house before the midwife arrived. Instead of saying that a woman was expecting a baby, adults would say she was sick and took to bed or that she had a bun in the oven.

One afternoon Mrs. Lambe came by to tell Mom that a particular unmarried girl was pregnant. When she took Mom aside and lowered her voice, my ears perked up like a puppy's. There was a lot of whispering and shaking of the heads so I moved a little closer to listen, but all I gleaned from them was that this girl was baking buns. I had just returned from that house, so I stuck in my two-cents worth and set the record straight. "Go on with ya, Mom...she's not baking buns...she got stuffed squid in the oven!"

Well, judging by the look on Mom's face, you'd think I'd slandered Joey Smallwood and the Missus looked like she was about to spit nails at me. "That youngster is gettin' some brazen!" she bellowed. "Saucy as a crackie she is, Lottie...and as far as I'm concerned, she should be seen and not heard!"

And without even knowing what I'd said wrong, Mom marched me upstairs and sent me to bed.

Shortly after that, a woman in the Cove and another in a nearby community both gave birth to twins. My sister Leona asked Mom how that could happen. "Did everybody double up like the sheep so they could get two lambs at a time?" she asked innocently.

Mom nearly dropped her cup of tea in her lap, and Leona took to her scrapers and ran upstairs with Mom at her heels.

"I thought Mom was going to yank the tongue right out of my head or wash my mouth out with lye soap," Leona told me. Not only that, she was drilled as to who was giving her ideas about babies and warned not to ever mention the matter again – to anybody.

Isn't it strange how curiosity peaks our imaginations? Even

babies are intrigued by moving objects and once they discover their little fingers, they are quite content to fit their them into their mouths or up their nostrils.

When my sister Helena was six, she got into Mom's personal things and opened a small bottle of perfume. She liked the scent so much that she poured it all over herself. Then she decided to see if the cork would fit inside her nostril. It did.

After several days, Mom noticed that Helena had a temperature. She was complaining that her nose hurt, so my parents took her to the Lamaline Clinic on the horse and cart. Once the nurse extracted the cork, Helena refused to say how it got into her nostril. After all, how can a child know why they do what they do in the name of curiosity? And who are we to question them?

Helena had an excuse ready for the cork. "It blew up m'nose while I was sleeping," she said defiantly.

Doing things in the name of curiosity leads to learning by trial and error. I remember only too well many years ago when my aunt got a new wringer washer. My cousin Lorraine and I were about 10 years old then, and we were intrigued by this new invention that replaced the wooden wash tub. We marvelled at the way the wringer squeezed the water out of the clothes...so much so that Lorraine stuck her hand into the moving wringer just to see how it worked.

Within seconds her hand got pulled into the wringer and she couldn't get it out. By then, both of us were screeching and Aunt Laura came running to see what happened. Thank goodness her mother had the presence of mind to yank the cord out of the wall. However, after the commotion died down, several days later Lorraine's curiosity got the better of her again. This time, she was leaning inside the washer watching the agitator go back and forth when a piece of her long hair got wrapped around the wringer and she couldn't move her head. By the time her mother got her hair untangled, some of it stayed on the wringer and the rest had to be cut off from the top of her head. Years later, Lorraine still remembers vividly how her curiosity got her into that predicament.

Oh yes, we humans are very inquisitive. It's in our nature. Sometimes when I think back on all the foolish questions I've asked in my lifetime, I have to remind myself that it was a good thing. After all, where would we be if curious minds didn't ask questions about why the world was flat? What if Isaac Newton never questioned why the apple fell from the tree?

I hope I will always wonder, ponder and speculate on the things I don't know. And as far as I know, no one's discovered a cure for curiosity. Thank goodness for that, eh?

# The Fitzpatrick Clan at School

"Mom... where's me blue shirt?"

"You mean the one that belonged to Marceline that Aunt Lena gave her that I made into a vest for Harve last year? Oh, I took that apart and made underwear out of it fer Leona, my dear."

That's how the conversation went around our house the day school reopened after summer holidays in Lord's Cove when I was a kid. The confusion, fighting and scratching must have been unbearable for my mother, because as she remembers it, some of us liked school and some hated it. "You must've had tears of pride in your eyes watching all of us go off to school, eh Mom?" I asked when we were reminiscing.

"Oh, yes... I had tears in my eyes all right," she said, "'cause I knew darned well that the torture was started fer me. The teachers dreaded to see the Fitzpatrick crowd coming, and I don't blame them, 'cause somehow ye all managed to get into trouble."

I can still see my sisters and myself running off to school with bookbags and brand new hand-me-down dresses. Kate loved to go to school, but she was so shy that when she'd get in the classroom, she would laugh hysterically. She'd titter uncontrollably every time the teacher looked her way and she'd pull her dress up over her head exposing her bloomers. Then she'd get sent home with a note telling of her unladylike behaviour in class. Now Helena was always so eager to get started that she couldn't sit still in her desk. Much to the annoyance of the teacher, she'd move constantly, fidget with her hair, snap the elastic garters on her stockings and make weird noises in her throat. "Why is it that you can't sit still for one minute, Helena?" she demanded one day.

Happy to be finally asked a question, Helena said, "Mom says I got a tape worm, miss, and me flea bites are so itchy I got to scratch them."

In actual fact, part of that was true, because Daddy would make us take medicine to prevent us from getting worms that sometimes came from eating fish and pork that wasn't well cooked. Every year, on the day school started, we all got de-wormed, whether we needed it or not. Helena was itchy, alright, but it was from hives, not flea bites, because she was allergic to eggs. Poor Marceline, the oldest of our clique, who always got the task of making sure we were all scrubbed clean till our freckles shone, came home crying that nobody wanted to sit beside her because we had fleas at our house. Then, of course, there was Leona, who refused repeatedly to use the outhouse at school and threatened to go on the floor if the teacher didn't let her go home. She spent most of her time walking back and forth from school to our house and Mom had to chase her with the broom to break her of the habit.

My brother, Harve, knew the feel of that broom well, for he hated school with a passion. As soon as he was out of Mom's sight, he'd run off and hide somewhere. Once she found him hiding in the chicken coop and his excuse for being there was that he was squeezing the hens to make them lay eggs. Even when he went to school, he tried his darndest to get a holiday, from knocking over the stove pipes, to stuffing up the chimney to smoke up the classroom. His biggest dread was having to take the cod liver oil that the teacher handed out every September to keep us healthy.

He was not above emptying the bottle before he arrived home. Fred, the oldest boy thought much the same way, too, except he told outrageous stories to the teacher. Once he brought his teacher and the whole class to our house to show them the "hundreds of strange white birds" that he had captured in the hayloft. Naturally, there were no such birds, but he insisted that they must have flown out through a crack in the roof. If it wasn't that someone's bull had held him at bay outside the school yard or that he couldn't find his bookbag, then he'd pretend to have measles or chicken pox. It's no wonder the teacher decided to give up teaching and left Lord's Cove to join the convent. Mom was convinced that Raphael, the mischievous one in our family, probably contributed most to her sudden departure. He simply drove her crazy with his pranks and jokes. He'd put worms in her desk and when she'd turn her back, he'd take the teacher's bloomers from the drawer and use them to wipe off the blackboard and make everybody laugh.

Louis was the quiet one in our family and we hardly knew that he was around... most of the time, Mom recalled. On his first day of school, he refused to wear a shirt because she had sewn bright yellow buttons on it and he thought he would look like a girl. Mom's broom convinced him otherwise, but when she was out of sight, he hid behind the wood pile and with Harve's help, they pulled off all the buttons. Suspecting something was in the wind, Mom followed them. Harve got such a fright when he saw her coming that he swallowed some of the buttons and Louis poked one so far up his nose that Mom had to get Mrs. May Isaac, the midwife, to get it out with a piece of wire. But that wasn't the last episode. That same afternoon, Louis arrived home from school with Fred leading him by the hand with news that he had gone blind. Mom was frantic as she watched him stagger around the kitchen, bumping into tables and chairs, bruising himself all over. Daddy solved the case of the mysterious blindness when Fred told him that one of Louis' friends had just gotten a pair of eyeglasses. Nobody could convince him that he wasn't blind, until Daddy made him a pair of glasses out of cardboard and colored them with a crayon. Louis' vision was miraculously restored the minute he put the glasses on and off he went to show off to his buddies.

As I listened to the stories Mom had to tell, I asked what her fondest memories were of the good old school days with our crowd. Without hesitation she replied, "The best thing about school back then was summer holidays."

# Me and Joe

"Lucy, did I ever tell you about the time me and Joe stogged up the stove pipes at school so the place would get smoked up and we'd get the day off to go trouting?" my brother asked.

I said I hadn't, even though I had heard it many times before because I wanted to hear Raphael tell it again.

"...And then there was the time when me and Joe sneaked into Mr. Harnett's chicken coop late one night and stole a hen so we could make soup," Raphael chuckled. "We didn't know where to cook it in case someone found out what we did, so Joe plucked the feathers, then we knocked on Mr. Harnett's door and told him we brought him a present. He was so glad to get it that he invited us in for a drink and his wife made a big boiler of soup for us. They had no idea that it was their own hen they were eating!"

That's the way the conversation went several months ago when I went to Vancouver to visit Raphael. For as long as I can remember, Raphael has been telling "Me and Joe" stories and vise versa, for the antics of those two when they were young lads growing up are well known in both families. I listened intently as Raphael retold the stories this time, for there was much more to it than having a good laugh. Now his stories have become cherished memories that are meant to be a tribute to a boyhood friend, for Joe passed away suddenly awhile ago.

At the time of my visit, Raphael himself was recovering from a quadruple bypass surgery just four months after Joe's death, who, coincidentally, had died from a heart problem. As often happens in life, their paths went in different directions and they hadn't seen each other in a few years, but they always kept their friendship alive across the miles through family and friends. I suspect that Raphael was feeling very vulnerable at that time, not just because of Joe's death and his own medical concerns, but he was still dealing with the recent loss of our brother, Harve.

"Life's so short you know. We never know what's gonna happen from one minute to the next," he said. "I just wish I'd gotten to see Joe one last time... you know, to reminisce about old times."

Ah, yes, I'm sure we've all been guilty of taking things for granted and I daresay most of us have wished we could turn back the pages of time or done things differently. I know I have in the past and I've always regretted that I never took the time to truly appreciate the people in my life. Hindsight can be a grim reminder of all the lost moments and missed opportunities in our lives, but it can also teach us that we should live each day to the fullest and never take a moment for granted. I know I plan to seize the moment and make the best possible use of each day from now on.

Raphael laughed as he thought about the old days with Joe. "We'd do anything for a laugh back then and we were always up to no good. It's no wonder Grandma Lambe called us scallywags and hellions, because me and Raphael lived up to those names."

Sometimes recalling the good times we've shared with someone helps keep them close to us and often the things we admired in a person's character are what we remember most. I suppose that's the way we deal with grief by celebrating their memory and the good things they brought to our lives. Now anyone who knew Joe admired his terrific sense of humour, for he loved to laugh, as does my brother Raphael. That's why the two of them got along so well.

There was one tale in particular that happened when they 18 years old that they were very fond of telling and retelling. Apparently Joe's Uncle Gilbert often gave the boys a lift to wherever they wanted to go and one night when they wanted to go to Grand Bank to see some girls, Gilbert was not at home. Joe discovered that his uncle had gone to work with somebody else and had left his car parked in front of his grandmother's house with the keys in the ignition. So, the boys decided to *borrow* the car. Under the cover of darkness, the two scoundrels pushed the car out of the yard and away they went with Joe in the driver's seat. It was a very windy night and on the way back home later, a gust of wind blew the hood off the car and it landed somewhere in the woods. Raphael and Joe panicked and kept on driving, trying to get the car back before Gilbert got home. They returned the car where they found it, making sure Joe's grandmother didn't see them, were about to make their escape before Gilbert came home when their conscience got the better of them. So they waited and not wanting Joe to get into trouble with his uncle, Raphael told Gilbert that he was the one who took the car. But instead of giving them a reprimand, Gilbert looked his car over and calmly told them to show him where they lost the hood of the car. Together they retrieved it and put it back in place. "Don't worry, boys," he said. "I'll get it fixed at the garage tomorrow and she'll be as good as new, no harm done at all."

I, too, have memories of Joe from when I was a youngster, for he used to come to our house to stay with Raphael whenever our parents went out somewhere. They used to sing, play guitar and arm wrestle 'til they didn't have any strength left, only to end up giggling and laughing until they were exhausted. And best of all, they'd let me stay up late and they'd take turns rocking me in the chair.

Believe it or not, those two rascals were altar boys at one time. Many times I've heard them talking about how they used to sip the wine in the church vestry and then water it down before they served it to the priest at communion. They were even known to sneak into the confessional box before the priest got there and listen to the confession of some of their friends. As penance, Joe told one poor fella he had to run around the back road three times, and since one was not at liberty to repeat to anyone what penance was handed out, he did what he was told, much to the delight of his friends.

Raphael told me about an incident when they wanted to scare their friend who was supposed to meet them after dark one night. Their plan was to play a trick on him by throwing firecrackers in his path, but it didn't quite work out that way. An elderly woman, whom I shall not name, happened to go visiting at the same house where the boys lay in wait. Mistaking her for their buddy, they tossed the lighted firecrackers in that direction and hid behind a rock. They realized their mistake when they heard the poor woman wailing and screeching as the fireworks went off under her long skirt. When the people in the house heard the commotion and came to her rescue, the boys were nowhere to be found. 'Course, they both swore that they stayed long enough to find out that no harm had come to the woman and neither would admit that the whole incident had their nerves frazzled, especially when they discovered that the woman they had scared was a friend of Joe's grandmother. Mrs. Lambe was determined to find the culprits who were responsible for the scandalous prank and just to throw her off their trail, the teen "angels" offered to accompany her around the Cove looking for clues. Naturally, nobody had seen or heard anything, so once again, their secret was safe and the boys came out of the whole thing looking like the good guys.

They must've had a guardian angel in their younger days because they never seemed to get caught in the act. 'Course, the fact that Joe and Raphael just happened to be able to charm the leg off a table might have had something to do with it. Both of them were always grinning from ear to ear and when you saw them put their heads together, you knew they were usually up to no good. At least that's what I heard from very reliable sources back home, and judging from the reaction I've witnessed whenever one spoke of the other, I'd say their laughter spoke volumes about their relationship. "We've kept secrets together that we've never told another living soul," Joe once told me, "and I'd bet my life that Raphael hasn't told anybody either."

And you know, seeing my brother's impish grin when he refused to tell all, I could only imagine what it might have meant to both of them had they actually gotten together one last time. I'd be willing to bet that one would be trying to outdo the other and the storytelling would go on forever. Still and all, a part of me realizes that even though the opportunity never came to pass, I know that their friendship will live on through the memories they cultivated over the years. It will survive because my brother will make sure of it. "Hey, Lucy, do you mind the time Miss Collins sent me and Joe home from school because she caught us under the step trying to look up under the girls' skirts..."

Perhaps, after all, some secrets are better left untold.

# Mind Your Manners Please

"Don't forget to say 'please' and 'thanks' and mind you wipe your feet before you goes into the house, you hear me, Lucy?"

For as long as I can remember, those were the usual parting words Mom gave me every time she sent me on an errand to somebody's house. I always tried to be on my best behaviour even when I was out of her sight because it was very important that you made your parents look the model of perfection. Every youngster was expected to be polite and respectful to their elders, for no parent wanted anybody thinking their offspring didn't have good manners. "I never raised my crowd to be a bunch of heathens," Mom used to say, "so you'd better behave yourselves when I'm not around, because you know I'll find out about it."

And heaven forbid if that should happen, for it was of such importance that if you didn't give adults the respect they deserved, they snitched on you to your parents. Mothers, in particular, took it upon themselves to correct each others' children and if that should happen, you were in for a licking when you got home. When company dropped into our house, we knew better than to make a noise or do anything that would get Mom's dander up. I think most of the parents back then gave new meaning to the idea that "children should be seen and not heard," because we were always warned not to speak unless spoken to. Can you imagine how hard that was on a youngster to have to sit still and not speak for hours on end when company overstayed their welcome? But keeping up appearances was very important to our parents and we obeyed the rules no matter what.

We've all been told by our parents since childhood to mind our manners and to maintain some semblance of etiquette. That is something we remember for the rest of our lives, for we all want to be socially accepted. Granted, we didn't have any rule book to go by, only what we learned from others. There were many times in my adult years that I wished I had invested in a book on manners and etiquette. My biggest challenge was learning the proper way to conduct myself at a dinner table in a restaurant. It boggled my mind when I first saw all the dishes, glasses and utensils at each place setting. I couldn't imagine what I was supposed to do with three forks because at home when I was growing up, you were lucky to get one fork and one plate. But I wasn't about to let the other people at the table know how inexperienced I was, so I just watched whatever everybody else did and followed suit.

And I managed very well, thank you very much. Other than being the only one with my napkin tucked under my chin and drinking the water from the finger bowl the waitress brought me after I ate my chicken, I did okay.

I found it all very confusing as a child, because it seemed that there were manners for every occasion and they changed depending on where you were or who you were with. It just seems like an awful lot of fuss to go through to get a bite to eat when you're hungry. I'm a simple person and I'm quite happy to eat my potatoes, meat and veggies from one plate using just one fork and knife. That method worked very well in our house when our family was growing up in Lord's Cove. Even to this day, I don't go out of my way in my own home to be formal. I taught my sons what is expected of them in public, but I don't stand on ceremony. Oh, the polite words are always said… you know, please, thank you and excuse me, but other than that, I don't expect anything more. Mind you, when I was a youngster, we seldom said please and thank you to each other. There was no need for it. At the supper table if your arm was long enough to reach over whoever was sitting beside you, you helped yourself, and if that didn't work, all you had to do was get someone's attention. "Pass the butter dish down, will ya, and hurry up about it!"

There were certain things you'd never do in public because you knew that if your mother found out, you'd get your ticky-thumps. Mom considered it the height of ignorance to lick your fingers, drink tea from the saucer, burp or put your elbows on the table in somebody else's house. Yet, in the privacy of our kitchen, it was acceptable – unless we had company, of course. There was always so many around the table that you were lucky to find room to squeeze one hand in to get your food off the plate let alone find a spot to rest your elbows. When you were eating breakfast or having a mug-up, Mom never minded if you curled your legs up under you on the chair, dunked your toast in your teacup or even poured your tea into your saucer. My, but the tea tasted some good that way, didn't it? It was a real challenge trying to balance both your elbows on the table and sipping the tea from the saucer so you wouldn't scald your tongue. 'Course if two or three of us got to making that "ahhh…" sound or smacked our lips after the sweet tea passed by our palates, Mom would holler at us when the noise got on her nerves. Nobody raised an eyebrow at home if you soaked up the gravy from your plate with a bit of bread or sucked on a pork scruncion or a bone at the table, but you dare not do it in anybody else's house. If we had to excuse ourselves every time our crowd bumped against each other or passed in front of somebody in our house, we'd be apologizing all day long. We had our own way of getting the point across. "Why don't you watch where you're going?"

And if our parents weren't within hearing distance, often as not there would be name-calling and a few choice words bandied about. No, we weren't too formal back then, but we did know what was expected of us and we behaved accordingly when the occasion arose. Every youngster was taught to address adults as Mister or Missus and although it wasn't required that we knock on anybody's door, there was an unwritten rule to follow if you went to someone's house. You'd stand just inside the kitchen door with your back against the wall and your hands behind your back until you were acknowledged. And you'd never be brazen enough to sit down unless you were invited to. If you just wanted to visit, you'd take a seat when it was offered, but if you were sent on an errand, you politely refused. "No thanks, I'm not staying."

I remember all the warnings Mom used to give us if she took us visiting with her. Before she'd lift the latch on the door, she'd give us her last warning. "Now sit down, be quiet and if you're asked if you wants something to eat, don't you dare say you're hungry!"

'Course, that was their pride showing through then, for even if you had your tongue hanging out from hunger, no self-respecting mother wanted anybody thinking she let her children go hungry. Oh, my, sometimes my mouth would be watering for something I was offered, but Mom would give me that look and I'd say, "No thanks... I'm not hungry."

If the lady of the house offered a second time, you could accept it because it would be considered rude if you didn't take it. Oh, yes, it was so important to parents that their children acted properly in front of other parents. Sundays, in particular, were the worst, because everybody was expected to wear their best fit-outs to church. None of our crowd could get out the door at our house unless Mom inspected us first to make sure every hair was in place, our shoes were polished and our ears were clean, inside and out. I hated sitting beside Mom, because she wouldn't let me move a muscle if I turned around to see who was behind me. She'd click me on the knuckles no matter who was watching. As I got older, I tried sneaking into the church late so I could sit on the far side of the pew away from her, but that didn't work. I'd pretend not to hear her hissing at me to move closer, but then she'd lean over the others to either straighten my collar or stick a pair of rosary beads in my hands. Lord help me if I had a piece of hair standing up because she had no qualms about licking her finger and plastering that bit of hair down flat on my forehead. Course, then I'd hear about it all the way home. "You had to go and make a holy show of me in front of everybody, didn't you? Now people are gonna think I never learned you how to behave yourself!"

Oh, my, yes, we had manners for all occasions and rules to follow for everything. Back then we just thought our parents were being too strict with us and were teaching us things that were unimportant. But over the years I learned that it was not all in vain, for what my parents had taught me stayed with me for the rest of my life. And it wasn't a matter of learning manners or even keeping up appearances in front of others; it ran deeper than that. And even though the message was sometimes hidden behind harsh words or reprimands when we were children, it came through loud and clear… be respectful to others.

Sometimes now when I'm out somewhere and I see people being rude or impertinent to others, it gets me all riled up. I get this uncontrollable urge to snock them on the knuckles and I have to bite my tongue to keep from telling them to mind their manners. Course that would have been quite acceptable in my mother's day to do just that, but I know its not my place to remind anyone how to behave in today's society. Pity, isn't it?

# Saints & Sinners

Have you ever sat on an insect nest when you were berrypicking and suddenly felt a swarm of angry pissmores run amuck in your pants? No? Well, perhaps it was just my bad luck, but I dreaded that feeling almost as much as I did the sight of a priest when I was a child. No disrespect intended to a man of God, but every youngster back home felt intimidated by any member of the clergy wearing a black robe. Religion was a big part of our lives, for our parents instilled that in us as children. It was evident in every Catholic home, for there were statues of saints in every room, prayer books in the parlour and rosary beads hanging on nails, hooks and doorknobs.

At our house, we had a wall of fame where every saint and martyr who ever lived kept vigil from their glass frames. There were holy pictures everywhere to remind us of our Christian faith and, I suspect, were meant to be used as role models for us poor sinners. No matter where you went in our house, you had at least three saints watching your every move. As a child, I was always aware of their presence. Mom kept a picture of the Pope up over the kitchen table and no one dared move him from his lofty perch. My father had the gall to do it once... but only once, because Mom kicked up such a racket that you'd think he'd given away our best milking cow. Apparently, he had brought home a picture of Joey Smallwood and believing that Newfoundland's first premier deserved the most auspicious spot on the wall, Daddy ousted the Pope and replaced His Holiness with the smiling face of Mr. Smallwood. Mom was so infuriated that she accused my father of being sacreligious and without a shred of respect for the Premier, she threw him face down on the table. Naturally that set off a heated argument with religion and politics being bandied about, but Mom got the upper hand and restored the Pope to his rightful place. Not to be outdone, my father got up on a chair and hung the Premier up over the wood stove on the opposite wall facing the Pope. "Now then," he said, getting in the last word, "Joey Smallwood can take the heat with the best of 'em and he can talk faster than the Pope, so let's see how long the two can stare each other down."

For as long as I can remember, the Pope and Mr. Smallwood maintained their respective positions in our kitchen until the wall behind the stove was removed during renovations years later.

So you can understand the position that we, as youngsters, found ourselves in when it came to religious duties and church. Today, fortunately, the clergy are much more approachable, but not in my time. When the priest stood on the pulpit preaching fire and brimstone, adults and youngsters alike would bivver in the pew because we believed that we could be struck down at any given moment without as much as a sign from above. It's no wonder we were nervous wrecks when we had an encounter with a priest. If he came to the school during religion class, everybody cringed, because he always asked questions from the catechism about religious doctrines of the church. If you didn't know the answer and he asked if you had studied it, you dared not lie to a priest, because then you'd have to confess it to him later. And believe me, nobody enjoyed kneeling in that dark confessional booth waiting for him to open the shutter where all you could see was the outline of his face. Goodness, when I think back about all the things we believed to be sins, I cringe. We heard the word "sin" so much that we felt guilty about everything. Most of the time, parents threw that word into the conversation out of habit. "It's a sin not to eat your dinner when there are poor children starving to death in Africa!"

'Course it was very common to hear mothers threatening their children numerous times in any one day, for they put the fear of God in us to keep us in line. It seemed that everything we did or said was being sinful and, being children, we believed everything our parents told us.

"Don't talk back to yer mother... it's a sin!"

"You'd better remember to say your prayers before bed, 'cause it's a sin if you don't!"

In the Catholic church, a child of seven is considered to be of the "age of reason" where you know right from wrong and from then onward, you have to go to confession. Innocent as babies we were and if I'm not mistaken, when I was seven I was still having trouble figuring out why my shoes wouldn't fit when I put them on the wrong feet. I can't imagine that I fully understood the gravity of committing a mortal sin. In elementary school, it was the teacher's obligation to see to it that pupils went to confession and we'd be herded off to church every Friday where we lined up outside the confessional box to examine our conscience. Now it was VERY important to examine your conscience, because you had to decide if the sins were considered little ones or big ones. Once you confessed your wrong-doings to the priest, he'd absolve you from your sins and you'd be given a penance, which was usually a few prayers to say as an expression of contrition. Your penance was doled our according to the magnitude of the deed. For instance, if you confessed to stealing a rope, that might be considered a small sin, but if there happened to be a horse or a sheep on the OTHER end of the rope that you stole, then that was a big whopper of a sin.

Oh, yes, I remember my friends and I waiting in the line to go to confession. We'd watch the ones ahead of us to see how long they prayed when they came out of the confessional and we'd speculate on what they must have done to deserve such a long time repenting on their knees. By the time your turn came, your nerves could be right raw. Not that we had much to confess at that age, but we had no choice because we couldn't take communion at Sunday mass if we had sinned. Sometimes a person would have a litany of things the length of your arm to tell the priest. Even though most of them weren't sins, we confessed anyway, just to be on the safe side. Why, one Sunday after the priest preached on the wickedness of adulterous behaviour, one young lad who ran out of material, confessed to committing adultery and was sent back outside to reexamine his conscience. Only the good Lord knows what he thought he was confessing to.

Terrible as it may sound, when we couldn't come up with new stuff to confess, we'd talk it over with friends. Sometimes we even argued. "You can't tell him that you sauced yer mother, 'cause that's what I was gonna say... and besides, you told him that last week!"

The poor priest must've been mesmerized listening to us, because we all confessed the same things. We had our spiel memorized. It was important that you told the priest how many times you did the terrible deed, so you started off with a low number and worked your way up so it didn't sound so bad. And you'd always say it in a whisper, just loud enough that the priest could hear, but low enough not to be heard by those standing outside the door. "Bless me Father, I have sinned... these are my sins..."

Then you'd rhyme off all the things you had rehearsed outside. "I disobeyed my parents two or three times."

"I took God's name in vain four or five times."

"I stuck my tongue at the teacher when she wasn't looking six times..."

And then, for good measure, you'd end with the one you felt was the biggest offense of all. "I told lies nine or ten times."

This is where you kept your eyes closed and hoped that he wouldn't ask what lies you told because you couldn't remember anyway and then you'd be forced into telling yet another lie to explain the ones you just told.

So you see, it was a vicious circle where we handled the situation to the best of our ability as children. We weren't saints by any means, but I'm not sure we were sinners either. Whether we were right or wrong is irrelevant, because we always followed our conscience, misguided as it was at times. When I think back about how I bared my soul to the priest when I was a youngster, I still blush at some of the secrets I divulged. I just wish that someone had told me that lighting up a broom straw and pretending it was a cigarette was not a mortal sin. But it doesn't matter now. I just hope God has a sense of humour.

# Sweet Temptation

I know from experience that I would never make a good martyr. Not that it was a possibility by any stretch of the imagination, but when it comes to self-sacrifice and self-denial, I'm sadly lacking in that area. I blame it all on a congenital defect, for I come from a long line of "sweet-toothers." As far back as I can remember, I've had a weakness for sweets, whether it be in the form of chocolate bars, candy or ice cream. I will devour anything in sight that has sugar in it and I can no more curb my passion for sweets than I can pass up a one-way ticket home to Newfoundland...and that's serious business to me.

As I recall, my Catholic upbringing had a big influence on that particular area when I was a youngster, especially during the Lenten season. That's when we had to quit eating sweets, for our spiritual beliefs were tried and tested by performing penitential exercises of self-denial which included fasting, prayer and reflection. Ash Wednesday marked the beginning of Lent and continued through the 40 days which lead up to Easter. The words "self-denial" and "forty days," made every youngster cringe, for that meant we had to give up something of importance for a long time. On Ash Wednesday, we went to church to receive the ashes on our forehead as a symbolic gesture of repentance and remorse as we reflected on the sufferings of Jesus. Adults usually restricted themselves to one meal a day and some made personal commitments to stop smoking or took a pledge to quit drinking alcoholic beverages. Youngsters, on the other hand, didn't have a big choice and "giving up something" as we called it, was a big sacrifice as far as we were concerned. No sooner were we out of church on Ash Wednesday when the burning question was asked. "What are you giving up fer Lent — candy or gum?"

Now sweets may seem inconsequential to youngsters in today's scheme of things, but money was scarce back then and precious little of it went toward candy and gum. We knew from experience that temptation would befall us along the way, but once the decision was made, we tackled the 40 days and nights of the Lenten season like crusaders wearing a badge of courage. Though the thought of what we had to give up nearly drove us foolish.

Perhaps it was the fact that we were naive teens or that we didn't understand the importance of what Lent was all about like the adults did, but I can't honestly say that I was committed to the cause. When the priest made the sign of the cross on your forehead with the ashes, then you dared not remove it, for it was supposed to stay there until it wore off naturally. If an adult saw you rubbing it off, you'd get the knuckles upside the head for such an unholy act. 'Course, once you went outside Lord's Cove where there were non-Catholics, there was a chance that you'd meet someone who knew nothing about holy ashes. Children, in particular, were targeted. "Look at the dirt on your forehead, my dear — come here and let me wipe it off before someone sees you..."

I remember as a teenager being embarrassed if someone stared at me and often I'd pretend that it came off accidentally if Mom asked me about it. I know that my brother Raphael used to wash his off when he went out sometimes and then he'd come home, get a bit of soot from the cover of the wood stove or from the bottom of the kettle and dab it on his forehead. Mom never knew the difference. Other than that, we did our duty as expected during Lent. That meant we spent a lot of time in church praying, making novenas and going to confession once a week whether we needed to or not. Every evening at home we prayed the Rosary and, of course, we refrained from eating meat on Fridays.

Now while all this praying and fasting was going on, the youngsters were as busy as little chipmunks hoarding up all the little treats that we were not allowed to eat. And trust me, every penny we got, we ran off to the shop to buy candy or gum and then we'd hide the goodies in a safe place, like under the bed, in a closet or in the attic. It was like an investment to us, for all we could think about was the feast we'd have once the 40 days and nights had ended. Oh, the anticipation of eating the forbidden sweets was almost as good as the real thing — and we were tested to the limit. Our parents didn't help one bit because they were always reminding us of our pledges and watching us carefully. "You knows it's a sin to break your pledge during Lent," Mom would say, shaking her finger at us. "And don't think you can sneak behind my back and eat the candy because I'll know — you mark my words, I'll know!"

For some reason, whenever parents reminded us of anything that had to do with church and religion, we believed everything they said, even though some of it was meant to put the fear of God into us. We thought that every word they uttered came straight from God's mouth. I used to think that Mom had a direct line to heaven because she seemed to know everything we did, but my sister Leona set me straight. "Didn't you know that Mom got eyes in the back of her head, my dear? She knows everything and she sees everything we do — even when we can't see her looking!"

Because I was young and impressionable, I believed her.

Nonetheless, when temptation came our way, we thought it was a sin and went off to the priest to confess our wrongdoing. Temptation can be bittersweet, as we all know, and despite the fact that we believed our very souls were in jeopardy, we often succumbed to our cravings. Parents often reneged on their promise of abstinence, too, and the men, in particular, fell victim to temptation when it came to booze. I'd heard many stories of husbands taking a little "nip" for various reasons, but I think the tongue-lashing they got from their wives was enough penance that they didn't need confession. It wasn't uncommon, either, for ailing older ladies to be heard trying to justify a little sip of brandy. "Just for medicinal purposes, you know — me arthritis is acting up."

I remember every night before going to sleep, taking out my little can and counting out every piece, sniffing it and savouring the scent, but I'd muster up the courage to resist the urge to eat it. I don't know which was worse, the thought of going to hell or the fear of Mom finding out that I had eaten something. I was so tempted one night that I opened up a stick of Juicy Fruit gum and licked the little powdery white stuff off, telling myself that I didn't actually chew the gum. For three nights before I went to sleep, I'd peel off the silver paper, have another lick and carefully rewrap the paper in case Mom came snooping around. By the time Lent was over, the paper was stuck to the gum so badly that it was impossible to get it off, let alone chew the gum.

Now I wasn't the only one who strayed from the righteous path. A Newfoundland friend of mine, Evelyn (Noseworthy) Riches who lives in Niagara Falls, told me that she recalls having the same problem as I did. She, too, couldn't resist her sweets. Candy was her downfall. She told me of a time 60 years ago when she was preparing herself for the long fast during Lent.

"I was just dying for candy and Mother didn't have a copper to her name to spare, so she gave me an egg to take to the shop to trade it for a few sweets," she said. "I was on my way to school and I ran all the way to the shop. Just before I got there, I dropped the egg and it smashed on the road. I was heartbroken and cried all the way to school, and on top of that I got into trouble because I was late!"

'Course, trading one thing for another was quite common everywhere, so the candy trade was a big business for us. My sisters and I spent a lot of time salivating over the things we had hoarded up — yummy things like bubble gum, jelly beans, peppermint knobs, suckers, lollipops, sugar daddies and penny candy. Leona loved the black licorice pipes we used to get at the Co-op store and we always knew she'd been cheating a little because there were always telltale signs of the black on her fingers or her lips. My other sister, Helena, would do anything for something sweet and she was known to fib a little on the pretense of getting a lemon drop that Mom kept for when one of us got a sore throat. She used to fein a tummy ache as well and managed to talk Mom into letting her have a peppermint knob to settle her stomach. Some of the boys who gave up drinking soda pop for Lent sometimes put water in an empty pop bottle and pretended that it was for real, while others kept changing their pledges after they'd given in to temptation. At school, the teachers kept us on our toes as well and during religion class, they'd sometimes ask every blessed one of us what we were fasting from. And heaven help us if we lied, because our conscience would get the better of us and we'd have to go to confession again.

On weekends, we had nothing to do as any form of entertainment was off limits. A bunch of us would get together to show off what we had collected and we'd swap one sweet for another. Often, if we wanted something badly enough, we'd trade four candy or bubble gum for just one item. Then we'd take it home and count everything — just in case someone might find our loot and be tempted to take it. Lord, the sweet temptation was more than we could bear sometimes, but we did our best. You can't imagine how relieved and happy we were when the end of the Lenten season rolled around. Finally we were free to go back to our regular lives without restrictions and rules, and as Easter approached, we looked upon it as a new beginning. It was by far the best reward any child could hope for after our long pilgrimage. And as for myself, the only thing on my mind back then was the anticipation of sinking my teeth into all that sweet stuff — stale though it was. I can say with a clear conscience that it was well worth the wait. Like I said — martyrdom doesn't become me.

# The Height of Style

I can still see a bunch of us teenage girls pouring through the pages of the Eaton's catalogue and marvelling over the beautiful clothes that we could only dream about owning. "Oh, luhhh... I wish I could buy that green dress for the garden party next month! I loves that stand-up collar... it looks right stylish, don't it?"

"Yis, my dear and that colour would look some good with your red hair. And luuuhhh... see that frilly blouse there? My, I wish I could get that for meself. We'd be right in the height of style, wouldn't we?"

"I wish... I wish..."

Seemed like we were always wishing for something we couldn't have back in Newfoundland in my younger days, but you know what we were none the worse for it. No, siree... wishing and hoping didn't stunt our psychological growth at all. It did, however, give us hours of entertainment and enjoyment, as well as teach us to appreciate the value of things.

Even though we had little connection with the outside world, we were still conscious of wearing clothes that were the latest fashion. Granted, styles came and went and often, by the time something new got passed down from one to the other, it had already gone out of style. But it didn't really matter. We wore it anyway, for we knew we had seen it with our own eyes in the catalogue, albeit several years ago. With the nine of us in our family, we didn't exactly have a choice but to wear whatever the oldest kids had outgrown. And with second-hand clothes, they came in three sizes... big, small and one-size-fits-all. With most of the families, it was the same thing, so it was difficult at times to tell if children were under-nourished or overweight. If you had to squeeze into something that was too small, your clothes puckered at the seams and rode up over the wrists and ankles. "My, what are you feeding that child?" someone might ask. "Sure he's getting so big, he's popping out of his clothes."

On the other hand, if you were tall, skinny and gawky looking like I was, you looked like a streel with the clothes hanging off you. I suppose that was why kind old ladies looked at me with pity in their eyes. "My dear girl, you're so skinny, a puff of wind would knock you down. Eat more and put some fat on your bones."

When I'd grumble and throw a fit because I didn't want to wear a pair of hand-me-down slacks that didn't reach to the top of my ankles, Mom would try to reason with me. "My dear, you're lucky you can wear slacks because you got nice long legs," she'd say. "Just pull your socks up a bit more and you'll be right in style."

Many years have passed since then, but now when I look around at the younger generation, I realize that they're wearing exactly the same fashions as we did back then. The only difference is that we didn't actually KNOW we were in style. We couldn't afford to buy new clothes all the time, but for special occasions, like Easter or St. Patrick's Day, Mom made dresses or outfits for the girls. Sometimes, when we weren't around, she'd look through the catalogue and duplicate a dress style at her sewing machine, but she'd never let on to us that she did it. Then she'd act surprised if someone pointed out the similarities in the Wish Book. "Well, look at that," she'd say. "That's almost like the dress I made for you, Lucy, except yours is a nicer colour. It looks right stylish on you, too."

'Course I'd be prouder than a peacock, to say the least. But she always made us feel that whatever we wore was the height of fashion and I supposed we believed her. And like all mothers, she couldn't keep her tongue still if she saw us wearing something that she thought wasn't appropriate. She hated the miniskirts when they were in style and when that changed over to the maxi-lengths, she complained that they were too long. But my favourite was the hot pants. You remember them, don't you ladies? It was an outfit, with a short dress worn over a pair of matching shorts. Mom disapproved of them vehemently and claimed they were unladylike because it looked like the dress was too short to cover the unmentionables.

Oh, my ... those were the days. I still have a snap of myself and my girlfriend posing in our beautiful floral hot-pant fitout and wearing paten-leather boots that came to the knee. I just wish I kept that outfit, because one never knows when it may come back on the fashion scene again. A lot of things from the past have been resurrected in the fashion industry. There really is some truth to that old saying "what goes around, comes around." Just this winter when I saw the teenagers wearing plaid pleated skirts, I rushed home and dug out my old reversible, pleated skirt and the mohair, boat-neck sweater I had in high school. I was in my glory as I dusted off my wedge-heeled shoes and I mentally patted myself on the back for having the foresight to keep them all those years. Not that I thought they'd ever make a comeback, mind you, because it really was for sentimental reasons that I kept it all. Still, it made me feel good. Then when I saw the bell-bottom jeans and trousers in the stores last year, I kicked myself for throwing mine away. 'Course the now-generation don't call them bell-bottoms anymore... now they're FLARES, but the idea is the same. And along with that, the girls are wearing the polyester, floral blouses with the big collars and the chunky shoes with the thick heels that we referred to as wedgies. Fact is, that word, too, has several different connotations these days. I understand, one of which is along the line of having your underwear creep up on you and wedge itself in a certain uncomfortable place that makes sitting a bit difficult. Worse still, I'm told, is having a prankster yank your undies up from behind in what they call a "wedgie," for I hear it can be very painful.

I think what pleases me most is that the younger generation are wearing their clothes with pride because they're not in the least concerned with what other people think or whether the clothes actually fit properly or not. They don't give a hen's tooth if it is too small or too big or that the loud colours may clash with their latest hairshade. All that really matters is that it is fashionable and, by golly, I admire their tenacity because their self-image will never be damaged by feeling insecure about their choice in clothes.

Truth is, I'm happy about the way the styles have made a comeback because I'm tired of having to buy new clothes just so I can blend in with everybody else. And no more buying spandex that can stretch from a size 10 to a 16 just so I can tell everybody that I can still fit into a size 10. Now that the trend is more liberal, I can go from wearing something three times too big to something that fits like a latex glove and nobody will blink an eye. And the best thing about it all is that I won't have to buy any more new clothes. I can just rummage through the boxes I've kept over the years and bring out the clothes I wore 20 years ago. If I feel like going to work with my hair standing on end or wearing bobby socks with my pumps or perhaps even piercing my navel, then I'll do it. From now on for me, it's out with the new and in with the old. No matter what happens, I'll wear everything I have with confidence because I know that I'll be right smack in the height of style.

# The Way We Were

Recently when I was visiting my sister in Kingston, we noticed an airplane flying low as we walked to her car. Leona and I grinned at each other and, in unison, we cupped our hands over our mouths and shouted up at the plane: "Drop me a baby! Drop me a baby!"

Then we cracked up laughing, for when we were youngsters back in Lord's Cove, we thought that airplanes brought babies and before that, we believed the stork delivered them. Every time we spotted a plane, we'd wonder which family was getting a baby. We'd run up on the hill behind our house and wave our arms or a bandanna and shout for the pilot to drop a baby at our house. Oh my, every time I think about how naïve we were back then, I blush. We believed everything we were told because we couldn't conceive of the idea that there could be another explanation for things. Blind belief, that's what it was, but we were young, gullible and sheltered from the outside world. That's just the way we were back then.

When my boys were younger, I used to tell them about the things I did when I was growing up in Newfoundland and they'd just look at me in disbelief. We found wonder and awe in everything around us, whether it was watching the rise and fall of the tide, the birth of a baby calf or a lamb, or the sight of a rainbow after a storm. The things that my sons took for granted were the very ones that boggled my mind at their age: simple things like a television, a toilet and indoor running water. When Tim was seven, he heard me talk about bringing buckets of water from the well to fill the wooden tub for my bath.

"Why?" he asked. "Wouldn't Grandma let you use the shower inside?"

It's hard for someone to understand such a different way of life as compared to what we're privy to in today's society. When you think of it, there's not a whole lot that can make us even raise an eyebrow anymore. Sometimes I think that we're exposed to too much for our own good, for television has had both a positive and a negative effect on our lives. I've never believed that ignorance is bliss. While the media has given us a wealth of information and knowledge, it has also exposed us to the good and the bad side of life in living colour. Sometimes I think that we may become too complacent about it all, for nothing is left to the imagination and certainly nothing shocks us anymore. We don't have to wonder what's going to happen, we just expect that it will. Still and all, I feel that the imagination is the best place to escape to when we want to retreat to a quieter, different place that gives peace of mind. It may not necessarily be a better place, but at least we can control what we think and have a space to mull over our thoughts. As we grow older, sometimes that's the one thing that keeps us focused in life.

It's amazing when you think of it, you know. One day you're seeing things through the eyes of a young child, dreaming about the future; before you know it, you are an adult, looking back at the past and wondering how you got from point A to B in such a short time. As a child, the only thing I dreamed about was growing up and leaving home to explore the outside world beyond the perimeters of the Burin Peninsula. I thought that was what life was all about. But I was mistaken. Once I became an adult, I realized that it was just a plateau in life that we arrive at. I learned that it is what's in between being a child and an adult that counts. It is not just one thing in your life, but rather the past, present and the future all rolled up into one big ball that bounces in every direction.

The last time I was in Lord's Cove, I was visiting with Eileen, a childhood friend, and we were talking about the things we missed from our younger years. Goodness, how we laughed at ourselves. "I loved playing in that shed beside your house where your father had the old pot-belly stove and a table and chairs," Eileen said.

"It was such a cozy place, especially on winter evenings when we lit the lantern and drank tea from that big aluminum teapot your father always kept on the stove. I used to feel so important and grown-up because your mom used to let us use cups and saucers and the table even had a checkered oilcloth on it."

Oh, yes, that old storehouse gave rise to many hopes and dreams, and it was there that we practiced being moms, teachers, entertainers, movie stars and whatever else we wished for. Our sights may not have been as broad as those of the present generation, but we let our imaginations stretch as far as we could or even dared. At that moment in time, it was enough for us. There was no doubt about it, we looked forward to the future, so much so that we were in a rush to grow up. Often in the summer, Eileen, myself and my cousin Lorraine would get all dressed up in adult clothes and go walking around the Cove on Sunday afternoons. Lorraine's mother would let us wear her dresses, high heel pumps, hats and beads and off we'd go, lifting our long dresses to keep them out of the potholes. We always headed for the back road where it was usually dry and hardened from the cars that passed through the Cove. There we could hear the heels of the shoes clicking on the road. I can't explain why the clicking sound made us feel like adults, but it sure boosted our egos. It even made us brave enough to assume different personalities and often if we met another adult, they'd play right along with us. "My, that's some nice dress you're wearing there, young lady. Now who might you be?"

'Course, we'd make up a name that we liked and sometimes, if we had our dolls and prams with us, we'd refer to ourselves as Mrs. So-and-So. We'd make believe that we were on our way home to make supper for our husbands...the imaginary ones that we hoped we'd meet in the future. I suppose the way we were back then didn't hurt us any, although I'm not certain that it did us any good either. But the one thing I'm certain about is that we always felt secure within the circle of family and friends and it played a big role in who we've become as adults.

We believed everything our peers told us, and as such, we were very superstitious. When I was about nine years old, my brother Louis told us that the ghost of a dead horse caused thunder and lightning and naturally we believed him. My father once had a white horse that died from colic after he went berserk and kicked out the side of the stable. 'Course, we had no idea how or where he disposed of the corpse, but Louis told us that Daddy took it to Job's Cove, to a spot where we were forbidden to go. We called it the blowing hole, for it was a deep cavern between two huge rocks where the sea swirled around in a whirlpool effect and made a deafening noise. We knew it was dangerous, yet we went anyway. When the tide went out, we'd climb up on the rocks, lie on our bellies and holler down into the hole so we could hear the echo of our voices. Being older than us, I suppose my brother thought he was keeping us safe by telling us that if we went near the blowing hole, the ghostly animal would try to rise from his watery grave and whenever he tried to get out, his fury caused thunder and lightning storms. The vision of it set the fear of God in us, and we were terrified to go anywhere near there.

There are times when I think back about my life and I wonder if I had the chance to live it over again, would I do it differently? I can't honestly say that I know the answer to that because I've come to realize that things are not always that simple. There are some things in life that never change, some should be changed, some can't be changed and sometimes when we do change them, we wish we hadn't. With that in mind, I'm not sure I'd be willing to risk losing anything of my childhood, neither the good nor the bad, for those days of innocence will never come again for me. Perhaps if I'm lucky, my memory will be like a hard drive on a computer and when I grow too old to dream or remember, I can retrieve a nostalgic file, delete things that I no longer want to keep and save the ones I want for future use. That way I can always look back and remember the way we were.

# Taxi, Please!

As far as I can recall, I was 17 years old the first time I actually took a taxi from Lord's Cove to St. John's. It was indeed a memorable occasion, not just because it was my first move away from home, but because it was the beginning of a new life on my own. It was the longest drive I'd ever been on and I think I probably drove the taxi driver crazy asking if we had reached St. John's yet. Six hours later when we arrived at a relative's house where I was going to stay, I was so excited that I could hardly get the money out of the envelope that Mom had pinned to the inside of my bra. I felt so independent and grown-up when I gave him the $10, that my hand began to bivver. He smiled and thanked me. "Well, so long, my dear. Take care of yourself," he said as he patted me on the shoulder. "Any time you want to go out home, just give me a call, all right?"

When he waved as he pulled away, I suddenly realized that the taxi driver was my last link to home and I wanted to get back in the car and go with him. But I didn't. Not that day, anyway, for over the next several years, the taxi cabs from the Burin Peninsula to St. John's provided a lifeline for many folks who left home, and that included my sister Leona and me. When we were going to school in St. John's, most of the time we travelled with Drake's Taxi, and Dave, the driver, was always very kind and accommodating. Sometimes when we got a little homesick or just wanted to taste Mom's home cooking, we'd call Dave's taxi. Even if he had a full load, he'd make room for us if he could possibly do it.

One time in particular, there were eight of us in his 1966

Meteor and because I was skinny, I got to sit in the front seat above the hump on the floor. Dave was wedged up against the window and my knees were almost touching my chin by the time two other men squeezed in beside me. I felt like a sardine in a can, for every time we hit a pothole on the dirt road, their weight shifted onto me and nearly squeezed the living daylights out of me. When the hefty man next to me fell asleep on my shoulder, I was afraid to wake him, and after an hour of sweating from the strain of holding him up, my foot went numb. I finally managed to get my leg out from under him, but the car was bouncing over the bumps and Dave's elbow kept hitting me in the face. Finally, I asked him to slow down a little.

"You're the one driving the car, my dear, I'm just steerin' her," he drawled. "In case you didn't notice, you've had your foot on the gas pedal for the last 20 miles now."

There were times, as well, when Leona and I would be flat broke and Dave would either let us go for half the fare or he'd take our word that we would pay him back whenever we had money. I wouldn't be surprised if we still have a few outstanding IOUs after all those years, for I'm sure he never kept track.

We always used Drake's Taxi back then; but for the record, there were many other taxi services from the neighbouring communities of Lamaline, Point May, Grand Bank, St. Lawrence and Marystown that provided exceptional service as well. No matter what the weather was like or where they had to go, these men got the job done. If they couldn't accommodate passengers, then they would arrange for someone else to take care of them. Not only did they give you service with a smile, but they did things that went far beyond the call of duty. They would take people to doctor's appointments and wait for them; and often when parents couldn't accompany their children to St. John's, they'd place them into the capable hands of the taxi driver to get them to their destination safely. It's a good thing they didn't have meters running back then, for they put many extra miles on their vehicles and did it on their own time. They'd run errands all around town, delivering or picking up packages, prescriptions, licence plates, parts for cars and they never charged a copper more than the regular fare.

There's no doubt that the taxi service was one of the most important connections to the world outside the Burin Peninsula. Back in the '60s, most families in the smaller communities didn't own a car or even have a telephone in their home. In fact, the taxi drivers were very resourceful, for they gathered information about everything they thought passengers needed to know. There was a local radio station in Marystown called CHCM that offered people the opportunity to send out messages on the air. Often, when a taxi left to go to St. John's, they would make a stop there, even if it was less than an hour since they left their destination. Sometimes folks just wanted to let their family know how they were doing, especially if a person was ailing and on the way to see a doctor. As I recall, first when this service began, there was a standard message to be read on-air for people who were too shy to say much. The radio announcer would name the person it was going out to, where they were from and then read the message which simply said the same thing all the time: "Passing through Marystown and feeling fine."

Once the novelty wore off, people got more relaxed and added to their messages. "Passing through Marystown and feeling fine. The baby only threw up once since we left home, but she's asleep now."

"Dear Mom. Passing through Marystown and feeling fine. I forgot to bring my jacket, so can you send it in to me by taxi on Friday? Love, your son."

If, on the other hand, the taxi was arriving from St. John's, people still sent out messages to let their kin know what time they'd be home. I still chuckle at the message I heard that a man sent to his wife. "Passing through Marystown and feeling fine, but I'm gut-foundered. Looking forward to a feed of salt beef and cabbage when I get home."

We also had a few local taxi drivers who took people from one community to the other. Being able to hire a taxi to go a short distance was a luxury, and it might have been the highlight of my life, had the circumstances been different. Let me tell you what happened...

For days I had pleaded with Mom to let me go to a dance in Lawn when they were having their Garden Party, for up till that time she had never let me go. Finally, on that occasion, she relented and off I went with my friends. What a time we had dancing with the boys from Lawn, for we always thought they were the best dancers whenever they came to our dances in Lord's Cove. During the night, I went for a romantic walk with a boy I was dancing with and when we got back, my friends were nowhere in sight. Somehow they thought I had taken a ride with somebody else, so they left without me. Had it not been for my friend, Sheila Haley, who took me home with her, I would've been quat up on the step of the hall in Lawn all night long.

Knowing that Mom would be furious with the turn of events, I asked Sheila's dad to call my father to let him know I'd be staying the night with them. I barely slept a wink all night worrying about Mom's reaction when I got back home. The next morning at 8:30, Mr. Bob Walsh showed up, unannounced, at the Haley house to take me back to the Cove. Naturally, I dared not mention that I missed my ride home because I was on a moonlight walk with a boy, for I knew I'd never get out of the house to go to a dance again. Mom was madder than a broody hen about having to send a taxi for me.

"That's the height of wastefulness for me having to spend 50 cents to hire a car to bring you home!" she said, with her hands on her hips. "Well, missy, I can tell you that you won't be setting foot in Lawn for a dance for a long time!"

It's funny how sometimes we take things for granted, for we don't always take the time to tell someone how much we appreciate the things they do for us. I'm sure Leona and I never said it directly to Dave, but his kindness never went unnoticed to us or to our parents. Even though I don't know any of the new drivers back home anymore, I'm sure they still give the same great service that we've all experienced in the past. Sometimes when I arrive at the airport in St. John's and I see the taxi drivers standing outside the door, I get this wonderful feeling of déjà vu. Once again, I see Leona and me standing on the curb with our grips in hand and the familiar, smiling face of the taxi driver opening the door for us. "You two get aboard the taxi now and we'll have you home in no time at all."

I think those were the most comforting words any homesick person could ever hear.

# Swinging

I thought I'd outgrown it, but I was wrong. The urge still hits me in the summer months and before I know it, I'm heading for the nearest park where I know all the swingers hang out. I look for a more secluded place where the adults won't notice me, and then when I get the chance, I sneak past the children and choose the swing at the farthest end.

As soon as I'm off the ground, I close my eyes tight and let my mind drift back to when I was nine years old in Lord's Cove. I am seated on one of the homemade swings my father made and my fingers are wrapped securely around the thick brown rope on the swing. One of my sisters is pushing against my back to get me started. "Higher! I wanna go higher!" I squeal.

I can still remember how it felt. I'm leaning back as far as I can, my long ringlets billowing out behind me, as my bony legs extend and retract to propel myself higher until I'm flying solo. My whole body is reaching out and up, over the top of the post that holds the swings and I'm feeling elated and afraid at the same time. I can hear my own shrieks of laughter as the wind carries my voice past my ears and I want to stop, yet I don't. I swoop down, then back up again and I literally lose my breath as my head comes dangerously close to the ground. Oh what a thrilling feeling that was, for I felt like I was flying. It was an exhilarating and invigorating experience that always stayed with me.

As children, swinging, was our favourite pastime, especially in the summer. We spent a lot of time whiling away the hours and entertaining ourselves by having contests to see who could swing the highest and who could jump the farthest. Mind you, jumping wasn't for the weak and whiny person, for it took a lot of courage to jump from a moving swing at its highest point. Make no mistake, it was a dangerous practice, but that only added to the excitement for us. One of the older ladies in the Cove who'd pass by would often warn us what might happen. "If you jumps like that, you're gonna drive your legs right up into your stomach!" she'd say.

We'd stop immediately, but as soon as she was out of sight, we'd do it again. Now the timing had to be perfect for jumping from a swing, for we knew there was a chance that we might never be able to land safely on our feet. We usually relied on our friends to coach us from the sidelines, for nobody wanted to get hurt. "Go on, go a bit higher, that's it! Now aim for a spot to land on, and when I counts to three, you jump!"

As soon as we heard "Three!" we'd let go of the rope and, screaming as loud as we could to bolster our confidence, we jumped. Even in midair our legs were moving and once our feet hit the ground, we were already running to hold ourselves upright until we skidded to a stop. God help anyone who got in our way.

I remember one time when I was all geared up to jump and a gust of wind blew my dress up over my face just as I let go of the rope. With arms and legs flailing, I hit the ground, tumbled head over heels and landed face down in a puddle of mud. The next thing I knew, Mom was hauling me up on my feet and wiping the mud off my face with her apron. I was dazed for a moment; but, other than a few nasty scratches on my knees and elbows, the only thing that was bruised was my ego. Apparently when I landed in a heap, my dress was up over my head and my underwear was exposed to all who came running to my rescue.

Now Mom was always warning us about getting hurt or injuring somebody else, so we can't say we weren't told often enough, especially after the incident with my sister Helena.

When she and our cousin Francis were playing around on the swings one day, they never noticed that Mom came out to the woodpile to pick up woodchips for the stove. As usual, she was bent over filling her apron with the kindling. When she backed up, Helena was swinging in midair and her foot caught Mom's elbow, sending the chips flying in all directions. Mom wasn't hurt, just taken off guard a little, but that didn't stop her from giving my sister a tongue-lashing about being careless. "You mark my words, young lady, you'll be sorry when you breaks a leg or, worse still, you breaks your neck one of these days," she said. "If you goes looking for trouble, then you'll find it!"

No matter how many warnings we got, it didn't deter us from having fun, which sometimes included two people sharing the same swing. We'd stand face to face with our feet planted on the seat and see how high we could make the swing go. If the swing happened to break from the weight, then there was nothing between us and the ground to soften the blow. And it certainly wasn't easy to find another rope for a swing, but one of the boys always managed to cut off a piece of somebody's clothesline when they were not looking.

My cousin Lorraine lived next door. She had several swings as well and our dads made the greatest swings for us. The wide, wooden seat was handmade with two holes at either end where the rope was threaded through, so the seat was always secure and comfortable.

We had two sets of swings at our house, one beside the sunporch and the other up on the hill behind our house near the stable. The two up there were the best, for my father made the posts much higher, which meant that we could swing farther out because the rope had a longer reach. And best of all, you got a panoramic view of the Cove from that point.

Once you started swinging like a pendulum, your feet swung out so far that you could look down over the roof of our two-storey house. 'Course we dared not jump from that height, for there was a rocky incline below and the girls weren't that brave.

The boys didn't use the swings too much because that was a girl thing, but they did when they wanted to show off to the girls. They'd jump no matter what consequences they suffered. Although a few came out unscathed, others ended up with sprained ankles or chipped teeth, or got the wind knocked out of them. Still, no matter how badly bruised they were, they got back on the swings.

I suppose back then, we didn't have many places to go other than each other's houses, so we usually congregated in groups outside somewhere. At our house, we used the chopping block to sit on, along with several seesaws. One of the seesaws was ours and the others belonged to Lorraine. It was just a plank shoved between an opening in the picket fence that separated our houses. So between the seesaw and the swings, we spent a lot of time there, singing and talking.

Most of the songs we knew, of course, were old ones we'd learned from our elders, songs that told stories of lost love, hardship and sorrow. Looking back now, I can imagine how someone today would wonder what in the world young children were doing singing such woeful songs. But for us, it didn't matter what the material was, for we just loved to sing. My favourite used to be "The Conductor's Song," a story about a young vagabond who drifted from town to town on a train searching for his long-lost father. Bernard Stacey from Lord's Cove used to sing that every time he came to our house and I'd get all choked up listening to him because he sang it so beautifully and with such feeling.

Then there was a song called "Mary of the Wild Moor" that my sister loved to sing. It told of Mary's sad plight when she walked across the moor to her father's house on a cold winter's night with her baby in her arms. When she arrived, he was asleep and never heard her knocking and crying for him to let her in. In the morning when the old man opened the door, he discovered that his daughter had perished on his doorstep, but the baby was still alive in her arms. Leona would be sitting on the swing, belting out the song at the top of her lungs. When she'd get to the part where the distraught father discovers his dead daughter, she'd get so emotional that her voice would squeak and her whole face would bivver.

"I couldn't carry a tune back then and I still can't," she laughs now, "but that didn't stop me from trying."

Leona recalls overhearing a comment from our neighbour as she chatted to Mom one day. "Lottie, my dear, that song is mournful enough as it is, but somehow whenever that poor youngster tries to sing it, it sounds right pitiful altogether," Mrs. Lambe said.

Goodness, how we loved swings. Even when we thought we outgrew them, we didn't really give them up totally, not even when we were teenagers. And romance was not lost on us either. What better setting could one ask for than a warm July night with the saltwater moon shining overhead and the smell of hay lingering on a gentle sea breeze? Picture it. A bashful young girl sitting on a swing, lounging against the rope while an adolescent boy gently moves the swing back and forth. Her giddy laughter resounds in the night air as he playfully catches the swing and holds her suspended in midair so that he can steal a kiss. Oh my, but that would make any girl's heart flutter, wouldn't it?

It may sound strange, but those swings were like security blankets that offered comfort as well as entertainment. There we could swing away the blues when we were feeling down, soothe a bruised ego or indulge in a private moment of pouting because we were angry about something. Motion was not necessary either, for we could just sit on the swing and ponder life in general, or amuse ourselves by twisting the rope around and then letting go so we could spin in a circle until we got dizzy or went cross-eyed. It was on those swings that we dreamed our dreams and made plans for the future.

Many years have past since that time, but memories of our swinging days still remain. Now whenever I go past a park and see children on the swings and seesaws, I get that old familiar feeling and I stop for awhile to watch them. On occasion, I slip into a swing just so I can relive those moments that were so dear to me as a child.

And I stay there as long as I can...well, at least until I'm asked to leave. "Hey, lady. Can I please have a turn on the swing now?"

Sheepishly, I relinquish my seat to the curly-haired little girl patiently standing beside me. I smile at her and walk past the children who are talking and laughing. Then I take one last look at the little girl on the swing with her hair flying in the wind. All the way home, the vision of her happy face stays with me.

# Young Love

Picture it. It is a warm June night and the moon is hung so low over the ocean that you can almost reach out and touch it. You're standing on the shimmering sand and Pat Boone is softly singing "Love Letters in the Sand" as he gazes into your eyes. Your heart is thumping in your chest and your legs feel so weak you can hardly stand as he croons sweet love words: "...how my broken heart aches, with every wave that breaks, over love letters in the sand."

Reaching for your hand, he pulls you into his arms and, giddy with the anticipation of his kiss, you close your eyes as his lips touch yours. Then, without warning, your eyes suddenly fly open as you hear your name bellowed in your ear. "Lucy, hurry up and fill up that bucket will you! You've been staring up at the moon long enough. What's the matter with you d'night, me child?"

That's when I realized it was my father's voice. I was 13 years old then, standing on the beach in Lord's Cove, with my rubber boots planted firmly amongst thousands of twitching silver-black caplin rolling in from the Atlantic Ocean where they came to spawn. I was holding a net and an empty bucket, staring up at the big moon and Pat Boone was nowhere in sight – except in my mind's eye, that is. But my, it was a lovely fantasy while it lasted.

Romance is wonderful, isn't it, especially when you are a teenager? Even though we were not exposed to the ways of the outside world in my day, we had no problem recognizing what romance was. We heard it in the songs we listened to and we saw it in the reaction of those around us. You know the kind of signs I'm talking about: the special look that passes between two people, a blush, a bashful glance or perhaps a flirtatious smile. Every time we heard a romantic song, we memorized every word of it. A song was not just a song and a dance was not just a dance, for we believed that every word and action meant something. If it was a love song that was playing and a boy asked you to dance, then you believed that he was sending you a message that he wanted you to be his sweetheart. "Oh my gawd, he's gonna ask me to dance! I'll just die if he sings the song in me ear when we're dancing."

Granted, most of the intrigue was in our imaginations, but that's where the seed of romance begins, isn't it? I admit, I had a crush on Pat Boone, but I was totally infatuated with Elvis Presley. I fell in love the moment I first heard him sing "Love Me Tender." I got so emotional that I almost choked when the slice of bread and molasses I was eating got stuck in my glutch. It didn't matter that I was in Newfoundland and he never knew I existed; but in my heart and soul, I knew he was singing that song for me alone and I swooned at the thrill of it all. I think William Shakespeare knew the ways of the heart when he penned these words in "A Midsummer Night's Dream."

"Love looks not with the eyes, but with the mind
And therefore is wing'd Cupid painted blind."

As I recall, many moons ago when I was in my teens, summer was the most romantic time of year. Most of the courting went on at night, for we didn't want our parents to know that we were consorting with boys. Goodness, we'd never get out of the house after supper again if they knew, for young love would be nipped in the bud before we even got nerve enough to hold hands. 'Course that never stopped us. We still took advantage of every opportunity. If it was a beautiful moonlit night, then we'd go for walks on the back road or down on the wharf. If it was raining, we found shelter beneath the roof of a stage on the beach, and on foggy nights we could walk the main road without worrying about the probing eyes of the adults.

That's not to say that the parents didn't believe in romance, but they always seemed to discourage it in our pubescent years. Call it tough love on their part, but I think they were merely trying to ease the emotional hurt that often comes with young love. I know Mom could detect the lovesick blues before we even knew we were smitten. 'Course, with nine youngsters to raise, I imagine she recognized the symptoms, for we all had loss of appetite, walking around in a daze and standing in front of the looking glass to practice how to kiss with your lips puckered up like a sculpin. My sister Leona recalls having a crush on a boy in Lamaline when she was 14. She never told a soul her secret, but yet Mom knew. There she was one day, lying on the daybed thinking about him, when suddenly Mom snapped the dishtowel across her backside. "Will you stop mooning around after some boy, my dear!" she said. "Now you forget all that old foolishness and make yourself useful. Go scrub the kitchen floor or bring in the clothes off the line."

I can still recall the first time I encountered a similar situation when I got my first kiss. Well, okay, so it was just a peck on the cheek, but it could've been more had the circumstances been different. 'Course, to protect the identity of my knight in shining armour, I won't name him, but it happened one night when we were walking up the road together as we'd done many times before. I was taken by surprise when he asked me if I wanted to stay and talk for a while and I immediately felt very shy. He went and sat down on the chopping block by the woodpile, and not knowing what his intentions were, I sat on the opposite end. I got so tongue-tied that I could hardly speak and I could tell he was feeling very uncomfortable as well. For almost five minutes, not a word passed between us and, as usual when I got nervous back then, I started fidgeting with the garters on my stockings. When he edged closer and whispered in my ear, I almost snapped my garter. "I wants to kiss you," he said.

I guess I must've said yes because the next thing I knew, he was leaning toward me with his eyes closed, so I shut mine, too, and puckered up the best way I knew how. Just then, the outside porch light came on and Mom stuck her head out the door. "Lucy, what are you doing out there?" she bawled. "You get in the house right now and do your homework, you hear me?"

His kiss barely landed on my cheek as I jumped up and before I realized it, I had knocked him off the chopping block. Oh, me nerves! I was so embarrassed that I ran into the house and left him there and neither of us ever spoke of the incident again. Who knows how our lives might have turned out had that romantic moment happened?

I think we all have recollections of the first romantic stirring of love that we felt. I know we found romance anywhere and everywhere and we took advantage of every opportunity, including playing the games of love that people play. Awkward as newborn calves, we found a way to get the point across if we were attracted to the opposite sex. Often we'd re-enact a scene from a western show, and under the guise of playing "let's pretend," we marched into a world of unknown adventure.

I can still see the boys now, red kerchiefs tied around their necks, brooms or mops tucked between their knees to imitate the horses and Carnation milk cans molded to their shoes to give the effect of thundering hooves. In retrospect, I realize that the whole experience was a comedy of errors, for we had no idea what happened in real life, so we just did a lot of play-acting. As we observed at the Sunday afternoon movies, we simply went along with the idea of the women welcoming their men back home with open arms. There was a lot of giggling and foolishness going on, but we did it anyway.

Caught in time between children and adults, we played child games with grown-up rules; games like hide-and-go-seek, where we got paired off with the opposite sex to find a hiding spot. In the summer, we'd hide in a haystack so that we could cuddle and do a little smooching, for we knew that nobody was in a hurry to be found. If we went to someone's house while the parents were away on a Saturday night, we played spin-the-bottle, for that offered the chance of being sent to the back porch or a dark closet for the sole purpose of kissing. For the inexperienced and the bashful, this was the perfect set-up, for the intrigue of discovering what young love can be like taught us many things about ourselves. Oh yes, keen as the wind we were. We may have been a bit naïve, but we weren't stunned.

When I think of the artists who wrote the lyrics to all the love songs, I suspect they knew it was a universal subject, one that would last for all time. When it comes to matters of the heart, we're all romantics, and I daresay that many relationships have been formed based on the words of a song. Every year, come Valentine's Day, people try to recapture that old familiar feeling in many ways. Some may wonder about what might have been of their first love, while others try to rekindle the flame or perhaps celebrate a lasting relationship. I know I still keep the memory of Pat Boone and Elvis Presley tucked away in my heart because it reminds me of what it was like to experience first love. Writer and cartoonist Norman Lindsay once said that the best love affairs are those we never had. I agree with him. Young love really is a many-splendoured thing, isn't it?

# Farewell to the King

A few years ago when I heard about Patrick Swayze's new movie, "Dirty Dancing," I could hardly believe my ears. I thought someone had written a true story about the dance that set Lord's Cove on its ear when I was a teenager. That's where it started, you know…the dirty dancing. I should know, for I was smack in the middle of the whole scandalous affair back in the early '60s. Let me take you back to the night of our first sock hop when the teenagers were reprimanded and the King of Rock and Roll himself was banned in Lord's Cove.

We lived very sheltered lives in our outport back then. Radio was our only link to the outside world for we grew up listening to the downhome music of the fiddle, the button accordion, the guitar and the mouth organ. The sound of my dad's fiddle was as natural in our house as the resounding pitch of Mom's voice above the din of nine bawling youngsters. Everybody in the Cove knew how to sing and step-dance before they ever went to school and we spent hours listening to radio, memorizing the words to every song as we emulated the likes of Kitty Wells, Wilf Carter, Hank Snow and Johnny Case. The planchions buckled beneath our feet at the square dances and we were like wild stallions, kicking up our heels to the rhythm of the Lancers, the American Eight, the Set and Kitty's Ramble.

For years we were content with our own kind of entertainment…until we heard about the new dance rage. The square dances suddenly paled in comparison to the two-step, the jive and the twist. Ricky Nelson, Del Shannon, Bobby Vinton and Roy Orbison became our new idols and we'd crowd around the radio like flies around a molasses dish to listen to them sing.

And then there was Elvis Presley, crooning his way into the hearts of every teenager with "Love Me Tender" and making us gasp with the brazenness of "Don't Be Cruel." We were stunned when we saw his picture, stuffed into those tight clothes, and overwhelmed at the thought of a singer moving a part of his body other than the lips.

Even the boys went crazy for him. They started to talk and dress like Elvis, walking around with their collars turned up, their hair slicked back, making their lips quiver and their eyebrows twitch every time they saw a girl. When Mom saw my brother bivvering and shaking in front of the mirror one day, she lugged him off to the doctor to have him dewormed.

The girls traded their ponytails for kiss curls and lipstick, and their rubber bottoms for high-heeled shoes. We pretended not to notice the halo of mosquitoes that hovered around the boys' Vaseline-slicked hair and they turned a bind eye to the girls as we practiced walking in high heels.

Then came our first teenage sock hop and it was the most exciting night of our lives. At first we all sat around listening to records, since nobody knew how to do the new dances. Finally, one brave couple tried to do the twist but it looked so painful that nobody else ventured out there. It took awhile before we dared to put on a little slow music and everybody was shy to try the two-step, for nobody wanted to look foolish. We stood around looking like a bunch of stun-poles and when Pat Boone sang about love letters in the sand, we all took to giggling. It looked to be a disastrous evening until someone turned off the bright overhead lights in a desperate attempt to get us past the awkward stage. There were still lights all around the hall – it was by no means dark – but slowly the dance floor filled with stiff-backed boys holding girls at arms' length, nobody daring to look at their partner. We looked like newborn calves trying to walk for the first time.

When Elvis' record was played, even I couldn't resist his charm. I kept stomping on my partner's feet at first and we couldn't get on the same beat no matter what we did. So, we did like all the other couples did... we counted the steps aloud. "One, two, three, step front... one, two, three, step side...one, two, three, step back..."

We were just getting the hang of the two-step without counting when all hell broke loose as one of our mothers walked in. The bright lights were turned back on, Elvis' voice came to a screeching halt and we were driven out the door like a herd of sheep. In no uncertain terms, we were accused of dirty dancing in the dark and displaying sinful, disgraceful behaviour in public.

The priest summoned everyone to the school the next morning and we were charged with performing what he called "the belly rub." The great inquisition lasted for hours and we were found guilty of dancing under the influence of the devil's advocate: Elvis Presley. Sock hops were forbidden for six months and the King was banned for life. When his records were played, parents turned the radio off and we got the knuckles upside of the head if his name was mentioned in their presence.

And that's what really happened. I don't regret my part in the big scandal because it was a symbolic moment for us teenagers. In a sense, it marked the death of our innocence and our emergence into modern times. After I saw Patrick Swayze's provocative movements in "Dirty Dancing," I felt a little disappointed... cheated, somehow. I couldn't help but wonder what we missed that night at the sock hop and how we might have changed history had we known the sexual implications of that dance. But I guess we'll never know now and we can only imagine what might have been. The only thing that makes my memory of that night less than perfect is the fact that I was dancing with my cousin Lorraine. But still and all... it was a night to remember.

# From Bobby Socks to Stockings

I remember vividly my first year of high school at Saint Joseph's Central High on Allen's Island in Lamaline. My friends and I were so excited our heads were spinning with high hopes and great expectations. We actually envisioned an overnight transition into adulthood and while we looked forward to meeting new challenges and deciding on careers, we were still apprehensive, fearful even, of both success and failure.

One morning, feeling especially grown up, I walked downstairs dressed in my new blue shag sweater and black skirt. My father smiled as he looked me up and down.

"Well, look at you dis mornin'... all dressed up like a new stick of gum!" he said. "Sure you looks like you're all growed up in that fitout you're wearing."

I felt so proud I could feel my elastic garters tightening up on my nylons. You remember the nylon stockings with the seam up the back, don't you girls? My sister had loaned me a pair of hers but I didn't want Mom to see them because I knew she'd never approve. I tried to keep out of her sight so she wouldn't see my legs, but the moment I opened the door to leave, she came up behind me.

"Glory-be-to-God! The nerve you got trying to sneak out wearing nylons at your age," she said. "You march right back upstairs, missy and take 'em off and don't let me see you wearing 'em again, you hear?"

I wonder if my mother had any idea how important it was for me to wear those nylons? They were a status symbol for teenagers. We wanted to fit in with the high school students and

to us, that meant dressing as maturely as possible. We were
prepared to leave everything behind that reminded us of child's
play. We discarded our hair ribbons and the denim book bags
our mothers made for us in elementary school, left our younger
playmates behind and literally traded our bobby socks and our
Lysle stockings for nylons. Besides, we wanted to make an
impression on the boys from the other communities of Point au
Gaul, Taylor's Bay, Calmer, Muddy Hole, The Meadow, Lories
and High Beach. Lamaline was only half an hour away, but it
may as well have been a thousand miles for us because, in our
minds, we were headed for bigger and better things in life.

I was devastated when my mother wouldn't let me wear
nylons but I wanted to fit in so badly, I found a way around it.
After all, Mom had only warned me not to let her "see me
wearing nylons" and I took it literally. For the first couple of
weeks, I'd put on the nylons and garters, roll them down to the
ankles and wear knee socks over them. As soon as I got on the
bus, I'd scoot down in my seat, pull up my nylons and take off
the socks. Naturally I made sure I reversed the process again
after school and Mom was none the wiser.

Just recently, my cousin Anne and I were reminiscing about
those days when we thought our nylons symbolized
womanhood. We may have been isolated from the rest of the
world, but we wanted to keep up with the styles in the catalogue.
I was used to getting hand-me-downs from my sisters or wearing
clothes that Mom had done a makeover on, but I always found a
way to make old clothes look different. We all did.

When we'd get tired of wearing a cardigan, we'd button them
up, wear them backwards and add a kerchief around the neck.
The summer before we started high school, we used to draw a
pencil line up the backs of our legs and pretend we were
wearing nylons. Then we'd practise how to walk, strutting up
and down the road with our hips swinging from side to side.

Anne and I were laughing about how it didn't matter to us if we got runs in our nylons or that those itchy garters kept rolling down to the knees. We were forever yanking them up and adjusting the seams at the back.

"I had a sore neck from looking over my shoulder to see if my seams were straight," Anne said. "To this day, I believe that's the reason I got arthritis in my neck."

"Tell me about it," I said. "My garters were so tight they'd cut off my circulation. Why do you think I have these ugly varicose veins now?"

I think it was about the end of the third week when Mom discovered I was wearing nylons. I'd forgotten to roll them down in my socks before I got home one day and she spied them right away. It wasn't the seams that alerted her, but the large run up the front of my stocking.

Once a girl changes from bobby socks to stockings, it's hard to go back, but Mom made me wear those itchy Lysle stockings that I wore in elementary school. "Pride must pay," she said.

It wasn't until my second year of high school that I was allowed to wear nylons and by then, the seamless ones were in vogue and garter belts were worn instead of the handmade elastic garters. I'm not sure which was worse, trying to keep the garters from rolling down or losing the little fastener on the suspender and having to put a button or a penny in there to keep the stockings up. Still, I didn't let it bother me much. I was wearing silk stockings and that was good enough for me.

Ahh, but the years have gone by so quickly, haven't they? Time and distance has since separated me and many of my classmates, but the memories of those days at St. Joseph's Central High School will always stay with us. Perhaps one day we'll have a reunion and we can catch up on everybody's news and reminisce about old times. If that happens, I think I'll get all dickied up like I did on my first day of high school. If I can find a pair of nylons with the seam up the back, I'll make myself some garters and wear them, just for old times sake.

# Lessons Learned

"If mistakes were horses, then many a fool would ride." I'm not sure who said that, but I thought it a wise observation. After all, who among us is perfect?

We all succumb to weak moments and do things we are ashamed of or cover up something we don't want others to know. I can only imagine how difficult it was for my parents raising nine children and how they coped with the lot of us is beyond me. As I recall, we all had great respect for our parents and we knew better than to sass them. Trust me, there were many lessons learned in our household when we did wrong and while at times there was a sprinkling of tough love, we understood that it was for our benefit. Mom's bark was worse than her bite, but we always saw through that. My sisters and I usually got a swat across the backside with her tea towel, but it was always gentle enough that only the ego smarted. Usually the boys got a tongue-lashing from her, but Daddy seldom ever raised his voice to us.

The only time I saw him getting all worked up was when my brother Harve was 15 and they had a few cross words. I was never sure what the disagreement was about, but when I overheard him talking back to my father, I was shocked. Apparently Harve told him that he was too old to be told what he could or couldn't do. "Getting too big for your britches now, are you?" my father shouted. "Well you're living under my roof now, so you'll abide by my rules!"

With that, Harve declared that he was leaving home and never coming back. "Suit yourself, m'son," Daddy said, "and make sure you closes the door behind you!"

Without another word Harve stomped upstairs and a few minutes later returned carrying his grip. I begged him not to go but he walked out and slammed the door behind him. When I started bawling that got Mom all upset, too, and when he hadn't returned by 11:00 p.m., my father began pacing the floor. I kept going outside and calling his name, but to no avail...until I saw a flicker of light under the cellar door. And sure enough, when I opened the door there was Harve, sitting on his grip in the darkness smoking a cigarette. Once I told Mom he was home again, she coaxed him to come inside and face Daddy.

"Now Harve, you knows yer father didn't mean for you to leave home," Mom said, daubing at her eyes. "I kept your supper warm in the oven, so come and sit down now. You must be starving."

"Yis, b'y. Forget all the foolishness now," my father said with a smile. "We both got our dander up over nutting at all."

And just as Harve opened his gob to shove in a hunk of baloney, Mom socked him upside the head with her knuckles. "Now don't you ever make me worry like that again, young man, you hear me?"

Once my brother and my father established the boundary of mutual respect between them, they never discussed the matter again. Many years later, I asked Harve where he went that night and he confessed that he never even left our yard. "As soon as I got outside I realized I forgot to bring my clothes, so I hid in the cellar," he said. "The only thing I had in my grip that night was a pair of socks."

Years later, our brother passed away at the age of 56 after a long battle with lung cancer. But even in his last days the story about leaving home still made him chuckle.

Mom always claimed that my brother Raphael was the mischief maker in the family. "I never knew what that rascal was up to from one minute to the next," she'd say.

Raphael was nine when my sister Leona was born, and on

that particular day, he had the poor midwife at her wit's end because he kept bringing worms and insects to show her. Finally Mrs. May sent him outside to play, so he wandered off to the stable where he discovered a nest of white mice. Thinking that Mom would like the cute little things, he put them into a can and crept into Mom's room where he found her sleeping. He sat quietly for a few minutes until, anxious to give her his present, he shook her awake. "Look, Mom. I got a surprise for you. See?" he proudly announced as he dumped the mice on her pillow.

To put it mildly, Mom nearly went foolish from fright when the little rodents scattered across her pillow and the midwife literally had to hold her down. "Jumpin' Moses, what a dido Mrs. May kicked up!" Raphael remembers. "She took me outside by the ear and then m'father made me sit on the chopping block for an hour!"

Despite Mom's doubts, Raphael still maintains that his intentions were good.

Even as an adult he was up to his old tricks. When Raphael had a job transporting fish and freight to Grand Bank, our uncle would occasionally go with him. One time, after they had a couple of beers in Fortune, Raphael was driving along when he saw a police car approaching in the distance. Worried that he might get stopped, he pulled off onto the roadside. "Quick, Uncle Dave! Grab a wrench and get under the truck!" he yelled. "Just bang on something under there and make some noise so they'll think we're having trouble."

Sure enough, the policeman stopped to see what was wrong. As they talked, the banging got louder and louder beneath the truck, and then the cursing started. After the officer left, Raphael was delighted that his little charade had worked. "You did a wonderful job with all that racket and banging you were doing, Uncle Dave!" he giggled. "And the cussing was a nice touch."

"I did what you told me to, m'son," Uncle Dave said, "but what do you want to do with these doo-jigger t'ings that fell off?"

At that point Raphael realized Uncle Dave Joe was holding the muffler and tail pipe.

Oh yes, that was a costly mistake for my brother and only one of many lessons he learned.

Recently my sister Leona and I were talking about the things we did as children when she suddenly brought up a question that made me flinch. "Do you mind that pretty blue cup and saucer that Mom got from one of our relatives in Saint-Pierre and Miquelon?" she asked.

My heart lurched, for in my mind's eye I saw a vivid picture of that gold-trimmed floral cup and saucer. We were never allowed to touch it because it was so delicate and the only time it got used was when the priest came for a cup of tea. I stalled. "Hmmm, a blue cup you say?"

"Remember? Someone broke the handle off the cup and Mom blamed it on me," Leona said, "but I didn't do it."

No matter how I tried to get her off the subject, she nattered on until my nerves were rubbed right raw. Finally, I confessed my secret of 40 years. "ALRIGHT! It was me who broke the cup and I was scared to tell Mom, okay!"

"YOU SLEEVEEN!" she hollered. "You let me take the blame all those years ago and Mom thought you could do no wrong!"

How I regretted sneaking into the house after Father Lawlor left that day and Mom went to the shop. I couldn't believe it when I saw Mom's prized possession sitting on the sideboard. On the spur of the moment, I picked it up. Holding the cup and saucer as carefully as I would a newly hatched chick, I carried it to the table. Then I filled it with water and sat on the chair beside the window where Father Lawlor usually sat. I felt like a queen sitting there as the sun glanced across the gold rim of the teacup when I sipped my water. I held the cup so tightly that when I tried to set it back on the saucer, my hands began to bivver and I banged the handle against the edge of the table. Horrified when the handle fell in pieces on the floor, I scooped them up, put them inside the cup and turned it around so the broken part wasn't visible.

Realizing what I had done, I ran to the nearest hiding spot – the chicken coop. Snivelling and whimpering, I endured the foul smell for several hours. When my legs started to cramp I crawled out, covered in hen droppings and feathers. I readied myself to face Mom, but when I got into the porch I heard her lecturing Leona about the broken cup. Like a coward, I crept upstairs and let my sister take the blame.

I was guilt-ridden for days and when the time arrived for our school class to go to weekly confession, I unburdened my conscience. A sin of omission, Father Lawlor called it. And just to make sure I was forgiven, I went and stood in the lineup a second time. I tried to disguise my voice so the priest wouldn't know it was me and after he gave me absolution, I felt relieved...until he reminded me that I only needed to confess the same sin once in a day. Suffice it to say that I made myself scarce every time he came to our house after that.

In retrospect, I believe I have learned by my mistakes and I'm glad now that I finally 'fessed up to my sister. The way I figure it, if I can stay out of the way of those fools riding horses, then there's hope for me yet. From now on, if I do something wrong I'm going to admit responsibility for my actions...as soon as someone drags it out of me.

# Leaving the Nest

It was the best week of my life and it was the worst week. That's the only way I can describe the experience of leaving home for the first time when I went to St. John's back in 1967. Like most teenagers, I had envisioned this event all through high school: making plans for college, meeting new friends and being on my own where I could do whatever I pleased. I was convinced that my future would be one big roller coaster of fun and merriment once I left my old life behind. When I got dropped off in St. John's at a friend of my mother's, I stood in the driveway with my battered grip in hand and $25 pinned to the inside of my training bra. Awed by the sheer size of the city I felt very small and insignificant in my unfamiliar surroundings, yet excited by the prospect of it all. I had finally done it. I had flown the coop… left the nest.

Everything was so different than what I was used to. I had never seen so many people in one place at one time or so many houses and cars. I spent most of the first morning at the College of Trades and Technology trying to find my way to where I was going to register for school. At the end of the day, I had to get on the city bus for the first time. Seeing a girl I recognized from my class, I took the same bus she did, although I was too shy to speak to her. Instead, I crept to the back of the bus, wondering how the bus driver would know where to drop me off because he didn't ask me where I was going. I must have driven around St. John's three times before I finally made my way up to speak to him and discovered that I was on the wrong bus. When I got off the second bus, I got lost and Mom's friend was frantic with worry.

Finally, after walking around the block a dozen times trying to find her house, I straggled in with blisters on my feet from the sparbles in my old shoes and so hungry I almost fainted.

Everything was so different from home that at first it scared me. I just couldn't get over the fact that people lived in basements. When I walked along the streets on my way to the bus stop, I'd see faces peering out through windows by my feet. I felt so sorry for these people because, at home, we only kept vegetables, barrels of pickled cabbage and old junk in our cellar. Everybody seemed so cold and unfriendly. I'd be walking to school, nodding my head and saying hello to everybody I passed like we did at home, but people either ignored me or gave me weird looks. When I mentioned this to the woman where I was staying, I got a lecture on the dangers of talking to strangers and then I was afraid to look at anybody.

I was so homesick by the third day that I wanted to head back home to familiar surroundings, crawl into my own bed and hear Mom nagging me again. "Now you be home tonight to do your homework if you knows what'd good for you, young lady!"

The only thing that kept me going the first week was the thought that I'd be seeing my sister Leona on the weekend. She was attending Memorial at the time, but I hadn't been able to contact her because she didn't have a telephone at the apartment where she was staying with two other students. When she finally showed up, I was ecstatic. I begged her to take me with her and once we got to the apartment, she reluctantly talked her roommates into letting me stay with them permanently. That small, three-room apartment with the oil stove in the middle of the livingroom was a far cry from luxury, but it looked like paradise to me. Mind you, I would have given anything to have my old chamber pot stuck under the bed, for we had to go down two flights of stairs to the bathroom that we shared with six other tenants.

Learning how to survive in the big city of St. John's was an

experience in itself, but naïve though I was, I got through
somehow. After I got to know all the girls in my hairdressing
course, I felt more at ease, for most of them were from small
outports like myself. They felt overwhelmed by the different
way of life, too, so we explored and learned together by trial and
error. Whenever we got together, all we did was talk about
"home" and reminisce about the good times we had with our
friends. Although nobody would admit it, being on our own
was not at all as we expected. It was probably the first time in
our lives that we realized all the good things we had taken for
granted. We were a bunch of homesick kids who missed the
security of our families and we grew up overnight.

Money was almost nonexistent for all of us girls at the
apartment, but we learned to stretch the few pennies we had for
miles. We gave new meaning to the word 'sharing'. We
exchanged, mixed and matched clothes every day and between
all of us, we were able to add a little variety to our wardrobe. We
even pooled our nylon stockings. Of course, that was before we
had pantyhose. We worked out this system so that we'd each
buy two pairs of stockings and whenever someone got a run in
a stocking, they'd take out the new stocking and save the old
one. By the end of several weeks, everybody's stockings had
runs in them, so we'd look for a perfect match from the pile. For
instance, if one of my stockings had two runs in it, then I'd pick
one from the pile that matched and so on until there were so
many runs in all of them we threw them out. We learned to be
very resourceful and whenever we ran out of food, we wrangled
an invitation for a meal. We sought out distant cousins who had
ever lived within 100 miles of Lord's Cove and even people we'd
never met before. Sometimes it wasn't easy trying to be tactful
on the pay phone, but hunger can do strange things to people.

"Hello. Is this Mr. Bishop? Well, you don't know me, but you
were in hospital with me father about 10 years ago... uhhh...
his name was John FitzPatrick (pause). Oh, so you DO

remember him? Well… I was just wondering if your lumbago is any better now… (pause). Come to supper, you say? Well… I think maybe I can find the time…"

Our parents would have disowned us if they'd known what my sister and I were doing. Our poor grandparents, God rest their souls, they would have turned over in their graves. Bold as brass we were. Oh, sure, oftentimes we treated ourselves to a movie or a good scoff of fish and chips at a restaurant, but we didn't make a habit of scrounging off the good nature of people. Still, we had a few tricks to pull out in emergencies. We'd accept dates for the sole purpose of getting a free meal. We usually double-dated so that at least two of us got fed, but we'd always order more food than we needed so we could bring home a doggy bag for the other two. That didn't always work to our advantage, mind you, for our dates were usually guys we met at school and they were in the same financial predicament as we were. Once when my sister and one of the other girls went on a double date, they thought they were going for dinner. After a two-mile walk downtown to Water Street, Leona and Grace were tired, hungry and thirsty. Every time they came to a restaurant, the girls stopped, thinking it was where they were going to eat. But the guys kept moving on. This went on the whole length of the street and the girls were salivating as they passed every restaurant. The guys didn't even offer them a Coke. When they realized they weren't going to get fed, they ducked into an ally when the guys weren't looking and headed for home. Later they heard via the grapevine that the guys were also broke and had asked the girls on a date hoping they were going to cook for them.

Oh, yes. Leaving home wasn't nearly as easy as I thought it would be. Lord's Cove seemed so far away to me back then and I longed to go home again. Suddenly the thought of scrubbing and waxing the linoleum in the kitchen didn't seem a chore anymore. Sitting at the table with a cup of tea was no longer a way to pass time, but a welcome opportunity to catch up on the news. And when the weekend was over, I'd find myself lingering on the doorstep, reluctant to leave what I thought I had wanted to get away from all my life.

My leaving home was a memorable occasion for more than one reason. Not only had I begun to embark on a future where I took control of my life, but it gave me the chance to spread my wings to see if I could fly alone. But I never forgot the reason why I was able to be strong enough to succeed in my solo flight. It was because I knew I could always go home if I failed. But more importantly, it made me realize that no matter where life's road might take me, I'd always have the recollections of those years to remind me of my roots and my family.

# The Gift of Gab

There are some people in this life who seem to be born with the gift of gab and their silver tongues can get them through any situation. My father always admired Joey Smallwood as a great orator and I often heard him say that our first premier was long-winded. "That man got a tongue like the clapper of a bell," he'd chuckle, "and he can talk the leg off a table without drawing a breath."

Now I'm not sure if that's a good or a bad thing. It has been said that talk is cheap because supply exceeds demand. I expect we all know people who monopolize the conversation when they're around others and they are often unaware of this vice unless someone brings it to their attention. While it may be an annoying or boring habit that's unacceptable to many, there could be a legitimate explanation behind all that talking.

For starters, nervousness can sometimes have the opposite effect on people. If they are normally shy or bashful, they can suddenly go off on a tangent and talk incessantly to fill in silences in an uncomfortable situation. Conversely, others can crack jokes or entertain an audience but are suddenly tongue-tied when they are offstage. Some talk nonstop because they want to be the centre of attention or they like the sound of their own voice, while others just need someone to talk to because they're lonely.

Call it what you will – gabbing, jabbering, chit-chatting or prating – when it comes to talking, we Newfoundlanders are able to hold our own. When you grow up in a household like ours with 11 people under one roof, you either ignored the nattering, shut your gob if you didn't want to talk, or joined in with the rest of them. I remember how our poor mother would get mesmerized with everybody talking at one time. "Merciful heaven...I can't hear m'self think with all the racket you youngsters are making!" she'd say as she stamped her foot. "Yer tongues are gonna fall off from all that chawing."

Apparently, as a young child I didn't even speak for several years or more. Mom said I couldn't get a word in edgewise because my eight siblings prattled so much and nobody really noticed that I wasn't talking. Seems that all I had to do was point to what I wanted and somebody got it for me. Perhaps that explains why I was a painfully shy child. I remember that when somebody spoke to me, I'd either run away or hide behind Mom's apron. In high school, if the teacher asked me a question in class, I'd almost faint; if I did manage to speak, I made no sense at all. I was fine talking to someone on a one-to-one basis, but if there were more than three people in a room, I'd be so nervous I'd get tongue-tied and end up looking like a stun-pole.

The hardest thing I had to do was leave home to go to college, for I had no choice but to speak up for myself then. Sure I remember the first time I had to use a public bus in St. John's. My nerves were rubbed right raw and I was afraid to speak to anybody. I waited until everybody got on the bus and then I mustered up the nerve to speak to the driver. "Sir, does this bus go to the College of Trades and Technology?" I asked timidly.

Relieved that I was on the right bus, I passed him the quarter that I was clutching in my clammy palm and without making eye contact with anybody, I made my way to the back of the bus. When I saw the Confederation Building coming up, I knew the college was just beyond so I stood up and waited...but the bus kept on going. I was so frightened that I was almost in tears, but when I got my wits about me, I watched to see how the others knew when to get off. Finally, on the second trip around, I clued in that I had to ring the bell and I yanked that string several times to make sure the bus stopped.

I'm sure any of my family will tell you that even though I didn't gab much as a child, I made up for it in years to come. As I got older I had so much to say that I became quite adept at joining in the conversations with my brothers and sisters. I could prattle and argue as well as the rest, but I was still bashful around people I didn't know. Our crowd had acquired a knack of talking all at the same time and we each tried to speak louder and faster than the others. The girls, especially, could jump from one conversation to another and pick up where the other left off and never miss a word being said. It could be very confusing for outsiders. The first time I took Murray home to Newfoundland before we were married, he nearly drove himself foolish trying to follow the conversation. It's a wonder he didn't get whiplash from looking from one to the other when we all spoke in unison. He had a befuddled expression on his face all the while he was in the Cove. "Pardon? What? What did she say? Tell me what she said, Lucy…"

I think some people come by the gift of gab naturally. Back in my time, we lived very sheltered lives. All the same, there was a lot of interaction between people in small communities. They knew how to entertain themselves through songs, music and dance, for their social lives revolved around family and friends. We had a radio in our house, but we didn't have a telephone or television until I was in high school. Word of mouth then was a powerful tool, for news was passed on from one person to another and then on to other communities. Women carried on conversations over the fence as they hung laundry on the clothesline, while old men reminisced about days gone by.

I daresay the elders in Newfoundland communities didn't even realize they were setting the stage as entertainers for our generation. In my day, we were blessed to have the opportunity to sit around the kitchen listening to the older folks spin yarns that they'd heard from their forefathers. Through them we learned to become good listeners as well as good talkers, for not only did we respect the wisdom of our elders, but we were captivated by their stories.

I loved it when older people came to visit on the long winter nights. Mrs. Lambe from next door was my favourite storyteller. Mom knew that I always had nightmares whenever I listened to ghost stories so she'd make me go to bed, but I'd sneak out to listen anyway. My father had cut a hole in the floor above the kitchen stove to allow the heat to go upstairs, so I'd bring my pillow and lay on the floor where I could look down into the kitchen. One time I got so caught up in the story Mrs. Lambe was telling, that I trembled in fear. She told Mom about a moonless night when she believed she was being followed across the beach by a sinister creature that dragged itself in from the sea. When she got to the part about hearing him rattle his chains and pound on her door, she demonstrated by banging on the ceiling with the broom handle. I let out a curdling screech and as I tried to scravel to my feet, my foot went down through the opening and my leg got stuck right up to the thigh. The next thing I knew, Mom was hauling me out of the hole and giving me a tongue-lashing I didn't soon forget. To this day, I still don't know who got the biggest fright, me or Mrs. Lambe.

Storytelling is indeed an art. A good teller of tales can make a big difference between boredom and amusement, for it's all in the way you deliver a story. If one person can hold the attention of a crowd who come away smiling and laughing, then that's something to be admired. Using your gift to entertain, persuade or comfort someone is not a bad thing as long as you use it wisely. So if someone should tell you that you have the gift of gab, don't be offended. As long as you're not told to please shut up, then prattle on my friends…prattle on. The world is full of gabbers.

# Love, Marriage
# & Kids

*"Children deepen, complicate and test
the 'I do's' of marriage."*

– Unknown –

# Nobody's Fool

When I was a young girl, I always dreamed about meeting my Prince Charming and being whisked off to Niagara Falls on a honeymoon. I wasn't interested in a fairytale wedding or going to some exotic island. I just wanted to go to the Honeymoon Capital of the World because it sounded so romantic. As fate would have it, I did meet the right man and we did go to Niagara Falls on our honeymoon. Matter of fact, the more I think about it, the more I wonder what my life might've been like had I not met Murray.

Considering our first meeting, it's a wonder we ever got together at all. It was on a night in April at a dance in Labrador City when I first clapped eyes on him. A few of us girls from work decided to go listen to a new band and just before midnight I noticed one particular guy who kept looking toward our table. He had dark hair and a moustache and from across the room, he reminded me of Sonny Bono. As I surveyed him from a distance, he suddenly looked my way and our eyes locked for a moment. Feeling a little embarrassed, I quickly looked away and then, a few minutes later, he was standing at our table. My friends stopped talking all at once and then he held out his hand to me.

"Would you please have this dance with me?" he asked, ever so politely.

I felt tongue-tied for a second and then one of the girls literally shoved me off the chair. "Yes, she'd love to dance, wouldn't you Lucy?" Pam said.

The slow dance was almost over by the time we got onto the

dance floor, but then the band swung into a faster song, so we began to dance. When he smiled a little sideways smile, my heart fluttered. At that moment I knew he was special – different even.

Then he started singing along with the band. I'll never forget the way he belted out the song to the top of his lungs. "I love bread and butter, I love toast and jam, I saw my baby eating, with another man."

His singing brought tears to my eyes. It was downright pitiful watching him flounce around in jerky movements as he sang off-key in a high-pitched voice that could crack the bottom of a jam jar.

Good Lord, I thought, what kind of a fool did I get tangled up with here? He sang so loud that he nearly drowned out the band and he never took his eyes off me. I was mortified because he appeared to be serenading me and he paid no attention to the dancers as they moved out of his way. That was the longest dance in history and as soon as it finished, I made a beeline back to our table without giving him a backward glance.

My friends were laughing hysterically.

"If this is supposed to be your idea of an April Fool's joke, I'm not laughing!" I snapped. "I'll bet you guys put him up to this and I don't think it's one bit funny!"

Turns out it wasn't a joke after all. They never saw him before and when he came back for a second dance, I politely refused. The girls could hardly keep a straight face as he introduced himself and they invited him to sit with us. I pretended not to be interested, until I heard him say he was from Ontario.

"Oh, so you're a Mainlander then," Pam said, as she nudged me in the ribs again.

Murray looked perplexed.

"Oh no, I'm from Wasaga Beach originally, but I came here from Niagara Falls."

'Course my ears perked up when I heard Niagara Falls

and I barely heard Pam explaining that we usually referred to people from Ontario as Mainlanders. Was this a coincidence, I wondered? Could my Prince Charming be sitting right next to me?

As soon as the other girls got up to dance, Murray and I chatted a little and he confessed that he had indeed tried to woo me with his singing. I thought it was rather sweet, because it had to take a lot of gumption for him to do what he did. Call me a fool if you will, but I think that was the moment I realized he had stolen my heart. Just three months later we were engaged and a year later on April 22, we were married.

That was more than 30 years ago and I'm proud to say that we're still enjoying our lives together. As I recall, we encountered a few little hitches along the way, but we didn't let that stop us. Take my parents, for instance. They weren't too thrilled that I got engaged after three months, let alone the fact I was making plans for a wedding and they hadn't even met him yet. That he was neither a Newfoundlander nor a Catholic was also a big issue with them. My mother made no bones about it and she warned me that there could be trouble in paradise.

"You mark my words, Lucy, mixed marriages never work, my dear. Couldn't you have waited a little longer until you found a good Catholic Newfoundlander to settle down with?" she asked over the phone.

My father, on the other hand, had a different objection. He was disappointed that I didn't find a man who had some musical talent, because most of our family could sing, dance or play some kind of instrument. The first time I took Murray home to meet my parents, my father played the fiddle and as usual, I danced a little jig. Murray was so impressed that he jumped up and tried to step-dance as well. Oh me nerves, what a disaster that was!

He looked like he had two left feet. No matter how fast or slow my father played the fiddle, my eager husband-to-be didn't even come close to making both feet move at the same time. He tried in vain to hop from one foot to another until Mom complained that he was going to make the middle of her cherry cake fall that she had just put in the over. Finally, when the stove pipes started rattling, my father shook his head and hung up his fiddle. Later, out of earshot from Murray, he told me what he thought.

"That poor man you got there put me through some misery trying to play the fiddle for him, my dear," he said.

"I thought he was gonna beat the face off hisself the way he kept getting his feet all tangled up. Sure he must have lead in his boots 'cause he haven't got a bit of music in his bones at all."

Oh yes, my parents voiced their concerns, but I think they were just afraid that he would lug their youngest offspring off to the Mainland and I'd never get home again. Murray promised them that he'd get me to Newfoundland as much as he could and in all those years, he never went back on his word. Once we were married and they realized how much he loved Newfoundland, they gladly accepted him.

Trust me, I was no fool – I knew what I was doing when I married "that fella from the Mainland," as my parents used to call him. I am very proud of him for putting up with me all those years, for he was the one who had to make all the adjustments because of my downhome background, not me. I have to give him credit for trying to pass himself off as a Newfoundlander, but to this day, he's never been able to get the accent down pat because he talks too slowly. He's always been very proud that he married a Newfoundlander and he's never tried to change the way I am.

"I had to go all the way to Labrador to find a good woman," he usually tells people.

I think he's done remarkably well over the years. Oh sure, he gets that little nervous twitch in his right eye when we go to Lord's Cove and he tries to step dance. He tends to repeat himself at least 10 times a day, especially if I get into a snit. He knows exactly what to say now. "Yes, dear, no dear, you're right dear."

The best thing I love about him is his sense of humour, for he always has something positive to say. Every year when an anniversary comes along, we joke about the fact that Murray made my dream come true when he took me to Niagara Falls for our honeymoon. 'Course I tell him that I only wanted to visit Niagara Falls, not move here, for we've lived here most of our married lives. And he always gives me the same answer. "That's because we're still on our honeymoon."

That says it all, doesn't it? Oh sure, he still sings off-key in that high-pitched voice and no, his dancing hasn't improved over the years. But every time I see him walk into a room, my heart still flutters. Asked once about an impending anniversary, he said with a straight face, "We've been married for 30 wonderful years. Twenty- nine happy ones for Lucy and one for me."

No one took him seriously, though, because in another second that little sideways smile of his gave him away. That husband of mine is nobody's fool. That's why I married him.

# The Perfect Marriage

I know Mom warned me before I took my vows there could be trouble in paradise if I married a Protestant. "You mark my words," she said, "mixed marriages never work. Couldn't you have waited a little longer until you found a good Newfoundland Catholic to settle down with?"

Well, that was 38 years ago come April and I can say with total confidence that after a quarter-century of being together, we're still talking to each other and can argue as good as the next couple. What's the secret to our marital bliss, you might ask? Well, I'll tell you. I don't have a clue. That's the gospel truth. Note well that I have not said we have the PERFECT marriage. That only happens in the movies or in fairy tales – and besides, that theory clashes with both our religious beliefs. Perfection, after all, is in the eye of the beholder. But if I have to comment on what constitutes a perfect marriage, then I'd have to say what comes immediately to mind: If a couple can get through a week without nagging each other about something or uttering the words, "when hell freezes over," then that's as close to perfection as any marriage can get.

Doesn't sound like the ideal marriage, does it? That's because I've edited the romantic trimmings and fast-forwarded to reality. We all know that the honeymoon is over when you unpack the suitcases and realize that one of you has to wash the dirty laundry and cook dinner. It's a rude awakening for newlyweds who start their lives together with great expectations of living on love the rest of their lives and clinging to the impossible dream of changing everything about each other that you don't like. I remember how it was. I had a list longer than my arm of things that needed fixing on Murray and I was convinced he'd be just perfect as soon as I made him over in my image and likeness. I even dared to hope that Mom would forgive him for not being Catholic or at the very least, that she'd stop calling him "stun pole." But I was dead wrong. Trying to change that man was like trying to get blood from a turnip. And thank goodness he didn't budge, because these 38 years would've been disastrous if I had to live with someone as stubborn as I am.

It was quite a shock when we first found out that we were not compatible and the words "for better, for worse" suddenly had a new meaning. It seemed that all the BETTER things took a turn for the WORSE overnight. Trouble was, we both wanted to sleep on the same side of the bed and neither of us was willing to give it up. He had a sports injury and needed to keep his right leg on the floor while he slept and I had this thing about not being able to sleep unless I was facing the door. Finally, after a week of snarling at each other, we came up with a solution to accommodate both our needs. We moved the bed to the opposite side of the room...our very first lesson in learning how to compromise. I think that's when we realized that although we believe marriage is a union, it wasn't going to work if we both thought we were management.

We couldn't agree on anything. He liked to sleep on top of the covers with the heat turned up in the winter and I liked lots of heavy blankets with the heat turned way down. It seems that every day we clashed over something. I liked to stay up all night and he liked to go to bed early. He liked sports and I hated them with a passion. My idea of romance was a candle-lit dinner with roses, while his was Kentucky Fried Chicken and flowers that needed to be dusted. He made decisions on the spur of the moment and I took days to deliberate. We saw a side of each other that we never knew existed and the only thing we had in common was the fact that we agreed to disagree. The time we spent trying to prove to each other that we were compatible was just not worth it, so we gave up trying and accepted the fact that we are different.

To me, marriage is like a seesaw. Sometimes you're up and sometimes you're down, but it takes two to make it work. If one or the other falls off, then you help the other climb back on again. There's no such thing as a 50/50 arrangement. Some days one spouse gives 60% and the other 40% and then there are times when the role is reversed. The thing is, once you uncover the weakness and strengths in each other, then you have to either overlook them or accept them.

Like my cooking, for instance. I was far from being a domestic goddess and I've never made a secret of that. I walked into our marriage with very little in my hope chest other than a can opener, my old diary and a dozen Archie comic books that I'd saved. I did my best to make the meals exciting, but there are only so many ways you can dress up beans and fried potatoes. I got really ticked off when his mother interfered and began sending him care packages every week. And when she sent me a cookbook, I was so devastated that I almost packed my grip and headed home to Newfoundland to live with Mom. Naturally I blamed Murray for complaining about my lack of culinary skills and I got very angry. "If you don't like my cooking, then you can do it yourself!" I snapped.

It took a lot of cajoling, apologizing and talking to get past that big hurdle, but we got through the arbitration stage. Once we established a few guidelines, things ran more smoothly and we decided to take turns cooking and agreed to eat whatever the other made without complaint. I promised to read the cookbook if he would tell his mother not to send food and to stop phoning collect to ask what he had for dinner. To this day, my husband does the grocery shopping and I put them away. If he wants something special to eat, he cooks it and when my turn comes, I open the cans of my choice. As for the cookbook, well I READ it, as promised. I put it to good use – to prop up the end of the sofa that had a missing leg.

Oh, yes, you have to be flexible in a relationship and learn how to work out your differences. And believe me, you learn the hard way...through trial and error. There are no rules to follow and since it is your marriage, you can run it the way you want. And if there are things you can't change, then you may as well live with that fact. That's why I finally got my own television because I knew I'd never get custody of the remote control when Murray was watching sports. If it means having a heated argument over something occasionally, then so be it. Most happily married couples argue and if they say they don't, they're lying. Life would be pretty boring if the two of you agreed on everything all of the time. I love bickering back and forth; and what's more, I think it's healthy. Now Murray may call it an argument if we have a difference of opinion, but I call it communication. Sometimes when I can't make him see things my way, he'll agree with me just to hush me up, especially if there's a hockey game on TV. There's nothing more infuriating to me than leaving an argument unfinished. An hour later, that man has already forgotten we ever had a discussion and by then, I've built up a grudge bigger than both of us.

He actually has to ASK why I'm mad at him. "You KNOW!" I say, fixing him with the hairy eyeball.

Now I know he doesn't have a clue why I'm so mad... sometimes I don't remember myself, but he's a husband, so a wife can always find something he's done wrong. You see, it doesn't matter which of you gives in first and says you're sorry, just as long as you can keep peace in the house. But I know that my husband hates it when I give him the silent treatment, so he eventually apologizes and promises never do it again, even though he doesn't know what he's done in the first place. Whatever works, right? 'Course, I've had 38 years practice to hone my skill, so I'd never recommend it to newlyweds.

I don't know...maybe we tackled things the wrong way and that's why we don't have the perfect marriage like other people seem to have. I see other couples holding hands and kissing in public and it looks so romantic, yet I know I'd probably give Murray a black eye if he tried that mushy stuff with me in the middle of the mall. Heck, sometimes you can't even tell we're a couple. We never wear matching T-shirts, sing duets at parties, finish each other's sentences, eat off the same plate or open each other's mail. But we do respect and trust one another, enough so that we feel confident to do our own thing, to be independent and function as individuals. We're always there for each other even though we may be in separate rooms, and when we sit with our feet touching on the coffee table as he watches sports and I read my book, you can't find a more contented couple. In other words, we suit each other. We're soul mates and we've grown accustomed to our style. And that little bit I mentioned about Murray apologizing when he doesn't know what for? I'll let you in on a little secret. He knows I'm too stubborn to admit that I'm wrong or say I'm sorry to him, so he pretends it's his fault just to let me off the hook. Now what couple in their right minds would spoil a good thing like that?

# 'Til Birth Do Us Part

A friend of mine recently became a grandmother for the first time and naturally I went to see her new grandson. As I was admiring the baby, the new mother asked me a question that made me bivver all over. "Would you like to see the video of the baby being born, Lucy?" she asked enthusiastically. "My boyfriend got everything on tape...me screaming my head off, the crowning... everything. It's awesome!"

I could feel the corner of my mouth twitch and the hives popping on my thighs. She said the words so easily that you'd think she was asking me to watch an episode of "The Young and the Restless." The thought of watching something so intimate on a big screen over cake and coffee made me blush and I politely declined, telling her I had to rush home to water my plants.

Let's face it, I know where babies come from. I've had two myself and even the thought of having my husband in the delivery room with me was a strain on my nerves 23 years ago. After all, in my mother's day, babies were born at home with the help of a midwife, but the men were never present at the actual birth. Oh, they participated alright because they had the important task of boiling water for the midwife. Mind you, Mrs. May Isaacs, the midwife who delivered all of my mother's children, once told me she never really needed all the gallons of water the men provided. It was more to keep them busy so they wouldn't get in her way and they wouldn't dare poke their noses in the bedroom door because that was a private matter...a "woman thing", if you will.

However, things change, so when my husband expressed a

wish to go into the delivery room with me, I reluctantly agreed. In all fairness, he was there for the conception, so I figured he was entitled to be there for the birth as well. As it turned out, he didn't quite witness our son's birth and perhaps it was just as well. If Murray had attempted to stick a video camera in my...er...face, in my heightened state of misery, I might have resorted to violence like Lorena Bobbit did. My chances of having a second son would've been very slim had I been able to get my hands on a scalpel. Since I was not in any condition to help police search for Murray's missing appendage, divorce would've been inevitable.

As I watched the new mother getting ready to go see a movie with her boyfriend, I marvelled at her recovery from childbirth after only three days. Was it just me, I wondered, or is this new generation of women physically and mentally stronger than mine? In my mother's day, after childbirth the woman stayed in for 10 days or more, so I thought that was normal. But I later found out from the midwife that it wasn't because the women were so delicate, but it was more for their mental well-being. "If it was a woman with a large family, I always told the husbands that their wives had to have complete bed rest," she said. "After all, that was probably the only chance the poor dears would get to get off their feet. God knows they needed that time for themselves."

Oh, yes, I liked her way of thinking. Fact is, I needed the time to let my body shrink back to normal. I had enough stretch marks to reach from Ontario to Newfoundland and permanent ring-around-the-buttocks from having to sit on a rubber doughnut ring. I hung on to the bed springs for three weeks before I was evicted and even then, I didn't go willingly. I'm not ashamed to admit that I took full advantage of all the pampering I got from Murray when I got home. He did everything...the cooking, cleaning, groceries, washing diapers and getting up for the baby's night feeding. I figured that I had done enough in the delivery room, so now it was his turn. After all, I gave him a son and a snap to put in his wallet to replace the old one of Marilyn Monroe, didn't I? And he did, after all, miss the actual birth.

You see, I was in labour for almost 40 hours before our son made his grand entrance. That's why we always celebrate his birthday for two days. Naturally, Murray was beside me every second and after the first 30 hours, I was exhausted from pain. The more he tried to help, the more frustrated I became. I didn't handle giving birth graciously, but Murray remained in complete control, holding my hand, giving me directions on how to breathe and telling me not to push whenever I tried to speed things up. I'll be frank with you, even in normal times I get my dander up when someone tells me what to do, so you can imagine my reaction under stress. My dark side emerged and I was like a raving lunatic. Between the panting and heavy breathing, I focused all my attention on the centre of my pain...HIM. I don't even recall the words I spit at him or the rotten names that flew like knives off my tongue, but the woman in the next room later told me that she knew every time I got a pain because I screamed at my husband, "I feel a cramp coming on and it's got your name on it, so get out of my face!"

When I threatened to rip out his mustache one hair at a time, a wise nurse who had given birth three times herself, sent him to have a coffee. And wouldn't you know it, before he got back, our son was born. I felt terrible about all the verbal abuse I showered on him then, but he was so wrapped up in our new son that he didn't even remember that just an hour earlier I was threatening immediate divorce upon delivery. Instead, he brought me roses, chocolates and all kinds of lovely gifts. I could tell by the proud look on his face when he held the baby that all was forgiven, but I worried that the trauma of childbirth had taken its toll on him. Perhaps it was my weakened state that made me feel the way I did, but I thought he was acting really queer the way he'd stand outside my room stopping passersby and dragging them off to see the baby. He took up permanent residence outside the nursery window, making goo-goo sounds and reciting nursery rhymes in baby talk. It was pitiful to watch a grown man with his face plastered against the nursery window showing sports equipment to a newborn who had barely had a diaper change yet. Thank God our son couldn't see the crazed look in his father's eyes when he held up the hockey stick and skates as he blubbered on about the Boston Bruins, or he might have been traumatized for the rest of his life.

It wasn't until three years later that our second child was born and Murray saw my ugly side emerge again during labour. This time he was prepared for any adverse reaction on my part. Since the first delivery was so long, we assumed that the second might be the same, so when Murray went to take our three-year-old to a friend's house, it happened. After only 24 hours of labour, I was whisked into the delivery room and by the time Murray returned half an hour later, I was sitting up in bed holding our second son. He was very disappointed and apologetic for not being there and just to make it up to me, he actually hired someone to come to our house for a week so I could rest up in bed. Naturally I accepted his gift because I knew I wouldn't get the opportunity of being pampered for a long time now that I had two children to attend to. I was ecstatic the first morning when he brought her to my bedroom. After he left I just lay there relaxing while the pleasant young lady went to meet my toddler. "You know what would be great to start the morning," I said to her as she looked in the door, "...a long, hot bubble bath."

Her response was immediate. "I'll run the bath right away," she said and before I could blink an eye, she was headed for the bathroom.

Now I knew Murray said she was supposed to do light housework, but drawing my bath water? I thought I'd died and gone to Heaven! I called Murray at work and thanked him for finding this wonderful gem. "She's going to work out great," I told him excitedly. "You won't believe this, but she's running a bubble bath for me as I speak. I feel like a queen!"

My excitement was short-lived, however, when I made my way to the bathroom and heard my "hired help" splashing and singing in HER bubble bath. I could've used a video camera then. Somehow this young college graduate was under the impression that she was supposed to be on the receiving end of the "pampering," because I ended up doing all the work while SHE rested. I knew I should've set her straight on the first day, but I thought I'd give her another chance to redeem herself and besides, I didn't want Murray to know. The poor angishore didn't have a clue about anything. Instead of two babies, I now had three to look after. She talked on the telephone while I made lunch and did laundry, lay on the sofa reading her Harlequin Romance novel while my toddler watched cartoons, and took longer afternoon naps than he did. Every time I crawled back in bed, she'd yell up the stairs to tell me the baby was crying or come into the bedroom to ask if she should pick him up. When she woke me up to tell me we were out of chips and dip on the second day, I lost my cool and broke the news to her that the health spa was closed for the season and sent her home in a taxi so I could get a rest.

But that's all in the past now and I've chalked it up to inexperience. Had I known then what I know now about love, marriage and babies, I might have rewritten our vows. The words uttered so willingly at the altar might have set a new trend for women had I altered one little word before he slipped that wedding band on my finger. "Till birth do us part..."

My, it has such a nice ring to it, doesn't it?

# The Art of Snoring

It is one-thirty in the morning and I know I'm in for another sleepless night because my husband is at it again. He's lying here on our waterbed snoring so loudly that the vibrations are sending ripples through the water and I'm feeling nauseous. There is nothing more annoying than lying awake at night listening to someone snore, especially when that person won't admit there is a problem. My husband refuses to believe that he snores and gets very irate when I mention it. "Don't be ridiculous! Don't you think I'd know if I snored?"

I've tried to stop his snoring, but nothing works. I've stogged dirty socks in his mouth when he's sleeping, put toilet paper up his nostrils and I've even clamped a clothespin over his nose. On occasion I've used the old dog routine of hitting him on the nose with a rolled-up newspaper, but he sleeps so soundly that nothing will wake him. I've propped him up in a sitting position and blasted loud music in his ear, but he just snored along with the beat of the music. I even put tennis balls under him to keep him from sleeping on his back, but that didn't daunt Murray. In desperation, I called Mom to get her expert opinion and she told me to try putting a pouch of garlic and sulfur around the neck. I don't know if it was the snoring, the odious smell or the stiff neck I got from trying to sleep with that contraption, but it sure didn't work the way it should have.

In all fairness, I must say that it's not just men who snore. Women do it, too…and in the oddest places. I was chatting to an elderly woman at the bus depot once and right in the middle of her conversation, she fell asleep. There she was, wearing her sunglasses, sitting primly with her elbows propped on the adjoining chairs, holding a magazine as if she was reading and snoring so loudly that people began to stare, not at her, but at me. The shrill, little twittering noises came fast and furious, but never once did she lose her composure. She seemed to have a smile painted on her face, so nobody would ever suspect the weird noises were coming from her. When she finished her nap, she just opened her eyes and continued talking as if nothing had happened.

I'm convinced now that snoring is an art, one that has to be cultivated and honed through years of practice on unsuspecting victims like myself. I wouldn't be surprised if snoring could be used as a probable cause for divorce, not to mention the possibility of spousal homicide. I'm sure there are probably all kinds of medical reasons to explain why people snore, like allergic reactions, sinusitis, tight underwear, emotional tension or even dentures that don't fit properly. Dear Abby once wrote in her column that snoring could be a substitute for crying or a necessary unconscious form of release that's important to mental and physical well-being. In my husband's case, I'd say it's a form of mental cruelty...directed at me. It could be his way of getting back at me for hiding his golf clubs or for insisting that he wear the birthday tie the kids gave him with the battery-operated neon light. I read somewhere, too, that researchers believe snoring to be a hostile reaction, a sort of allergy to one's mate...a neat way of hitting one's spouse without leaving visible marks. I tried that theory once, you know, giving Murray the gentle budge in the rib cage, just enough to make him sit up and say, "What...what's all that noise?"

It worked for a week or so, but I finally had to fess up when he made a doctor's appointment to check out the bruising and soreness in his rib area. I guess if you've never been around someone who snores, you cannot begin to imagine what it is like trying to sleep with all that ruckus in the bedroom. As soon as Murray closes his eyes, the ree-raw starts.

I've had a lot of experience with snorers over the years and I believe there is a rhythm or pattern to snoring, because each snorer has a distinct tone, pitch and volume. Take my husband, for instance. He makes a powerful HKOHK-KHOHK on the intake breath and a thunderous VROOM-M-M-M on release with intermittent sounds similar to the call of tickelace. It's downright embarrassing when you have overnight guests. You haven't heard anything until you have guests who also snore, like my sister and her husband. Naturally, they both vehemently deny that they are in any way involved in such torturous behaviour and my sister gives me the cold shoulder if I mention it. The house is filled with the cacophony of bizarre snoring. Murray starts off the symphony with his *hkohk-hkohk...vroom-m-m-m* and my brother-in-law pitches in with a little vibrating number that sounds like *twoo...twoo...phew*! And my sister breezes in with her light, airy *aw-pooo-o-o-o*. This goes on all night, with the three of them snoring in discord, sometimes two taking up the slack while the other is building up steam for the next number. When they all reach the vibrating point, it sounds like an opera house with everybody singing off-key. The only way I can stand the noise is to find a song that fits the rhythm and hum along with the symphony until the noise lulls me into an exhausted, semiconscious sleep.

Now I'm getting desperate for a solution. If I can just get Murray past the denial stage and forced him to say "I AM A SNORER," that would be a start. Judging from the rumbling noises here beside me now, it sounds like he's reached an all-time high because my cat is dangling from the ceiling fan in a stark terror. The way I see it, the timing is perfect right now and I'm determined to get all the proof I need...even if I have to dangle this microphone in his face all night.

# Love is in the Air

I wonder if any of you who grew up in the 1960s remembers how teenagers in Newfoundland celebrated Valentine's Day?

In Lord's Cove, we would make our own heart-shaped cards and write notes that said "Will You Be My Sweetheart" or "Be My Valentine," but we never signed our name. Goodness no. Not knowing the identity of your admirer was the most exciting part. We called this little romantic gesture "dropping valentines."

Sometimes boys specifically put a girl's name on the cards and others just said "Guess Who." When that happened at our house, chaos erupted. We'd drive Mom foolish with our arguing as the three of us girls would claim that the card was meant for the other. "It's mine...I got it first!"

"No, that was s'posed to be for me."

"Mom, make Leona give back my valentine!"

'Course, Mom would lose her patience then. "Will ye stop that racket!" she'd say. "If those young men knew the way you girls are acting, they'll never come calling to court any of ye!"

I suppose there's not a woman around who doesn't enjoy being romanced by a loved one, myself included. Every year come Valentine's Day you'll see enamoured men buying chocolates, flowers, jewellery, perfume and romantic cards to express their love. They plan secret hideaways and reserve expensive rooms with heart-shaped tubs to woo their sweethearts. After all, passion blooms even in the dead of winter.

Of course, not all men are romantic. Some take love for granted; others don't seem to be able to express their emotions, so they buy cards embossed with the appropriate words that they can't say out loud.

My own dear hubby is not the most romantic man in the world, but he's always reminding me how much he cares by doing little things for me, like getting out of bed to go buy junk food when I'm watching a late-night movie. Now if that's not love, I don't know what is. He may not always express his love in words, but his heart is in the right place. The following true story is case in point.

A few years ago, one of my friends had booked a lovely room at a hotel here in Niagara Falls for Valentine's Day. When she had to leave town suddenly on business, she offered it to me. Naturally I accepted, for it was the perfect opportunity for a romantic rendezvous with hubby, especially since his birthday falls on February 15. I decided I would keep the room a secret till the last moment.

I had a week to think about it and wanting to make sure Murray would get in the mood for Valentine's Day, I wrote little love notes and drew hearts on the serviettes I put in his lunch bag. When that didn't work, I began flirting with Murray when he got home from work.

After supper one evening, while he watched a Boston Bruins game, I sidled up to him and sat on his lap. "How would you like a little bit of action later tonight?" I whispered in his ear.

"Sure, but can you move your head so I can see the TV, please?"

Then I wrapped my leg seductively around his. "Wanna play Doctor? I'll make it worth your while," I purred.

"I don't need a doctor," he said, trying to see over my head.

I nuzzled his neck. "Maybe we can spice things up a little tonight?" I suggested brazenly.

Suddenly Murray jumped to his feet and I nearly fell on the floor. "YES! YES!" he shouted. "It's about time you did something!"

I smiled, thinking I'd finally gotten the reaction I'd hoped for, but then I realized he wasn't looking at me. His eyes were fixed on Glen Murray from the Bruins. And, yes I can tell you it certainly was NOT me who scored.

When it comes to romance, that man of mine is right stunned sometimes. I gave up the advance flirting and concentrated instead on my plan to surprise him at the hotel. Let me tell you, it certainly WAS a surprise because he never showed up.

Earlier that day, I left him a message in a sexy voice inviting him to come to room 234 at exactly 8 p.m. I had everything set for romance: the lights were dimmed, the wine was chilled, dinner for two was ordered and I was all dickied up in my new black negligee awaiting his arrival. Eight o'clock came and went, but I gave him the benefit of the doubt and waited a little longer. Then I tried calling him at home but the line was busy for over an hour. Thinking he was probably on the phone with our son talking hockey as they usually do, I decided to get dressed and go home. To my surprise, I found Murray sound asleep in his chair with the telephone still beeping in his hand.

I shook him awake, none too gently. "Don't you ever listen to your messages?" I hollered.

He looked befuddled. "I've been on the phone all night looking for you. What happened to you?"

"I was waiting for YOU, of course!" I said sarcastically.

By now I was mad enough to spit nails. "So you're saying you DIDN'T get my message about the hotel?"

"What hotel? What message?" he croaked. "The only message I got today was a crank call from some drunk woman with a bad accent!"

That's when I realized he hadn't recognized my voice. With the mood I was in, I had no intention of telling him the difference. I felt my bottom lip bivver. "Never mind. You've ruined the surprise so let's just forget the whole thing!" I snapped.

As I walked past the dining room, I noticed a flicker of light. You could've knocked me over with a feather when I saw what was in there: a table laden with a beautiful flower arrangement, a bottle of wine, chocolates and a candlelight dinner for two that had long gone cold. Then Murray came in behind me. "Happy Valentine's Day, m'love!" he said as he planted a kiss on the top of my head.

"What a surprise!" I said, honestly shocked.

"And you thought I wasn't paying attention to the hints you were dropping all week!"

I was so happy that I decided to tell him about HIS surprise at the hotel. Though sheepish, I even fessed up about the phone call.

I'll leave you with one more of my memories about love. When I was 14, I fell for the most handsome man I'd ever seen. Though he was 10 years older than me, the moment I clapped eyes on Pat Boone singing "Love Letters in the Sand," I felt as if I'd been hit by a thunderbolt.

My heart thumped. I felt breathless and my knees went so weak I could barely stand. My heart melted like a Popsicle on a hot day and I fell head over heels in love. I'd go down to the beach and pretend he was writing love letters in the sand just for me. Oh yes, my head was in a cloud and Mom's concerned eyes honed in on the way I was sighing.

"What's wrong with you, Lucy? You looks awful pale, my dear," she said as she looked inside my eyelids, ears and throat.

Embarrassed that she might guess I'd been bitten by the love bug, I fibbed and said I had a stomach ache.

"Well maybe your bowels are bunged up again," Mom said. "What you needs is a good dose of castor oil to fix you up, my dear."

Lord almighty, I had no idea that falling in love could be so hard. Even though I'll never forget my first love, I'm sure Pat Boone will forgive me for moving on to find Murray, the true love of my life.

Love is indeed a many-splendoured thing, isn't it?

# Garage Sale Anyone?

Up until a few years ago, I've always found the idea of garage sales distasteful, for I couldn't imagine why anybody would want to buy other people's junk. Lord knows we had enough at our own house, because my husband is a hoarder and he hates to part with anything. As far as I'm concerned, if something can't be used, it should go in the garbage...but not Murray. Oh, no, he just keeps everything "...just in case I need it."

Then, one sunny day in May, when I was doing my yearly house cleaning, I had a sudden change of heart brought on by the frightful sight of junk crammed into every nook and corner of the house. I made the decision that it was all going to the dump, no matter what Murray said. When he saw that I meant business, he suddenly announced that he was going to have a garage sale.

At first I balked at the idea because I didn't want our neighbours to think that we were desperate for money. But then I decided to keep my mouth shut, for I was willing to sacrifice anything that would give me the freedom to walk through the house without getting my shins bruised. I actually got excited about the whole thing as I watched Murray gather up all the things I wanted desperately to get rid of. For almost four hours, he carted 20 years of junk from the house to the backyard and when he was finished, we both stood back and surveyed the enormous pile. My excitement was overwhelming and all I could do was prattle on about my plans for all the extra space in the house. When he didn't answer me, I turned and saw the expression on his face.

He looked like he had a heavenly vision, for his face was all aglow and his eyes were glazed over. When he finally spoke, my enthusiasm shrunk to the size of a pea. "I had no idea I had so much stuff...and it's all mine," he whispered as he beheld the shrine before him.

I should have known better than to believe a man who still has boxer shorts he wore 25 years ago. He was never going to part with any of his loot. It was a losing battle to begin with, so I decided to gather up another pile of things for the garage sale. You'll have to trust me when I say our two sons are cut from the same cloth as their father, for they suddenly became very possessive of their "STUFF" and didn't want to part with it. Most of the things have been condemned, broken or outgrown anyway, but as soon as I touched them, everything suddenly looked better than it did before and they insisted on keeping all of it. After hours of indecision, they finally parted with a decapitated Cabbage Patch doll, a broken baseball bat and a frayed jock strap that they used as a slingshot. Naturally, that went in the garbage, but I managed to weasel a few things from Murray's pile when he wasn't looking. I spent days cleaning and polishing items, for I had no intention of letting the neighbours think I was selling dirty junk. When I set up the tables in the garage, Murray began repairing everything that was broken. And the rest is history. Once he fixed everything, he refused to part with them and started carting them back into the house.

"Guess what?" he'd say. "I fixed that old purple lamp Aunt Olive gave us for a wedding present. It's just as good as new...do you want it in our bedroom or the living room?"

By the time my dear hubby finished, there was nothing left to go out in the garage sale. Two broken door knobs, a few hinges, an old pair of his football cleats and a box of popsicle sticks. I was at wit's end because he had been running a newspaper ad for a whole week advertising a GIANT THREE-DAY GARAGE SALE. The contents of the one remaining table looked pitiful, but still Murray insisted on going ahead with the sale. I resorted to sneaking things out of his pile while he slept and the next time I'd look, they'd be gone. The day before the sale, I was so distraught that I started putting out my good dishes from the kitchen cupboards. That was when I realized that I'd have to do something that I vowed I would never do.

Hiding behind sunglasses and a big hat, I hopped in my car and went to my very first garage sale, praying that I wouldn't meet anyone I knew. I cleaned out the first three sales I came upon, loaded up the car and headed home with my loot.

Murray was like a kid in a toy shop when he saw what I'd bought and he actually wanted to keep all of that stuff, too, but I was adamant. "After this sale is over," I sputtered, "don't you ever mention a garage sale to me again. From now on, anything that's not being used is going in the garbage and God help the person who brings it back inside this house!"

So, we ended up having a garage sale to sell other people's junk. I was determined to at least get back the money I had spent on that heap of trash. It was more like a nightmare. People were ringing our doorbell before we were even out of bed and when we opened the garage door, they practically ran over us. You'd think K-Mart was having a blue-light special the way they grabbed things from each other. I was amazed that they would negotiate and hassle over items priced for a quarter and after one hour of this, my temper was starting to rise. I just wanted to end the whole fiasco with my dignity still intact, so I started throwing things in boxes and put a FREE sign on them. Throngs of people who had been browsing converged on the boxes and we nearly got trampled in the stampede. It was terrifying to watch grown people arguing over who got what first as they pushed and shoved each other. And just when I had almost lost faith in the whole human race, an elderly man pushed his way through the mob and handed me a loonie. I gestured to the Free sign, but he just smiled and said, "I couldn't possibly take anything for free."

"God bless you sir," I sniveled, thankful that I had made one sale without having to make change for a quarter.

When everything was over, we didn't even make enough money to pay for the newspaper ad, let alone what I had spent buying the other stuff. And still there was all that junk of our own that Murray refused to part with to be put back in the house. Nothing had changed, except my frame of mind. Depressing is the only way to describe it. And that's what it's been like every summer at our house since that first garage sale. It's a vicious circle. I gather up the junk from the house, clean it up and Murray takes it all back. Then I have to start going to garage sales again to get enough stuff for the one that I know Murray will insist on having next year. I keep praying that he'll get over his urge to hoard things, but I'm not holding much hope. You see, now Murray has started going to garage sales and judging by the size of the storage shed he's building to put all his newly acquired junk in, I'd say my chances are...well slim, to say the least, wouldn't you agree?

# Getting Back to Nature

Many years ago I swore that I would never again let anybody persuade me to go camping or take part in any kind of outdoor adventures. I'm just not the type who enjoys anything remotely associated with getting back to nature.

I still haven't recovered from my first experience sleeping under the stars when I was 11 years old. One summer evening, my sister Leona and I decided we would spend the night outside, so we went up behind our house and fixed up a makeshift shelter. We draped blankets across the top of two big rocks, laid a mattress of hay on the ground and packed a Carnation box full of food, a deck of cards and a flashlight. We thought we were brave little souls sleeping under the stars – until sleep time came and folks around the Cove turned out the lights.

It was the first time I was aware of how forlorn and frightening the outdoors could be on a moonless night, for that was before the advent of streetlights. Even the roar of the sea rolling in sounded sinister and, as the night dragged on, our vivid imaginations conjured up visions of ghosts and creatures from the depths of the ocean. Leona and I nearly drove each other foolish every time we heard a dog bark or cats fighting somewhere in the darkness. We were afraid to close our eyes and by one in the morning, when we heard a noise up over our heads, we were cowering under the blankets. "Did you hear that noise, Leona? Listen...someone's out there!" I whispered.

Before we could react, the blankets we had draped overhead on the rocks fell down on us and when we looked up, all we could see was a big, black figure towering above us. We were so terrified that we scravelled out on hands and knees and ran down the hill to our house. We burst into our parents' bedroom, screeching and blubbering about a big, black creature trying to carry us off into the night. Daddy took a lantern and went to investigate. He found the culprit – Dick, our horse, was calmly eating the molasses buns and potted meat sandwiches we had left outside in the box.

It was many years later in Ontario when I finally let my husband and young sons talk me into another outdoor venture. I'd been on a day trip with them once before and come back full of mosquito bites and with swollen eyes. When Murray came home one day and asked if I wanted to take a week's vacation, I was excited...until I saw the brochure. I stared at the beaming faces of 10 people standing in front of a small tent and holding up dead fish, and immediately my dander went up.

"You want to take me CAMPING in a remote area of northern Ontario where the only sign of human life are fingernail scratches that say HELP or BEWARE OF BEARS?" I screeched at him. "Are you stunned 'er what?"

As usual, my husband and boys coaxed me into going despite my apprehension. But I went well prepared: I packed gallons of insect repellent, allergy pills, ointment for poison ivy – and my chamber pot. There was no way I was going to the bathroom behind a tree and getting pissmores in my pants. My husband kept assuring me the entire time that I'd enjoy the whole experience like he did. "I love camping and getting back to nature where I can rely on gut feelings and common sense for survival," he said. "You'll feel the same way after this trip, you'll see."

On the big day, all four of us crammed into our hatchback – the one that didn't have any air conditioning – and drove 300 miles in bumper-to-bumper traffic to camp out in the wilderness. By the time we arrived, I had already broken out in hives and was ready to go home.

The first day was humid and the mosquitoes came out in full

force. On the second day, the rain started. Murray and the boys insisted we stay, so there we all were, sitting in an 8x10-foot tent waiting for the rain to stop. Let me tell you, there's nothing like togetherness on a wet day, watching mould and mildew grow on each other's running shoes. My nerves were rubbed right raw lying in a leaky tent counting the raindrops as they plinked in the pots and pans. "Just relax," Murray said. "The rain will stop tomorrow."

But it didn't.

As soon as Murray lay down, he fell asleep. When the boys got bored, they'd amuse themselves by decorating the tent with toilet paper or testing their strength by trying to lift me out of the rollaway bed while I was still in it. When they weren't getting up and down to use my chamberpot that was chained to my wrist, Scott and Tim were either arguing or trying to punch each other out. We had to take turns standing up to stretch our legs to get the cramps out and once darkness fell, we sat in a circle around the flashlight and sang songs until the batteries died. It was so damp in the leaky tent that we wrapped ourselves in garbage bags before we got into our sleeping bags. There we'd all lie, just like sardines in a can, listening to the crackle of our garbage bags as we turned over, trying to get a little comfortable.

My husband and sons loved every minute of it, but not me. By day three, I began to daydream about taking a bath in a real tub, blow drying my hair and wearing clean, dry clothes.

"At least you don't have to cook and clean," Murray offered one day. "Isn't that what you've always said you wanted?"

He was lucky I didn't have the energy to crawl out of my sleeping bag, for there was no telling what injuries I might have inflicted upon him at that moment.

I longed to wake up in the morning and hear the boys argue over the last bowl of Cheerios, instead of waking to the sound of buzzing mosquitoes trying to squeeze a stolen wiener through a hole in the tent. I wanted to turn over in bed at night and not have damp socks that smelled like skunk sticking in my face, or to know that the fur I felt in the darkness was my son's teddy bear and not the real animal.

No matter how hard I tried, I couldn't sleep at night; it was very unsettling the way the animals hung around watching my husband shinny up a tree to tie up bags of food or salivating as they watched him bury it. Having to dig up a package of Kraft Dinner every time the boys wanted lunch was not my idea of getting back to nature, but my husband doesn't understand that. To him "roughing it" means sleeping in a tent with the insects, spending six hours standing in a stream trying to catch trout for dinner and shaving out of a coffee mug. To me it means a motel room with a black-and-white television and no room service. I ask you, what kind of husband takes his wife on vacation where there's no indoor plumbing, no television and no stores within a hundred miles?

By the end of that hellish week, when the rain stopped falling, we were out of food and the kids were eyeing each other hungrily, so my husband decided to drive into town for supplies. And that was the best part of the vacation for me. The sight of real houses and another human being was overwhelming as I staggered out of the car smelling of insect repellent and smoke. My hair was standing on end, my eyes were swollen from mosquito bites, there were bird droppings on my jacket and my track pants were all lumpy from being stretched on a stick to dry over an open fire after the rain stopped. The lady in the grocery store stared at me as I approached the cash register. "Do you have a rest room here...with running water and a real toilet?" I whispered hopefully.

When she led me to the restroom I began to blubber at the sight of the toilet. "You've been camping, haven't you," she said as I touched the flush box. "Go ahead, dear, flush it as often as you want. I understand."

I wonder how she knew?

# The Second Time Around

Well, it finally happened. My worst fear was realized recently when my youngest son crossed the fine line that separates the child from the adult. Tim turned 16.

In all honesty, I must say that I had been dreading that milestone in both our lives since he became a teenager. I knew things would never be the same since his 13th birthday, when he miraculously discovered hair on his upper lip, which he claimed was definitely NOT there when he went to bed the night before. It jolted me for a minute, but when he straightened up long enough to close the fridge door, I realized how tall he'd grown and I had to accept the inevitable: my baby wasn't a baby any more.

It's strange how time just slips by and you don't even realize it. I was just getting over a similar "hair-raising" situation with his older brother. I felt happy for him because I knew how long he had looked forward to his 16th birthday, but yet another side of me felt sad. I wanted him to be enthusiastic, because being a teenager is such an exciting time of life and there's so much to look forward to. Still, there was a part of me that didn't want to let go. It's selfish, I know. It's not that I wanted to keep him from growing up, it's just that I knew I was going to miss that inquisitive little boy who asked me on my 35th birthday what I wanted to be when I grow up. As I watched him slip into his designer jeans and jacket on his birthday, I found it hard to believe how he could suddenly look and act so mature. I couldn't decide if it was the mustache he was trying to grow or the size 11 shoes he was wearing, but something was different. "I hope you like your present," I said, handing him a gift.

Without hesitating, he said, "As long as it has wheels and roars when I turn the key in the ignition, I'll like it!"

It took me a second to realize what he was talking about, for I'd forgotten that driving a car is a status symbol for a sixteen-year-old nowadays, just as getting my first pair of high heels and nylons was my symbolic gesture of womanhood back when I became 16. "Can you take me to get my driver's permit after school, Mom?" he asked.

I could feel my hormones exploding inside me at the thought of TWO teenagers fighting over the car. I don't remember feeling so depressed since I did his homework for him when he was in fourth grade and he got a C on it.

As a parent, I can honestly say that I don't adjust well to change. I've always believed that it would be so exciting to grow up again with my children and experience life through their eyes. That's not to say, of course, that I wanted to LIVE through them, because that would be unfair to my sons, but I did want to learn along with them. But Lord, things sure have changed since I was a teenager.

For the past 19 years, I've been running faster than my legs can carry me trying to keep up with each of my boys in turn and since they've become teenagers, I feel like I'm lagging way behind the finish line. Just as I got them through the teething, tummy aches and the temper tantrums, it was time to put away the playpen and catch up with them before they outgrew me again. I can't tell you how much I miss the security of that playpen, because whenever I needed to get away from the kids, I'd sit in that thing for hours and watch them through the bars, hoping they'd wear themselves out before their father got home from work.

It took a lot of adjusting to get them through their rebellious period. I thought I'd never be able to function properly again when they hit that obnoxious phase that children go through. I still haven't recovered from the time when my husband's boss and his wife came to dinner. I had warned Tim, who was six at the time, to be polite and not ask too many questions. After he had told our guests that we only used our good dishes when we had company and that his mom said this dinner was costing us an arm and a leg, he decided to clear the table before we'd even finished eating. "What a nice boy you are, Tim!" my husband's boss said, patting him on the head.

Without hesitating, Tim said, "My dad says I got to be nice to you 'cause he's gonna ask you for a raise."

Funny, that seems like only yesterday and before I realized it, he went smack into puberty overnight. I wasn't sure how to handle going through puberty a second time, because my older son changed completely when he hit that stumbling block. He spent a lot of time trying to "find himself," and I spent most of my time trying to find out where he'd been. For the first two years of his life, I tried to get him to talk, then I spent the next ten trying to keep him from talking. For the rest of his adolescent life, I tried to decipher what he meant when he did speak. His answers were always so vague and ambiguous. "Where are you going this evening?" I'd ask.

"Out."

"Who are you going with?"

"The guys."

"When will you be back?"

"Later."

I asked my mother's advice on puberty because I couldn't imagine how she raised nine children and lived to tell about it. "My dear, there was none of that stuff going around in Newfoundland when you youngsters were growing up!" she said. "Everyone makes too much fuss about it these days... just leave the youngsters alone and they'll outgrow it in their own time."

So, that's what I decided to do with Tim, just ride it out until he comes to me for help. After all, I got his brother through puberty, so how hard can it be?

Just to be on the safe side, I decided to have a little talk about sex again, just to get him started on his journey to manhood, and let him know that the lines of communication were still open. But when I tried to look him square in the eye, I was suddenly aware of how big he'd grown, and I couldn't get the right words out. "Tim, I need to talk to you about, ahh... something... well, something private..." I began.

He raised his eyebrows and said, "Oh boy! I can feel a talk about the birds and bees coming on! I do sex education in school, you know, Mom."

With a sigh of relief, I said, "Yes, that's exactly what I want to talk about... all that... that stuff you've learned in school."

He looked at me with such understanding in his eyes, that it took me quite unaware for a moment. Then he patted the chair beside him and said, "Have a seat, Mom. I'll tell you everything you need to know."

# Teen Angels

Every now and again I get to wondering if my life would have been different had I given birth to girls instead of boys. My mother raised nine children and she said that she'd pick boys over girls any day, because the five of us girls were harder to get along with than the boys, especially during the teenage years.

Well, I haven't had the experience of dealing with girls, but I've certainly had my share of ups and downs with my boys. As far as I'm concerned, the sole purpose in life for teenagers during those adolescence years is to test the patience and endurance of the unsuspecting parents. I'm still reeling from my first ordeal of dragging Scott through his teenage years and he's 21 now. But I still have a ways to go, because his brother, Tim, just turned 18 and God willing, both of us will get through this one unscathed.

I wasn't at all prepared for the telltale signs of puberty the first time around. With girls, the physical changes are more obvious, but with boys, it is much more subtle. I had no idea what to expect and, as I recall, it was Scott himself who told me about the facts. He was 12 when it happened and it came as a total shock to me. For a whole week I had been forcing cough medicine into him and when I insisted that he see a doctor, he looked at me and rolled his eyes. "Don't you get it, Mom?" he croaked. "I'm not hoarse... my voice is changing, that's all."

I think of puberty as a metamorphic change for both sibling and parent. Neither is ever the same again. There's so much to deal with: the emotional turmoil, the mood swings and outbursts of temper. I'm still not over mine.

I thought after the first time I went through puberty with

Scott, that I'd be well-equipped to handle Tim's adolescence, but I was wrong. My boys are totally unalike in every aspect and nothing I learned in dealing with Scott applied to his brother. It was like starting from scratch again.

Dealing with boys has been a whole new experience for me and over the years, I've learned a lot about the opposite sex. And I mean "opposite", because their way of thinking and doing things are definitely different from the female point of view. Take bathrooms, for instance… toilets, in particular. It never ceases to amaze me how they can aim for such a big target and miss it every time. Are all males naturally uncoordinated or are the toilets in my house too small? And I ask you, is it too much for a mother to ask that they remember to put the toilet seat down after they've finished? I hate it when I stumble into a dark bathroom at night and get rudely awakened when I sit in ice-cold water. I've now concluded that males enjoy the challenge of aiming for the opening between the cover and the seat and that is their peculiar way of establishing territory.

Sometimes I wonder if puberty destroys a boy's ability to grasp certain things, I mean little things that females take for granted. Neither of my teenagers ever mastered the concept of putting a roll of toilet paper on the spindle. No matter how often I demonstrated, the mechanics of inserting roll over spindle evades them completely. There would be a carton of paper hanging over the toilet and one of them would shake me awake in the morning and yell in my ear, "Mom, there's no more toilet paper on the roll!"

Given the fact that my husband is an engineer, I assumed that our sons would at least have a propensity for gadgets and the way they work, but I was wrong. Their father can't seem to figure out how that little spring works either, so the toilet paper is usually left sitting on top of the spindle until my cat streels the stuff from one end of the house to the other.

My boys could take apart a stereo system and put it back

together, but they couldn't figure out how to open the door of the dishwasher, turn off a light switch or put the lid back on the toothpaste. My teen angels were always hungry. The food in the fridge never stayed cold because the door was always open. My fridge still lists starboard because one or the other was constantly leaning on the door while they looked for something to eat.

Untidiness is a way of life for teenage boys. Unless it was the telephone or the remote control, neither of my sons would raise a finger to pick up anything without being asked to. They'd look totally surprised when I'd tell them that their rooms look like a disaster area, for they saw nothing wrong with unmade beds or having clothes strewn on doorknobs, chairs and windows. And they still do it. 'Course, they have a perfectly logical explanation. Why waste time making the bed in the morning if they're going to sleep in it tonight? Why go to the trouble of folding clothes and putting them away when they have to wear them every day? Their concept of cleaning up and mine are miles apart. Blowing dust off the coffee table with a hair dryer and letting the cat lick the food off the plates is NOT my idea of cleanliness.

Yes, it took me awhile to adjust to living in a male-dominated household, but when all is said and done, it wasn't so bad. Sure, there are times when I'd like to hear a conversation that doesn't deal with sports or be able to sit on the toilet without getting my feet wet. I like being the only female in the house. I like being around my sons and I don't think I've missed out on anything by having boys. After all, they can be every bit as considerate and thoughtful as girls. Boys just have a different way of showing their feelings, that's all. I mean, how many times have I been outside mowing the lawn and one of the boys would come out to remind me of something. "Mom, you left the kettle on and there's smoke coming out of it. Do you want me to unplug it?"

On more occasions than I can count, Scott has stood holding

the door open with his foot while I brought in groceries, giving no thought to catching a draft from the doorway. And they're always patient with me when I have to make a dozen trips to the car for the groceries. Just the other day when I was struggling with two cases of pop, Tim took time from playing his video game to direct me up the front steps. "Be careful you don't hurt your back with that heavy pop, Mom… here, let me hold your purse."

I've come a long way with my boys and I've grown with them. But my sons were good teachers. They taught me the importance of being a parent, how to communicate and how to smile instead of frown. And it was worth every wrinkle and grey hair that I got along the way. Now, every time I look at them and see what terrific young men they've become, I feel sad knowing that soon they'll be starting new lives for themselves.

I'm going to miss my teen angels and the noise and bustle around the house. I'll miss their little displays of affection… the way they'd hold me in a headlock or pat me on the head for no reason. But they know I'll always be here for them, just as I know they will come home again… they have to come back to get all the junk they left behind. Yeah… they'll be back. I'm counting on it.

# Shoo, Shoo Little Bird

It was inevitable, I know, for all parents have to face it one time or another. When my youngest son made the big announcement, it took me by surprise. "Mom," Tim said, "I'm thinking of moving out of the house."

For some parents, this may be the best news they've heard since an offspring acquired a job for the first time; for others, it may be very traumatic. Mothers in particular, I think, have difficulty adjusting to the idea, for instinct compels them to protect and hold on to their children for as long as possible. Some offspring leave home at an early age and others stay longer, depending on the circumstances. Like most boys, I'd heard Tim talk about this moment from the time he hit puberty. However, his decision to make his solo flight came at an unexpected time. For awhile there, I was afraid I'd have to give him a little nudge to make him spread his wings and fly, for my 23-year-old "baby" had outgrown his nest long ago. That's why I had mixed emotions about the whole thing. I was surprised, relieved and saddened at the same time.

At first I thought he was joking because he's still attending university, but when he held up a big envelope with APARTMENT FUND written on it, I knew he meant business. I listened intently as he gently broke the news of his imminent departure. And I say gently because he seemed to think he had to prepare me for the shock. "Now Mom, before you get all upset and try to talk me out of moving out, listen to what I have to say, okay? In case you hadn't noticed, I'm old enough to be out on my own. I can't stay home forever, you know."

At that moment, I didn't know if I should shout for joy or cry, but when I saw the sympathy in his eyes as he sat down beside me, I could tell that he was expecting the latter. I tried not to react until I'd heard him out, so I listened as he delivered his well-rehearsed speech about moving into an apartment with a school buddy. I was flattered that he had taken so much time for my benefit and even more impressed that he felt he needed my permission to take his leave. This whole move, he informed me, would be in MY best interest. "It'll be better for you if I move out, Mom, because you'll have a spare room for company and you won't have to put up with all the mess around the house or me eating you out of house and home," he said. "Besides, it's about time you and Dad had a little privacy, don't you think?"

I couldn't believe that my youngest son had become so perceptive so soon after turning 23, and I was so proud of him that I could literally feel the elastic fibres snapping in my spandex sweater. I wanted to phone Murray at work and tell him that his son's three years of psychology study had finally paid off, but I didn't want to spoil the momentum for Tim. I hung on to his every word as he talked about needing his own "space" and I was reminded of all the hopes and dreams I had when I was younger.

Mind you, things were different for me way back then, for we had such a crowd at our house all the time that we never had an inch of space to call our own. Everything was OURS, not MINE. I was lucky to find a spot in a bed let alone have a room to myself.

Still, I understood my son's need to be out on his own and by the time he had finished telling me about this great apartment and the carefree lifestyle he was about to embark upon, I was longing for that ideal life myself. "It sounds wonderful," I told him. "Can I come with you?"

While I waited for Murray to come home from work, I let myself imagine what it would be like after Tim moved out. I thought about converting his room into a den for myself, where I'd have the privacy to listen to my music and read. I even entertained the idea of buying a new house and new furniture, but reality set in when the door opened and Scott, my oldest son, walked in with an armful of books. That's when I realized that I had just repeated the same words to Tim as I said to him five years ago when he left home to go to university. "Just remember that our doors will always be open for you and we'll always be here if you need us."

. Scott was gone for three years and then one day he lugged all his stuff home again. "Mom, Dad ... I'm back!"

Matter of fact, last year, he decided to go back to university again, this time near our home and by the looks of it, he's settled back into his old nest for at least another three years.

Later when Tim repeated the news of his departure to his father, the subject of money came up and Tim assured him that he could afford an apartment because he'd be working full time during the summer. Murray was skeptical. "So, you'll be making enough money to take care of the monthly payments on the new car you just bought, pay insurance, rent, the utilities, buy furniture and food as well as save money for tuition fees, books for the next semester and still have pocket money to spare?"

Tim was undaunted. "Don't worry, Dad. I know exactly what I'm doing."

And Tim had the perfect plan, all right. He was going to do some home shopping ... which meant taking the furniture and the television set from HIS bedroom, the sofa, table and chairs and whatever else he needed from OUR family room. As for a washer and dryer, he planned on getting an apartment close enough to our house so that he could come home to do his laundry. "I'll be home practically all the time, except on weekends," he said. "So don't worry, Mom, it'll be like I'm still living at home!"

It's strange, isn't it, how much they want to get away from home and be independent, yet they want to take everything familiar they have with them? When Scott first left home, he set up in his new place just like it was at home. I noticed, too, that he did things

I used to do for him, like rolling his T-shirts so they wouldn't wrinkle, cooking the same kind of meals and ironing only the collars on his shirts the way I do with his father's. Now that the time had come for my youngest son to leave, I realized how much I would miss him, but I was happy that he had made the decision on his own. I knew, too, that I'd worry about him, but I couldn't let that get in the way. It was just part of life, that's all.

Someone once told me that the greatest gifts parents can give their children are roots and wings. Give them proper roots and when they're ready to leave the nest, they'll fly in the right direction. I knew in my heart that we had given him all the love and support he needed to face the future ... and there was no doubt in my mind that he'd make it. It was time for us to let go.

Everything seemed to be going well with Tim's plans for about a week and then one day, he sidled up to me in the kitchen. "Mom, I need to talk to you," he said.

When he dumped out the contents of his APARTMENT FUND, I saw a toonie and two dimes roll across the table, I got this feeling of déjà vu. Somewhere in the back of my mind, a line from a song came to mind. "Shoo, shoo, little bird, go on, take your flight..."

I had difficulty concentrating on what Tim was saying. "Mom, did you hear me? I said I've made a decision ... I'm not moving out after all."

"But I thought you wanted to get away from home ... have your own apartment...?"

He looked at me and shook his head. "Do you know what it costs these days to rent an apartment, Mom? I can't afford all of the expenses! That's why I decided to stay put until I finish school. You DID say your doors were always open for me, didn't you?"

I looked at the unopened bag on the floor that held the pink wallpaper and curtains for the spare room and sighed. I wasn't looking forward to the "empty nest syndrome" anyway.

Be it ever so humble, there's no place like home.

# Cathouse

I'm still not sure when or how it happened, but it was my husband who made me take a closer look at the role our beloved felines play in our lives. After the incident in March when we pointed out that our house had gone to the cats, I have to concede that our furry little felines, Yoko and Ono, were spoiled rotten and that they had us right where they want us – between their furry little paws. It happened one cold, rainy night when Murray came home from work and discovered he didn't have his house key. I was in the basement doing laundry, so it took awhile before I finally came upstairs and heard him knocking. When I opened the door, there was Murray, standing in the pouring rain holding our older cat, Ono, in his arms. "Quick, run and get a towel," he said as he deposited Ono on the mat.

I darted to the bathroom, grabbed a towel and ran back, "Oh, you poor darling, you're drenched! Come here and let me dry you off before you catch your death of cold," I said.

I barely heard a word Murray said because I was busy rubbing vigorously with the towel, but when he repeated himself, I knew by the tone of his voice that his nose was out of joint. "I meant for you to get a towel for ME, not the cat," he said coldly, as he watched me cuddle Ono in the towel.

"Don't be so foolish, my son," I said. "I'll get you a towel just as soon as I give Ono something hot to eat and get her settled in our bed with the heating pad. The poor little dear must be freezing."

At that point, he shook his head and walked away. "I think the cat gets more attention in this house than I do," he muttered.

After I thought about it, I had to admit there was some truth in what he said. We humans can be real pushovers when it comes to our pets, for there's a special bond between people and animals that nobody can dispute. We humans tend to see ourselves as caregivers when we adopt a pet, but I think it's the other way around. As soon as the adoption is complete, the people training begins and from then on, they lead and we follow. Animals are very skilled at communicating their needs when they want something, for they rely on body language. Cats, in particular, are very cunning and resourceful. My felines beg, cajole, coax and charm their way into our hearts with a soft purr, a touch of the tail across the ankle or an insistent meow at the fridge door.

The more I think of it, the more I realize that my husband was right. Our cats have taken over completely. It seems that the role of ownership has shifted in the past few years, and the change was so subtle that I didn't even notice it until recently. Before I went out of the house to work, Yoko and Ono were honoured guests who lived with our family and they were content to hang around the house just being cute and cuddly. But now that we are both at work every day, we don't have the time to spend with them and they've become finicky, petulant, demanding and devious. I'm beginning to feel that we are mere guests in THEIR house, for they have us catering to them as if they were queens. The McFarlane house is now officially the cathouse.

I've always had a weakness for cats and in my day, I've known and loved many. There's one cat in particular that I recall fondly, Blackie, who had a yen for fresh milk. Every time my brother Harve went to the barn to milk the cows, Blackie would sit beside him and Harve would direct a stream of milk in his direction every few minutes. Harve made it into a game by squirting milk in every direction to test the cat's agility; and true to form, Blackie would stay in motion while keeping his eye on the cow's udder. Then when the moment came, he'd spring into action, sprinting into the air and catching the stream of milk without even getting his whiskers wet. He never missed a single milking. Even when the cows were grazing in the meadow, he'd chase them around and swat at their udders as if he could get milk on tap. Oh, yes, Blackie sure had a personality, just like the cats that I have now.

Yoko has a superiority complex and Ono is just the opposite. One minute they're civil with each other; and the next, they can't pass each other in the hallway without snarling and swatting a paw across the other's head. Because Ono was the first in our house, she was very jealous when Yoko invaded her space and at times, tempers flare and fur flies. And don't think Yoko doesn't know that, for she taunts Ono by planting herself in her path, knowing full well that Ono is afraid to walk past her. Mind you, I sympathize more with Ono, probably because I see something of myself in her. Some days, she is as contrary as a dog on a Popsicle stick and other days she lazes around or sleeps for hours. She limps when she walks, drools and snores when she sleeps, throws up fur balls and has to be lifted up and down on top of the dryer where she usually sleeps when the clothes are drying.

Yoko, on the other hand, never stops moving. No matter where I go, she gets there ahead of me and she seems to anticipate my every move. Even when I take a bath, she sits on the side of the tub, dabbles her tail in the water and tries to catch every bubble that floats her way. And she's very inventive when it comes to sleeping quarters, for she's chosen a lofty place where she can watch everybody from a safe distance. We have a huge, stuffed gorilla that sits on a chair in our family room, and Yoko has burrowed a spot on top of his head where she curls up to sleep with her favourite fuzzy tail. Oh, yes, I do mean a tail other than her own, one that she pulled off a battery-operated ball that we gave her for Christmas a few years ago that she now uses as her security toy. She rubs her lip across this tail until she falls asleep and is very possessive of it. If someone comes into the house, she hides it and when she knows we're going out, she gets her tail and sits in the doorway with it in her mouth, hoping to persuade us not to leave her behind. Once, when my niece was visiting from Toronto, Yoko hid her tail in her suitcase and she nearly went crazy searching for it. I thought I was going to have to make an appointment with a psychiatrist until Darlene called to say she found it. "You found her tail? Oh, thank goodness! Yoko hasn't slept or eaten for several days and she's driving me right cracked tearing the house apart looking for it!" I said.

At my request, Darlene sent it by courier that same day and it brought tears to my eyes watching Yoko's reaction. She purred, tossed it in the air and for two days, her bottom lip was swollen out of shape from rubbing it on the tail.

I've been noticing, too, that my cats do things now that I would never tolerate from my boys when they were younger; and what's more, I seem to have more patience with my furry litter critters. For instance, there are four open cans of cat food sitting in the fridge because Yoko and Ono have decided that they no longer like the brand I buy. I've bought at least six different kinds to see what they like and each can I open, they just sniff it, put their tails in the air and wait to see if I'm going to open another. Now, if my kids had done that when they were younger, I probably would've made them sit at the table until they ate it.

The only time they come together for a common cause is at night. Being the nocturnal creatures that the little dears are, they hate it if we sleep and they're awake. They hate the sight of a closed door. They take turns clawing underneath the door trying to force it open and if that doesn't work, they try to play on our sympathy. Yoko makes funny little noises like a whimper, and Ono literally stands up and rattles the doorknob until one of us gets up and lets them in. My, how they love to get under the covers of our bed. Often I find myself crawling into bed very quietly so I won't wake them.

I have to admit that sometimes Murray gets upset with me because I let our cats take over our bed. 'Course he'll never admit it, but he loves those critters as much as I do. When he comes home from work, they're both waiting at the door for him, because they think he's their meal ticket. He talks to them and feeds them whatever they want from his dinner plate. Yoko waits for him to watch TV, then she lies in his lap and goes all googlie-eyed when he scratches her head. Ono, in particular, spends a lot of time in our bed, and if she wants to get on Murray's side while he's still in it, she'll stand on his chest until he either moves to the edge or simply gets up and goes to the spare room to sleep. If I'm first in bed, Ono follows me and claims Murray's side of the bed. By the time he comes in, Ono is snoring her little heart out. "Oh, look at her, she looks so peaceful! You don't really want to disturb her now, do you, Murray? Can't you just sleep at the foot of the bed for tonight?"

Now, that's the part that irks him most, and I can understand that. But I'm a fair person, so often, I'll take a turn sleeping in another room so he can have my spot. If truth be known, I could never sleep with BOTH of them, because Ono snores just as loud as Murray does and me nerves can't stand the noise.

I guess there's always a price to pay for everything, but when I think about the reward we reap from the happiness they bring us, I think my cats are worth their weight in gold.

# Paws for Thought

I should have recognized the telltale signs before things changed around our house, but I didn't see it coming. We already had a five-year-old cat named Ono when my youngest son brought home a three-week-old kitten. I didn't have the heart to say no to him. Besides, Ono had proudly embraced the wee one as her own, so we decided to keep her and name her Yoko. It never once occurred to us that this green-eyed little feline was plotting a takeover.

Oh yes, that angelic little fur ball established her territory faster than she could lick her whiskers. She managed to manipulate all of us, and I'll be dipped if I know how or when she became the boss. Before we realized it, she had us wrapped around her paws. Without as much as a meow, Ono stepped aside and Yoko crowned herself Queen of our house.

From the beginning she had a mind of her own. She insisted on sleeping in a china bowl on the kitchen cabinet. Yoko never meowed like other cats, but when she'd eat her food she'd make a low, guttural sound like someone savouring their meal.

She sure pulled our strings, for she lapped up all the attention she could get. All she had to do was put her head to one side, blink her beautiful eyes, and we'd do anything for her. Goodness, she was so cute that she reduced me to talking baby jargon. "Ahh...come here my precious wittle baby girl! Give momsey-whomsey kisses and I'll scratch your fuzzy wuzzy little tummy, okay?"

That was 14 years ago. Last year, Ono went to kitty heaven at the age of 19. Suffice it to say, Yoko is still ruling the roost and we're still catering to her every whim.

There's no denying it: when you have pets, there's only one boss in the house and it's not you. You never really own an animal. They own you – and what's more, they train us humans. Pets are very smart, for they make the rules and we follow their lead. Sometimes, I ask myself, "Is it just Yoko, or do all cats act like they're superior? Could it be that it is a female thing or do cats really have a superiority complex?" I don't know the answers, but I believe our whole outlook on life changes when we have these adorable little creatures.

Who among us has not attributed human qualities to our pets and forgotten that they are animals? Not that I personally would do that with my Yoko, of course, but pet owners often do. Sometimes, though, I worry if Murray and I raised her properly – especially when I see her tearing off strips of wallpaper with her teeth, or scratching the corners of the sofa. Maybe we should've sent her to a Feline Behavioural School, because she sure gives me attitude. Much as I love her, she's arrogant and stubborn and I have no choice but to discipline her sometimes. "Now this is gonna hurt mommy more than it'll hurt you, Yoko, but you won't get any treats today," I tell her, "and you won't be allowed back in the living room if you swing on the drapes again, you hear!"

I swear that cat watches way too much television. As soon as she sees me raise my finger at her, she assumes a kung-fu position and walks sideways toward me with her ears flattened. In a blink of an eye, she'll leap into the air and land a blow on my hand with her hind legs before she runs off to hide somewhere. A feisty cat is our Yoko!

I don't know...maybe we pampered her too much when we allowed her full run of the house, or perhaps we didn't pamper her enough. It's hard for parents to know what to do for our pets anymore, but we make sure she has the best of everything. When we take her to the vet's office, we use her proper name,

Yoko McFarlane, so she doesn't develop an identity complex since she never knew her real parents. We keep the vet's name and phone number programmed into our cell phone in case of an emergency. We've opened an account at the clinic in her name and she has a routine checkup every six months. Seems like we spend more money on her than we do on ourselves, for we make sure her teeth are cleaned, her nails are clipped and her fur is well groomed.

If we have company, I introduce her by name. If someone sits in her favourite chair, she'll stare them down. I have to ask the guest to move before she pounces on them. We put up with her hair on all our clothes, and carry a lint brush everywhere. We allow her to sleep wherever and whenever she chooses. We even hang her stocking at Christmas and wrap her new toys. When we get groceries, she rummages through the bags to see if we've brought her a treat. In short... Yoko is a spoiled brat of a cat.

Sometimes we go overboard with Yoko, but we get so much joy in having her around. Sure, she has bad habits, but don't we all? Ono, in her time, was not entirely innocent, either. When we first got Ono, she used to sleep in some of the weaved baskets I collected. Others, of course, I kept separate for bread and rolls. Once when hubby's boss and co-workers came over for dinner, I had the table all set up and Ono was nowhere in sight, so I announced that dinner was ready to be served. When our guests went into the dining room, I heard them laughing. "Are we trying something different on the menu tonight?" Murray's boss asked.

There was Ono, stretched out in the basket of buns on the table, contentedly licking butter off her whiskers.

Cats sure have a mind of their own, don't they? I mean, they strut around like the world is at their feet and no matter how much we try to change them, they never abide by our rules. I know Yoko is a totally free spirit. She snores, drinks out of the toilet and throws a hissy fit if I don't pour a bit of cream in her bowl. She hates it when friends come to visit and I swear she can sense when someone doesn't like her. She'll watch them for awhile to see if they're leaving. Then she'll cough up a hairball half the length of her tail and deposit it on their shoes. Talk about embarrassing!

That cunning little imp will sit on the chair beside me and beg for food. Fact is, Yoko likes to steal it, so I indulge her by putting a bit of food on the edge of the table. She hides her head under the tablecloth, sticks one paw up to feel around for food, then snatches it and gobbles it up. She's always hungry and if she hears the hum of the can opener or someone opening the fridge door, she comes running. She even has a sweet tooth. She loves doughnuts, chocolate bars and cake, but her favourite is ice cream. "No, no Yoko...you shouldn't be eating ice cream," I tell her. "You'll ruin your teeth!" But she ignores me anyway. She'll dip her little paw into my bowl when I'm not looking, lick off the ice cream and then come back for more.

Somebody once asked me why I like cats so much. The only way I could make them understand the bond between my cat and me was to ask them a few questions in return:

Have you ever sat in your chair until your leg went numb because your cat was sleeping on your lap? Do you ever call home to check on little miss meow to make sure she had her din-dins, or leave on the light and the TV so she won't be lonely? And have you ever asked your husband to sleep on the couch so he wouldn't disturb the cat's rest because she was up all night chasing dust bunnies? If the answer is yes, then you are indeed a cat lover.

My cat is my companion. She keeps me company, she licks my face when I cry at sad movies and she keeps me warm when we cuddle. Matter of fact, if I was to be reincarnated, I'd like to come back as a cat. Who wouldn't? After all, cats come with an excellent warranty. They have nine lives...and that would be just purrr-fect for me.

# Mothers & Sons

Have you ever stopped to think about what our offspring think of us – as parents? No? Well, I didn't either until my two sons and I went to visit my sister in Kingston. As usual, Leona and I were gabbing in the kitchen over a cup of tea so Scott and Tim went into the living room to catch up on the news with Leona's sons, Matt and Jed. We didn't pay much attention to them, but after awhile, the conversation got louder and we kept hearing the word MOM being bantered around. Jed was telling my sons that his mom always cons him into going shopping with her and it ends up being an all-day event.

"My mother does that, too, and then she expects me to go into the women's stores with her while she tries on clothes," Tim said.

"Man, that's so embarrassing when she comes out and asks for my opinion in front of the girls who work there!"

I felt my bottom lip bivver in indignation.

"Hey, you guys!" I shouted. "We can hear every word you're saying in there!"

There was complete silence for a few seconds, then laughter.

"Hey! We're just telling things the way they are," Tim called back.

"You and Aunt Leona are so much alike that it's scary! Is it a sister thing or did you guys make up the same rules for raising kids?"

That's when it dawned on us that our sons were comparing notes on our roles as mothers, so we marched right in there with the intention of defending ourselves. Despite our presence, they prattled on about us as if we weren't there and as

I listened, I had to admit to myself that some of the things they said were true. Even though Leona and I never lived anywhere near each other after we were married, it was obvious that our method of "mothering" was very similar. As we listened to their comments, we realized that we were seeing ourselves through the eyes of our sons for the first time. We felt like we were part of the TV show "This is Your Life," except we didn't know if we should be flattered or insulted.

Our sons made it sound like we were overprotective, interfering mothers who spent all of our time and energy trying to make them do things OUR way. They each put in their two cents worth and told stories about how their "dear mothers" embarrassed them by making them wear what they considered weird clothes and how my sister and I always cut their hair. They dredged up things that neither of us had any memory of and embellished other incidents for their own amusement. Scott maintained that because I was a hairdresser, I took it as a licence to control the style so he couldn't get funky hairstyles like the other kids, while Tim said I gave him brutal haircuts.

Of course, Leona's boys maintained that she did the same thing with them, except her haircutting was so bad that they always had to wear hats to cover up the bald patches.

"If you thought we gave you such bad haircuts, why is it that the four of you big, burly men still come home to get your mothers to cut your hair?" Leona asked.

Matt grinned sheepishly. "Because it's cheaper than going to a barber."

Tim got in the last word. "Hey, but our moms were way ahead of their time, you know. After all, we were in style with the bad haircuts and shaved heads long before everybody thought that it was cool!"

We couldn't help but notice how much fun they were having at our expense, so we gave up protesting and just listened. They talked about our driving habits and they laughed at the fact that we always gave them advice when they took the cars. Seems that they thought we were both worrywarts, especially after the first snowfall.

"Did your Mom tell you guys to be careful in the snow, not to drive fast and to call when you got to wherever you were going?" Matt asked.

Both my sons nodded their heads at the same time. "And watch for pedestrians on the sidewalk, wait for the light to turn green and, Mom's favourite, don't forget to wear clean underwear in case you're in an accident," Scott said.

That last remark drew a few giggles, especially since Matt said that even though he's 25 and his brother is 23, his mother still buys them boxer shorts with cartoons on them every Christmas.

"I just hope I don't get into an accident while I'm wearing my Tweetie Bird shorts," Jed snickered.

'Course, Leona's nose was out of joint then and she told them that there was a time when they thought she knew everything, and in their eyes, she was the greatest mom in the world. I said that my sons were the same way and when Tim rolled his eyes, I reminded him that when he was six years old, he would always tell me he was going to marry me when he grew up. Leona took pleasure in telling Jed about an incident in second grade when she was parent/teacher chairperson at his school. Apparently Jed insisted on ignoring the rules that he didn't like, so his teacher took him to see the principal. Jed was told that he had no choice but to follow his teacher's rules.

"My mom is god of this school and when she hears about this, she'll be changing the rules," he said defiantly.

When we got to their teenage years, our sons started ragging on us about how strict we were. All four of them said we never let them be normal and do the things other moms let their sons do.

"Mom always had the same answer for everything," Tim said

as he put his hands on his hips and mimicked me.

"If your friends jumped off the wharf, would you do the same thing, too?"

A burst of laughter followed and then Matt piped up. "Hey, Tim, it can't be any worse than my mom going with me on my first date. She actually came into the movie theatre and sat behind us all night."

Leona pretended not to hear him.

"Did you notice, Lucy, that mothers spend the first few years of their children's lives trying to get them to walk and talk, and the rest of their teenage years trying to shut them up? Life's funny, isn't it?"

"Yup, mothers can do no wrong when our kids are young and we can do nothing right when they are teenagers," I answered.

By the time everybody had thrown in a few stories, my sister and I relaxed a little. We talked about the places we took them as children, the exciting hockey games they played, the hours we spent in cold arenas and the times we traipsed around with them or sat in the hot sun to watch their baseball games.

When they started talking about all the great vacations they had in Newfoundland, it gave Leona and I a great deal of satisfaction to know that they had the opportunity to learn about their roots. Somewhere too, amid the conversation, we became aware that things had changed, that we had come full circle in our role as mothers. Even though our sons enjoy poking fun at us and they tell us we act like kids when we giggle and laugh on the phone, we know in our hearts that it is done with love and affection.

They don't realize it yet, but our sons have become very protective of us. They don't let us drive in the snow, they get upset if we go somewhere without informing them first and they scold us if we don't call to let them know that we've arrived safely.

At the end of the night when the guys went to watch a movie

on TV, Leona and I looked at each other and smiled.

"We must've done something right with our boys, Lucy," she said, "because they always find their way back home again, don't they?"

"Yeah," I said. "We've got to stop putting out those bread crumbs, you know."

I guess it's true that the stories of childhood always leave an indelible impression and even when they become adults, they never outgrow or outlive those images. I hope our sons will never outgrow us and that they'll always remember us with a smile on their faces.

Sons and mothers – what a combination. Now that's some kind of wonderful, isn't it?

# Life in General

*There are no mistakes in life,*
*there are only lessons to be learned.*

– Mark Twain –

# Dropping In

I had the most wonderful surprise the other day when friends of ours from Toronto, whom we hadn't seen in a couple of years, dropped by unexpectedly. I was in the middle of house cleaning and hesitated to answer the door, but when I peeked out and saw Annette and Wally, I was ecstatic. I didn't care that my house was a mess or that I looked like something the cat dragged in; all that mattered was that they had come to visit. Goodness, it had been so long since anyone dropped in without calling or being invited that I'd forgotten how nice it was to have someone surprise me like that. We had a grand time catching up on news and their unexpected visit made me feel like I was back home in Newfoundland again.

There was a time when I was younger that people around home just visited each other all the time without having an official invitation. But here in Ontario, the custom of just dropping by someone's house is not a common practice and that's something I never got used to. I just assumed that it was quite normal for people to visit their neighbours and friends without standing on ceremony. But I found out differently when I first arrived in Ontario from Newfoundland.

A couple of days after we were settled in our new place, I was feeling a bit lonely after Murray went to work, so I decided that since I didn't know anybody, I'd go next door and introduce myself. I didn't want to go empty-handed, so I made a few molasses buns to take with me. When I rang the doorbell, a frail, elderly woman opened the door a crack and peeked out from around the safety chain. "Good morning! My name is

Lucy," I said. "We just moved in next door and–"

"I'm not interested in buying anything, thank you," she interrupted as she started to close the door.

Hurriedly I explained who I was and told her I had just dropped by to meet her. "Here, I brought you a few molasses buns ...they just came out of the oven so they'll be lovely with a nice cup of tea," I said.

She opened the door a little wider and sniffed at the buns. "Thank you," she said with a shy smile as she took them from me.

Then she closed the door. Thinking she was taking off the safety chain to let me in, I waited...and waited some more, but she didn't return. Baffled at her behaviour, I went back home and called Murray. "Well, the nerve of the Missus taking the buns and not even inviting me in for a cup of tea!" I said. "Not very neighbourly, is she?"

'Course Murray explained that people weren't used to doing things like that in the city and that it wasn't safe to invite strangers into their homes, especially for older people. "You probably scared the poor woman half to death," he said.

Well, my nose was right out of joint by then and I didn't want to risk giving the poor lady a heart attack, so I never went back again. After that incident I was afraid to approach anybody, so I kept to myself.

It just seemed peculiar to me that people were so skeptical of each other, and what was even stranger was that you had to wait for someone to invite you into their home. In Lord's Cove when I was growing up, if someone's door was unlatched then it was understood that anybody was welcome to come in. Nobody raised an eyebrow if a person just walked into the kitchen to say hello. We didn't have telephones and, besides, the houses were so close together you could stick your head out a window or call out from the porch door to say you were dropping in for a spell.

Not that people didn't invite each other to their homes. It was just very informal, that's all. "Why don't you drop in for a cup of tea d'night after the youngsters are in bed?"

"Good 'nuff, my dear…p'rhaps I'll drop by later on then."

Nobody minded if the plans had changed and you were unable to come for a visit. The words dropping in, dropping by and later on meant that it was an open-ended invite where both parties understood that there was a possibility they may or may not come to visit depending on the circumstances. I suppose to people outside Newfoundland, that may sound like a strange practice and if one was not aware of the connotation, then it could pose a problem.

My husband had a similar experience when we moved to St. John's many years ago. Just after we arrived, some friends telephoned to see if we had settled in okay and they promised they'd come to visit soon. No specific date was made, so about a week later Lorraine and Wilbur Dyke just showed up at our house one Saturday morning. We had a lovely visit and as they were leaving, Lorraine said they'd come back when they had more time to visit. "All right, my darling," she said. "We'll drop in to see you later on."

"Indeed we will," Wilbur added. "We'll come back to see how you're getting on."

Later when I suggested to Murray that we go to the grocery store, he insisted that we couldn't leave because Lorraine and Wilbur were coming back. That's when I realized that he thought they meant they were coming back the same day.

Times sure have changed since I lived in the Cove; nobody knocked on doors in my day, unless it was late at night and you didn't want to frighten someone. People used any excuse at all to drop in to one another's houses. They'd stop by to see how things were, to talk about the weather, to see a new baby or to check on someone who was not feeling well. Friends dropped by to have a yarn and discuss things happening around the community, or just to pass the time away on a rainy night with a friendly game of cards. That's just the way things were in our tight-knit communities.

'Course nowadays the pace of life has become so fast that people don't have time to visit what with their jobs, looking after children and their homes. Besides that, there's the distance they'd have to go, because in big cities it's not easy to get from one place to another. Just dropping in on somebody unannounced is almost impossible now and sometimes it can even have repercussions.

A couple of years ago when my sister Leona travelled from Kingston to Barrie for a niece's wedding, she mentioned to our sister-in-law in Toronto that she was going to drop in on the way. Leona assumed that Helen would remember, so she never bothered to telephone and took a taxi from the train station to Helen's apartment. Well, when she arrived, it was already after midnight and Helen wasn't home. My sister tried to call Helen's cell phone, only to find that her own phone was dead. There was no sign of a telephone booth around and she didn't want to wake the people in the adjoining apartment at that time of night. Besides, she had her luggage with her and she couldn't walk too far, so she had no choice but to sit on her suitcase outside on the sidewalk and hope that Helen might show up.

But she didn't come and by 2 a.m. Leona was tired, hungry and a little nervous, so when she spotted a cab driving by, she took chase and flagged it down. Leona asked the driver to take her to a hotel and the cabby stopped at a few places until he found a room for her without a reservation. Apparently Helen assumed that since Leona didn't call her, she had changed her mind. So she decided to spend the night at her daughter's.

As you can see, dropping in on someone when they're not around can make for an expensive visit. Leona ended up paying a $30 taxi fare from the train station to get to Helen's, then a second $80 cab ride to find a hotel and $180 for a room for the night. "Now that would never happen in Newfoundland, because back home the door would always be left open for me,"

Leona said afterwards.

Let's face it, those days will soon be gone. It's a pity, really, for that's part of the charm and hospitality that keeps the spirit of our communities alive in Newfoundland. Sometimes now when I think about the little lady who didn't invite me into her home years ago, I wonder what she was thinking. In my heart, I want to believe that she really did appreciate my gesture of goodwill and that maybe she might have invited me in for a cup of tea had I returned. My mother always used to say that an act of kindness never goes astray and if that was the case, then I'm glad I had something to share with that lady.

And if you think that I'm planning on giving up dropping in on friends and neighbours when I go home to Newfoundland, then forget it. It'll never happen in my lifetime.

# Back Seat Driving

It's strange, isn't it, how something can stir a memory when you least expect it? The other day when my neighbour was showing me his new car, he insisted that I try out the comfortable seats. As I slid into the back seat something familiar flashed to mind.

I was back in Lord's Cove again, sitting on the side of the road with my cousin Lorraine as we patiently waited to see if her Uncle Bill and Aunt Selina would be going for their usual Sunday outing. It may not sound exciting now, but cars were scarcer than hen's teeth in the Cove 45 years ago. For two 11-year-olds, going for a drive was a big deal.

The Harnetts had no children, so often they'd invite Lorraine and I to go with them. We usually had a plan to make sure they saw us after church and I can recall sidling up to Mrs. Selina to drop a subtle hint. "Lovely day for a drive d'day, isn't it?" I'd say as I walked past her.

Then Lorraine and I would hurry home, gobble down our dinner and run outside to keep an eye out for Mr. Bill's car. "Oh luh…here they comes now," Lorraine would say. "Let's make out we're going for a walk and see if they'll pick us up!"

We'd act very nonchalant as we strolled along, pretending we didn't see the car until they were almost beside us. With bated breath, we'd smile and wait to see if they would stop. "We're going for a ride up to Taylor's Bay…hop in if ye wants to come," Mr. Bill would say.

Quick as the wind, we'd scramble into the back seat and press our faces against the window so we could show off to our friends. Mr. Bill seldom drove faster than 20 mph on the dirt roads because his wife was nervous. "Mind that sheep up there in the meadow, Bill," she'd say, "and watch out for the big rock on the side of the road!"

Mr. Bill would look back at us and wink mischievously, and we always knew what was coming next. We loved going over bumps and potholes on the dirt roads so he'd purposely speed up to make us bounce up and down on the back seat. 'Course that always got us tittering and laughing...and it usually prompted his dear wife to bless herself and utter a prayer.

I think I've always loved riding in the back seat because I could enjoy the view more. Whenever my brothers came home for a visit, I made sure I was always the first one to get a ride in their cars. Sometimes when there wasn't room for everybody, I'd resort to bartering with my sisters for the coveted spot in the back seat...even though it meant taking over a chore that I hated, like waxing the kitchen floor or churning butter.

Strangely enough, I never had the inclination to drive a car until my second son was born. And it's a wonder I ever got my licence at all, after what happened the night before my road test: believe it or not, a transport truck ploughed right into me while I was stopped at a red light. The whole front of my car was demolished. I ended up with whiplash and had to wear a neck brace for weeks. My husband eventually talked me into taking the road test and getting my driver's licence.

Shortly after that, my parents came to visit us in Ontario and one day when I was taking my mother shopping, she marched out to the car and got into the back seat. "Mom, there's only you and me here. Come sit in the front seat," I said as I opened her door.

She nearly took the fingers off me when she slammed the door. "Oh, no, me chile. I'm not getting in the front seat with you in case you gets into an accident!" she declared.

Mind you, I wasn't surprised by her reaction; back then, a woman driver around home was unheard of. When my sister Marceline unexpectedly drove from New York to Newfoundland in 1961 with her five children, including twins, but without her husband, Mom nearly fainted when she showed up! She wasn't very impressed, but my father thought Marceline was really brave to drive all that distance.

When I visited my brother Raphael in Vancouver this past summer, he told me about the time he came home in his new car and Dad asked if he could "try out his car." Naturally, Raphael asked if he knew anything about driving. "Yup…it's no different than steering a skiff or a dory, me son," Dad assured him. "Just give 'er a bit of gas and off she goes."

Since it was dark and there were no cars around, Raphael stopped on a straight stretch of road outside the Cove and they exchanged places. My brother showed him where the gas pedal was and before he could say another word, Dad put the pedal to the floor and the car took off like a firecracker. "Slow down! Take your foot off the gas!" Raphael yelled at him.

My father was hanging onto the wheel and weaving from one side of the road to the other. "She won't stop! Where's the brake?"

As the car veered toward a trench, Raphael grabbed the wheel and jammed his foot on the brake, bringing the car to a screeching halt. My brother was shaken, but not my father. He just grinned. "She got some pluck in 'er, haven't she?"

Raphael was about to get back in the driver's seat when a police car pulled up alongside them. The Mountie instructed my father to turn off the ignition and step out of the car. Not knowing where anything was, Dad turned the lights on high beam and then started pushing and pulling buttons on the dashboard. Raphael giggled as he told the story. "The Mountie leaned down and peered into the windshield to see what he was doing and at the same time, m'father switched on the wipers and the water squirted right up in the poor man's face!"

Why, we don't know, but the Mountie let both of them off with a warning and it was many years later before my father ever attempted to get his driver's licence. He was in his late 60s before he took his road test and even then he mowed down a snow fence outside St. Lawrence when he hit a patch of ice. I can't say he was a good driver and most of the time when my parents went for a drive to Lamaline or to visit my sister in Grand Bank, Mom became a "back seat driver." Oh, yes, she made sure he knew when it was safe to turn and reminded him to slow down. Although she never said it aloud, I know she really didn't trust his driving. A couple of years before he died, I was driving his car and he asked me why I was staying on one side of the road all the time. "Because I always follow the rules and stay on my own side, except when I have to pass," I said. "Why...don't you?"

"Naw, me chile, only when I have to," he said casually. "You see that silver ornament on the hood of me car that looks like an airplane? Well, I lines that up right smack in the middle of the yellow line on the pavement and I don't move over till the other fella gets right up to me."

Oh, me nerves! It's no wonder I've never liked being a driver. I seldom drive anymore unless I have to, for my husband usually chauffeurs me everywhere. The way I see it, I have the best of both worlds: I can relax and keep an eye on hubby's driving as well. And like my mother, I'm becoming an excellent back seat driver.

# Glimpses of Yesteryear

Where has the time gone, I wonder? Seems like I just get settled into a New Year and before I can blink, last year is already old news. Call me sentimental if you will, but I'd like to halt time for awhile so I can take pleasure in the past before it eludes me.

I was never more aware of the passing of time than during a recent trip home to Lord's Cove, when I suddenly realized how few people of my parents' generation are left. Whenever I met younger people from the Cove or the surrounding communities, they'd look familiar yet I couldn't place the faces. "Now who do you belong to?" I'd have to ask.

Then I'd discover they were the offspring of those I went to high school with and some of them already had children of their own. Lord, that made me feel older than God's cow! That got me thinking about all the older people who have long passed on and wishing I could go back in time and get to know them all over again.

When my brothers and sisters began swapping tales about when we were growing up, I asked them to tell me about our grandparents, for I was too young to remember any of them. As I listened to their stories about my grandparents and parents, I was intrigued – and envious – of all the things that I had missed in not knowing them. That's when I decided to start writing a journal and record all the things I learned for my own sons, so they can trace our roots and so they'll always feel a sense of belonging and perhaps get a glimpse of yesteryear.

I think autograph books, diaries, journals, scrapbooks and old photo albums are wonderful keepsakes. No matter what form the memorabilia, they are great reminders of the past, for they represent life and times that most of us don't even experience anymore. Whether it is a diary filled with romance or a journal of life stories or a scrapbook of old snaps, it is pure history that should be preserved.

A few years ago after my mother passed away, I visited Mary Hunt (Collins), a dear old friend of my mother in Montreal. She talked incessantly about their friendship when they were teenagers and how sometimes in the summer they'd walk the 20 miles between Lord's Cove and Lamaline to visit each other. As Mary reminisced about their escapades, I saw my mother through her friend's eyes and I caught a glimpse of Lottie Herlidan as a young, vibrant girl before I even existed.

"Your mom was a bit shy but full of fun, and I was the mischief-maker," Mary chuckled. "Your mother could keep a secret like nobody else and if my poor mother ever knew the things I did, she'd turn over in her grave!"

Mary told me about the time when she coaxed my mother into going to a dance so she could meet a young lad of whom her parents disapproved. She told them she was going to a dance in the Cove, but instead she went to the neighbouring community of Lawn. She had already walked to Lord's Cove and was tired, so she and my mother got a ride on a horse and cart with someone carrying a load of hay. "I had such a crush on your father's brother, Herb, the fiddle player! I got all dickied-up in my best dress and French perfume and halfway there it rained! After two hours of bouncing through the potholes, we arrived soaked to the skin, hair stuck to our heads and reeking of manure!" she chuckled.

Not wanting anybody to see the mess they were in, they peeked through a window…and saw Herb dancing and flirting with another girl. "I was right heartbroken over it so we decided to walk back home, but fortunately the man with the cart picked us up on his way back to the Cove." Mary laughed. "How foolish we were back then, eh?"

After the stories were told, she brought out her autograph book and showed me what my mother had written the day before Mary left to go to summer school at Littledale in St. John's. When I saw her familiar handwriting and the little blob of ink she dropped on the pastel pink page, it touched me. At that moment, I could visualize this young girl dipping her pen into the inkwell and saying goodbye to her best friend. The words were few but the sentiment was heartfelt:

*Dear Mary,*

*When you are far away*

*And your friend you cannot see,*

*When in some chapel you are praying*

*Will you sometime pray for me?*

*Lottie Herlidan, April 28, 1928*

Mary was kind enough to give me a copy of her autograph book as a souvenir and I gladly accepted it. During our conversation, I mentioned to her that I had an autograph book that looked identical to hers and was given to me by a 92-year-old woman who also studied at Littledale. When I asked if she knew a Mary Foley from Tilting, Newfoundland, she did indeed remember her well.

"The last time we saw each other was on the SS *Argyle* on September 1, 1929, and we exchanged notes in our autograph books," Mary said. "See what she wrote?"

*When you are married and have children happy*

*I hope every one of them will chew tobaccy!*

Later when I got home, I found the note that Mary Collins had written in return on that same day:

*If writing in notebooks*

*True friendship endures*

*With the greatest of pleasure*

*I'll scribble in yours.*

The writings in the books intrigued me. On every page there

was written some kind of sentiment or memorable saying from family members, good friends, classmates and people that both women met throughout the years. I know in high school we used to enjoy writing sentiments and good wishes to each other on the last day of school. Some of us who didn't have autograph books would write notes on scribblers or on the back of an exercise book. When I talked to my friends when I was home, they recalled some of those quotes:

*Think of me in the morning*
*Think of me at night*
*Think of me when I'm far away*
*And don't forget to write.*

Many penned sentiments about friendship, as written here by Harrie C. from Lamaline Meadow on February 5, 1928:

*If there's room for me in your album*
*There's room for me in your heart*
*There's room for us both in heaven*
*Where loved ones never part.*

Although it was mostly girls who did this, the boys were happy to enter something in their books. Mostly, it was a little rhyme or a saying that teased:

*Do you love me or do you not,*
*I told you once but I forgot.*

There were all kinds of beautiful poems, verses, quotations and witticisms inside those pages, such as this one:

*Here's to the train that runs on wheels*
*That never runs into danger*
*Here's to the girl that sticks to her love*
*And never flirts with a stranger.*

S.B. of Witless Bay, August 11, 1930

Naturally there was lots of humour and advice to impart:

*When your husband at you flings,*
*Knives and forks and other things*
*Seek relief and seek it soon*

*In the handle of the broom*
Kathleen from Tilting,
September 1930

And the ways of the heart were not lost on Gwendolyn, either, who wrote these words on September 13, 1929.

*A boy is like a little bird,*
*That flies from tree to tree,*
*But when he sees another bird,*
*He thinks no more of thee*

Maybe we should all invest in an autograph book or journal, for the written word is a powerful tool. Often I wish that I could share the words with the families of those who wrote the sentiments, for sometimes people will write things that they would never say aloud to each other. Whenever I see the names of the people who penned quotations and nonsensical little rhymes in the books that I have, I wonder if their families even realize that they exist. Do they know, I wonder, that within these worn pages their parents, grandparents and other relatives have left this beautiful gift of themselves?

I fear that in this age of technology the art of penmanship and the autograph book itself will disappear, and that would be a pity. As I see it, every piece of the past is stitched together in our roots and they hold moments of our lives that we should never forget. For the sake of those who have gone before us I hope that these glimpses of yesteryear will live on for someone else to enjoy.

# A Delicate Subject

Underwear. Now there's a topic that would never come up in a conversation back in my day. Frankly, I don't remember anybody openly discussing something as delicate as underwear. Good heavens…there'd be dead silence in the room if that happened – our undergarments were something we tried to cover up. It was a private matter that never went beyond the washtub and the clothesline. Mothers and grandmothers referred to their undergarments as "unmentionables," after all.

So why am I bringing it up now? Well, nowadays it seems that showing off your undies in public is the "in" thing. Lord almighty, it makes me very uncomfortable when I see young girls and grown women wearing pants that barely cover the pelvis, not to mention belly-button rings, tattoos and itsy-bitsy thongs. They don't even blink an eye at exposing their underwear in public. Even worse, some don't wear any at all. Whenever I go to a restaurant and see females of all shapes and sizes sitting in front of me with their rear ends hanging out, I avert my eyes. Such displays not only put me off my food, but make me feel uncomfortable, too.

Now I'm not saying that young folk are risqué; just that they are a little more daring than I'm used to and, frankly, I'm having a bit of trouble adjusting, that's all.

My mother maintained that there was great dignity in wearing good underwear – and she ingrained that into the nine of us throughout childhood. Every time one of our crowd went out, Mom always stood at the bottom of the stairs and imparted her infamous words: "Make sure you got on good underwear, in case you're in an accident and have to go to hospital!"

Now the chance back then of even seeing a car in Lord's Cove, let alone getting struck by one and sent to hospital, was a remote possibility. (You might get injured by Mr. Anthony's bull, for he was so ornery that if you looked at him scow-ways he'd take chase after you.) Perhaps I misunderstood Mom's intentions, but I gleaned from her words that it didn't matter if you got struck by a car or how badly you were injured…just as long as you were wearing good, clean underwear. I've never forgotten her words and, yes, I found myself saying the same thing to my sons when they were growing up.

I can only imagine the reaction of folks a generation ago if they saw someone walking around half-naked in public. Seldom did we ever see a woman with her bare legs exposed, and God forbid if someone saw a woman's cleavage. They always wore blouses or dresses with long sleeves that buttoned up beneath the chin.

But like everything else, ladies' apparel has gone through plenty of changes over the years – many of them necessary, in my opinion. Thank goodness we got rid of corsets, suspender belts, nylon stockings, and elastic garters that cut off your circulation. I hated those pesky things because my bony legs were like sticks and no matter how hard I tried, the stockings would still roll down around my ankles.

I'm grateful that I didn't have to wear the bloomers and knee-length drawers, or the shifts and petticoats, that they had in my mother's day. Our generation fell between that and having cute brand names for our bras and panties, such as La Senza, Victoria's Secret, Calvin Klein and Sweet Nothings. We wore "step-ins" – a brief panty with elastic around the waist and the top of the legs. As I recall, they came in two sizes at Rob Lambe's shop – big ones for women and small ones for children.

Our mothers and grandmothers were very modest people. My mother told me that, believe it or not, the older women used to wait for the men to go about their work before they'd hang their undies – and even then, they had to be pinned at the end of the clothesline so they couldn't be seen from the road. I doubt some husbands even looked at their wives' bloomers on the clothesline, let alone saw them being worn. When it came to women's underclothing, men seemed uncomfortable about the whole matter...and some still do.

Take my friend Pearl, for instance. She told me that before she married her husband, John, he had been a bachelor for 43 years and had lived with his mother, who did everything for him. Not long after they were married, Pearl was sick one day and John offered to hang her laundry out on the clothesline. Knowing he'd never done this before, Pearl watched him through the window. When he reached into the basket and pulled out one of her bras, John looked totally bewildered and tried to figure out which way to hang it on the clothesline. At first he hung it lengthwise to the ground. Then he took it off and stretched it across. Pearl saw him step back to look at his handiwork, then shake his head and quickly wrap her bra around the line in a secure knot.

"It was so funny watching his reaction when he picked up a pair of my panties," Pearl said, laughing at the memory. "He held it up between his thumb and forefinger, turned his head away and pinned it on the clothesline. He didn't even look at the others. He just stooped down, felt around in the basket and pinned them up. Poor man, what a shock treatment that was!"

When I was a teenager, we girls weren't as uptight about our underwear as our mothers were, but that didn't mean we showed it off, either. Older women called it scandalous the way the Eaton's catalogue boldly displayed women's briefs, especially since devilish lads would sneak a peek whenever the girls weren't around. Heaven's above, if your bra strap showed you'd blush to the roots of your hair if a male was anywhere in sight. And whenever I put out the wash, Mom watched me like a hawk in case I hung the underwear on the line any which way to get it all done.

"For the love of God, Lucy. Haven't you got no shame hanging your step-ins out for everybody to see?" she'd yell from the porch. "Now you go right back and hang them at the end of the line like I told you!"

I remember going to a dance wearing a blouse buttoned up to my chin. When I saw the other girls with their necks exposed, I undid two buttons. I was sure Mom wouldn't see me from the back kitchen, where she was serving food with the other women. I was wrong. Within minutes, she appeared out of nowhere and pulled me aside.

"Don't you think you can pull the wool over my eyes, young lady!" she said as she took a large safety pin out of her apron pocket. "You cover up your neck right now before someone sees you!" she added, pinning the collar under my chin. I could hardly glutch, but I was not about to disobey her. Instead, I sat in the corner all night so nobody could see me.

My sister Leona recalls a time some 44 years ago when she was leaving home to go to Memorial University. Somehow in all the confusion, she packed her suitcase but forgot to take her underwear off the clothesline. Just minutes after Stacey's Taxi drove away, my father spied Leona's underwear flapping in the breeze. He grabbed her step-ins off the line, clothespins and all, and chased after the car, waving them to get the driver's attention. When the taxi finally stopped, Daddy dumped all her underwear into her lap and declared, "It's a good thing I spotted 'em or else you'd be in St. John's with not a pair of drawers to your name, m'chile!"

Mortified, Leona stuffed her undies inside her jacket as the four male passengers sharing her taxi pretended not to notice her predicament.

"Looks like the sun's gonna shine later on," one said.

"Yup… yup… gonna be some day on clothes d'day,"

replied another.

That was back in the day of modest briefs, before skimpy undergarments were the rage. At first I wasn't keen on wearing a thong – small enough to fit into a thimble, a scrap of material wedged between my buttocks. That sounded downright uncomfortable. But once I tried one on, I have to admit it really wasn't so bad. And it's ideal for avoiding the "panty line" showing through clingy outfits. So like I said before, some changes in underwear fashions are good.

Yes, I've come a long way over the years. I don't even hide behind catalogue shopping for my underwear anymore. Now I hold my head high as I lay my purchase on the counter. With a confident smile, I look the salesperson in the eye. There's barely a quiver in my voice when I speak:

"The underwear is not for me, you know. It's for my sister."

# Golden Oldies

"Turn the light off in the parlour before you switches on that contraption because it's going to burn up all the juice with the two things on at the same time!"

That was my mother's reaction when we got our very first television back in 1965. She was skeptical of anything new and had opposed my father's decision to get it from the very beginning, for she was afraid it would use up all the electricity. Tonight as I watched hubby flick through the 60 channels with the remote control, I was thinking about how much things had changed since I was a teenager, for television opened up a whole new world for us outside Lord's Cove.

I suppose it was because we were young and impressionable, but we embraced change with open arms and looked forward to the future with great expectations. It was the sign of the times – we wanted to forge ahead with the new while our parents, being more skeptical, fought to hold onto the old. My mother, in particular, was never very comfortable with anything that was new and tended to either not use it at all or "keep it for good." I'm not sure what her reasoning was, but even when the television wasn't in use, she kept a blanket over it and for the first few weeks after we got it, we were only allowed to watch it at night. Come to think of it, it was around that time as well that we got a new chesterfield and she kept the plastic on that for almost a year. Even after my parents bought a washer, stove and fridge in later years after all of our crowd left home, they didn't consider it a necessity. It was functional, yes... but it was bought to be used just in case they needed it. In reality, even when the appliances were old in terms of years, they were still brand new because they were seldom used. Mom still insisted on using the outside clothesline and wouldn't let my dad plug in the dryer because it wasted electricity. But she found a practical use for it just the same. She set it in the corner by the kitchen door and adorned it with a lace tablecloth and a plant. Then, in the winter after my father insisted on connecting the dryer vent, she found yet another use for it... she stored her bread in it because there was no room in the freezer.

When it came to appliances, neither of them could even remember the names of them. They referred to one or the other as "chummy dinger," the "machine" or "that t'ing" and what was even more strange, each time they used those words, they knew exactly what the other was talking about. "Put the box over on the chummy dinger there where that t'ing is beside the machine..."

Let's face it, there are few things in today's modernized world that can make us raise an eyebrow anymore because we've been privy to so many new innovations and inventions that we've grown accustomed to it. We even take it for granted. I mean, have you ever stopped to think how people felt or reacted upon seeing something for the very first time... something they had no prior knowledge of or that they could never conceive in their lifetime?

Whenever something new came to the Cove, there was always mixed feelings about whether it was good or bad. I remember folks around home talking about the reaction of an elderly woman who saw a car for the first time in her life. When she saw it moving slowly down the road toward her house, she hurried outside to alert her husband, blessing herself as she went, "Glory be to God... look at that big t'ing coming down the road." She yelled, "Quick... shut the gate before it gets in the garden and eats the cabbage!"

Oh yes, the transition from the old to the new can be an unforgettable experience. I found that out the hard way when I was a youngster. Before television came to Lord's Cove, we had shows (or films) in the parish hall and I couldn't comprehend how the people got up there on that little screen. I knew what a train was, but had no idea what one looked like or how it sounded, so when I saw one film, the noise of the clanging wheels and the whistle scared the bejeepers out of me. When I saw that monstrous piece of steel barrelling down the track, I thought it was coming right through the screen and that we were all going to be killed. I screamed and instinctively ducked down, banging my forehead on the chair in front of me and my sister had to take me home because I was bawling and screeching so much.

Now, I wasn't the only one in the family who had a bad experience when I was a child. Take my sister Leona, for instance. When she was nine years old, she had to go to the Grand Bank hospital to have her tonsils removed. She had never seen a flush toilet before and refused to sit on it because she was afraid she would get sucked down inside. A nurse brought her a bedpan, but she flatly refused to use it. "I can't make my water lying down... I wants a chamber pot!"

'Course, they didn't have that in the hospital and eventually Leona did her business, but only after the nurse put the bedpan on top of the toilet seat.

Sometimes when I look back at the past and recall the way we used to live, I often wish that some things had never changed. I'm not saying that I'd actually give up the comfort of indoor plumbing or that I'd want to go back to lugging buckets of water or even having to do laundry by hand in a wash tub... not on your life I wouldn't. But there are times when I miss the old way of life I knew as a child. I'd give up anything, for instance, to curl up on the daybed in our old kitchen beside the wood stove and smell the aroma of bread baking in the oven, or just lie in the old wrought iron bed with the feather mattress like I used to have and listen to the wind whistling and rattling the windows. Those are comforting thoughts that I don't think will ever leave me, I know. I know there's a chance I'll enjoy some of those things again, but maybe not in the same way.

As time goes on, I'm beginning to realize that the more things change, the more they stay the same and the more new things we get, the more the old ones make sense. Every time I go back home to Newfoundland, I notice that the trend is changing again. I see a revival of the past being combined with the present and the things that were once considered old are fast becoming new again. It warms my heart when I see furniture or relics of bygone days. Many of us, I know, remember things that were relegated to the attic or the store room to make way for the more modern conveniences... things such as the old wooden wash tub and wash board, the butter churn, the oil lamp, the spinning wheel and the hand-operated sewing machine. These things we left behind stood the test of time, and I daresay they would again if necessary, but yet they took a back seat to more useful things like indoor water pumps, electric kettles, toasters, irons and wringer washers. Change was inevitable, and it was, after all, a sign of the changing times.

When I think of all the things that I should have or could have kept from my childhood days, it frustrates me that I didn't have the foresight to realize the sentimental value attached to it. Oh, sure I still have a few of my favourite things I've kept all those years, but not enough. As I look around my house now, I see little reminders of Newfoundland, like the pictures on the wall, my books, old albums and photographs, several school desks, homemade quilts and blankets, my diary, prayer book and a few dishes. Oh, yes... and two beautifully hand-painted chamber pots. I can't forget those, although there was a time when my parents would gladly have insisted that I forget I had them.

I remember back when we were living in St. John's about 18 years ago when they came to visit us for the first time after we moved. I was very proud of my two treasures because one belonged to my mother from her younger years and the other was given to me by an elderly lady in Lord's Cove before she died. Wanting to share their beauty with everybody, I decided to put plants in them and I displayed one as a centrepiece for my dining room table and the other on the living room windowsill. Everybody who came to our house admired them... except my parents. It never occurred to me that they might feel embarrassed by them, until I saw my father stop dead in his tracks and stare at the table. Mom hadn't noticed them yet and as I went into the kitchen, I overhead my dad talking to her in a low voice. "The Lord save us, Lottie... I've seen it all now! Lucy got your old pee pot sitting right smack in the middle of her table!"

I thought Mom was going to faint. "Haven't you got no shame at all putting something that private out for people to see?" she demanded. "We're not back in the pot auger days no more, you know, so shove that t'ing up under the bed where it belongs for heavens sake!"

Well, I tried to explain that I was trying to preserve the past, but she wouldn't hear of it and I had to put them out of sight until they went back home. But I still have those golden oldies and I don't plan on letting them out of my sight. Besides, who knows when an emergency might arise or a sudden storm will put out the electricity or the bathroom will be occupied when nature pays me a visit in the middle of the night? As far as I'm concerned, there's room for both the old and the new, each taking a place of prominence in their own right.

# Crossing the Border

"Citizenship?"

The Canada Customs Officer directs the question at both of us.

"Canadian," my husband answers.

I open my mouth, but not a word comes out. The man in the booth peers at me through the car window and redirects his question curtly. "Where are you from, ma'am?"

"Newfoundland… I mean Niagara Falls. I'm Canadian," I manage.

He raises his eyebrow and again speaks to Murray. "How long have you been in the United States?"

"About an hour."

My heart is beating so fast I can hardly breathe. I look away, afraid to make eye contact with the official in case he suspects something because I know what his next question will be. "Did you buy or receive any goods while you were in the United States, sir?"

Oh me nerves! I squeeze my fists shut, praying that he won't ask me that question because I'm afraid I won't be able to outright lie. Dear Lord, whatever possessed me to do something like this today? But now I was already wearing those stupid earrings and I told Murray not to declare them. I hold my breath as Murray answers. "No, I didn't buy anything, except gas for the car."

There, now I forced my husband into telling a lie. Oh, please, I pray silently, don't let the officer ask me that question. Suddenly a terrible thought crosses my mind. Did I remember to take the price tag off my earrings? Quickly I glance in the side mirror to check and I see that my face is flushed. Don't hyperventilate… just take a deep breath and smile. Smile. Who am I kidding? My face looks like a can of worms because the facial muscles are totally uncontrollable. From the corner of my eye I see the officer looking at me. I can feel his eyes on my earrings. Now my earlobes are burning. Oh, no... my red ears will be a dead giveaway! My hands go up to cover them, but then I change my mind and sit on them to keep them from shaking. Don't want to look suspicious. He's still staring at me... I can feel it because the hives are popping out all over me. "Would you mind opening your trunk, please, sir?"

I almost stop breathing. He didn't ask me after all. Instead, the officer steps out of the booth and walks to the back of the car.

"I should've told him about the earrings!" I hiss to Murray. "Did you see the way he was staring at me... I'm sure he knows! I'm going to tell him..."

"Okay, folks, you can go ahead. Thank you and have a nice day."

Drained and totally ashamed of myself, I sink back against my seat as we drive past the Canada Customs building. Thank God... we're across the border at last.

A guilty conscience is a terrible burden to lug around, isn't it? All that anguish and for what? I needed those earrings like I needed more freckles. From now on, when I cross the border to shop, I will declare my purchases. A clear conscience is worth any amount of money, even with the exchange on the Canadian dollar. Besides, I'm just not cut out to be a criminal because my bizarre nervous behaviour would give me away every time.

When you live so close to the United States like we do here in Niagara Falls with just a bridge separating us, people tend to cross-border shop. That means many a thrifty shopper wants to save money by not paying duty on their goods when they come back to Canada, and sometimes they take chances by concealing things in their car or on their person. But that can lead to a lot of embarrassment in some cases. Take my girlfriend, for instance, she had a habit of buying clothes in the U.S. and never declared anything. She used to wear old clothes going over, discard it and wear new ones back. And she got away with it for a long time, until one day, both her luck and the supply of old clothes ran out. She actually went over the border wearing nothing under her trench coat but her underwear. Now, I'd never have the guts to do that, because with my luck, the police would stop me and I'd get arrested for soliciting or indecent exposure.

Well, Darlene took full advantage of the sales and confidently pulled up to the Canadian Customs wearing two pairs of shorts, a skirt, a dress, a tank top, a blouse, a sweater and a pair of slacks under her trench coat. Without batting an eyelash, she told the lady officer she had nothing to declare, but the officer wasn't fooled. She took one look at Darlene sweating in the 100 degree August heat and sent her directly to the authorities for a strip search. Need I go on?

One of my friends, Brian, who works at a toll bridge, says that often people are caught smuggling things across the Canadian border and most of it is detected through routine spot checks. "You wouldn't believe what people do," he said. "I remember a young woman in a sports car being pulled over for a spot check. When the Customs Officer opened the trunk, out popped this huge man like a jack-in-the-box. I don't know who got the biggest surprise… the illegal immigrant stuffed in that little space or the officer."

Another time, Brian watched a car being waved through customs and before it got a few yards away from the booth, smoke began pouring from the car engine. The two young men in the car pulled over, popped the hood and when the Customs Officer came to help, he found the source of the trouble. Apparently the men were smuggling cigarettes and had stuffed them under the hood of the car… which ignited from the heat of the engine. Just another few hundred yards and they would've made it safely. But, as Brian pointed out, not everything is picked up by the officers in spot checks either. Sometimes, they make HUGE mistakes, so to speak. He remembers a young official who checked the back of a transport truck one night and seeing nothing unusual, he gave the driver clearance to go through.

When the driver asked if he wanted to check the papers on the elephant he was taking to the zoo, the astonished officer sheepishly admitted he hadn't even seen the elephant.

Of course, it's never a good idea to lie to an official when you have a child in the car. Chances are, they'll set the record straight in no time. My neighbour learned her lesson recently when she took her granddaughter across the border for new shoes. She had the child wear the shoes coming back and told the officer that she had nothing to declare. And she would have gotten away with it if the six-year-old hadn't put in her two cents worth. "Grandma, you forgot to tell him about the new shoes you bought me!" she yelled. "Look," she said, sticking her feet up for the officer to see. "Aren't they pretty?"

After I heard our friend, Shirley Laslo, talk about her mother's reaction to a guilty conscience, I felt somewhat relieved that I'm not the only one who overreacts under stress. One year, Shirley took her elderly mother out for dinner across the border and since it was her mom's birthday, she bought her a new hat. Her mother liked the hat so much that she wore it to dinner, so when they came back into Canada, Shirley decided she wouldn't bother declaring the hat. Repeatedly, she told her mother not to say anything about the hat, for her mom had a tendency to chatter to everybody who spoke to her. All went well for the first few questions and Shirley was very relieved that the officer didn't question her mother. Just as they got clearance to go through, her mom leaned across Shirley and spoke to the officer. "You see this hat I'm wearing? Well, it's not new, you know. Oh, no... I've had this old hat for a long time, haven't I, Shirley? Oh, sure it might LOOK brand new, but it's not... no, indeed it's not. Shirley didn't buy this new hat at Wal-Mart for me today..."

The officer was trying hard not to smile and when her flustered mother finally finished talking, he said, "And may I say, ma'am, that old hat looks just lovely on you."

Like I said, a guilty conscience can be a dead giveaway.

# To the Moon and Back

July 20, 1969. I can still recall the intense drama, the mind-boggling danger of that momentous voyage, the immense relief when feet first made contact with solid ground. That was the day that me and four other poor mortals braved the perils of the sea in a small boat from the French island of St. Pierre to Fortune… and, coincidentally, the same day that man first set foot on the moon. As 600 million people all over the world tuned in to the triumphant adventure of the Apollo 11's flight from pad 39A in Cape Kennedy, a bunch of us stun-poles back here on earth were being tossed from here to eternity in a raging storm, just praying for the sight of land. It's true that historic trip to the moon and back was hailed as a stunning achievement and a "Giant Leap for Mankind," but with all due respect to the astronauts, our adventure on the high seas was nothing to be scoffed at.

Let me backtrack a little here and tell you how we got ourselves into that situation years ago. There were five of us: my sister Leona, her new boyfriend, two of our roommates from St. John's and me. On the spur of the moment, we decided to pool our money and take a trip to St. Pierre, so we set off on the ferry from Fortune. Everything went just fine the first afternoon of our arrival, but the next day little things began to go wrong. The landlady at the boarding house where we stayed was kind enough to enlist her nephew to escort us around the island and to take us dancing that night. By mid-afternoon, my sister was beginning to feel poorly and complained of stomach cramps, for she had ignored the warning not to drink the water. When the young Frenchman came to pick us up that evening and the five of us tried to cram into his small car, I accidentally slammed the door on his hand and he had to go to the hospital. Diagnosis... broken index finger. He didn't feel too much like going dancing after that, so we walked to the club ourselves.

The music had barely started when Leona got short-taken and made a hasty retreat to the bathroom. Matter of fact, she spent most of the evening there until, finally, we took her back to our room. Somebody forgot to lock the front door and during the night a Portuguese sailor came in, walked upstairs and tried to get into the bedroom where the four of us girls were sleeping. We thought that some kind of axe murderer was trying to kill us, so we all started screaming and bawling for help. When the landlady heard the commotion, she woke up just in time to find the sailor about to get into her bed. When all the racket subsided and the gendarmes found that the poor drunken sailor had mistaken our boarding house for the one next door where his sweetheart was still waiting, everybody's nerves were frazzled. To make matters worse, Leona was up and down to the bathroom all night and kept everyone awake, so we were more than ready to get back home the next morning.

Unfortunately, a storm had brewed overnight and by mid-morning when we got to the dock, the ferry was cancelled. Now we couldn't afford to stay another night, so when a businessman from St. John's offered a fisherman a large sum of money to take him back to Fortune, he told us we could come as well... for free. Fools that we were, we clambered on board, never giving it a thought that if the weather was too bad for the ferry, we shouldn't be setting out in a fishing boat with an outboard motor and nothing but a makeshift roof covering a bench for shelter.

We were barely 20 minutes out when I began to worry, for the sky turned black, the wind got higher and thunder ripped through the sky. By now, the four of us girls were huddled together in the stern of the boat, wishing we were still back in St.

Pierre watching the news about the Apollo II spacecraft as it roared toward a rendezvous with the moon to see what mysteries it held in store. While astronauts Neil Armstrong, Edwin Aldrin and Michael Collins were preparing for touchdown on the Sea of Tranquility on the moon's surface, there we were, being tossed around like a matchstick on the Atlantic Ocean. Worse still, no one even knew we were out there.

As the sea got rougher, Leona began throwing up. Then the rain started and the waves began to sweep in over the boat with a force that had us all hanging onto whatever we could find. I wrapped my legs around my suitcase, tucked the loaf of French bread I had promised to bring to my sister under one arm and grabbed on to the leg of the bench with the other. One of the other girls, Grace, began to panic and started yelling that we were going to be drowned. Terrified now, I was struggling to hang on to my suitcase and hold on to Leona's feet whenever she hung over the side to throw up. We begged the skipper to take us back, but he said it was too late to turn around. Leona's friend, who had never been on a boat before, opened up a bottle of rum and drank it down straight in record time, as he happily sang at the top of his lungs.

I started reciting the Rosary, for it was all we could do to keep ourselves and our suitcases from being washed overboard. The sea became more ferocious as the wind heightened in intensity and the overhead covering offered no protection from the waves. We swallowed so much sea water that we all got sick and pardon my language, but everybody started barfing as we rolled around on the bottom of the boat. The small outboard motor was useless against the high seas, so the skipper turned off the motor, dropped anchor and began bailing out the water. At the very moment when the whole world was holding its breath at the Apollo prepared for touchdown on the lunar surface, I was mumbling the Sorrowful Mysteries of the Rosary for the fifth time and desperately hanging on to the loaf of bread. For some unexplained reason, that French loaf seemed the most important thing in the world at the time, so I shoved it under my jacket to try and keep it dry.

The terrifying hours dragged on. While the astronauts were making their historical two-and-a-quarter-hour walk on the moon, Leona's boyfriend was making feeble attempts to propose marriage to her, but she couldn't hear his words above the din of the storm. Every time he tried to kneel up straight, a wave would knock him over and he'd try it all over again. But Leona was none the wiser because she was too sick and frightened to pay any attention to him and I didn't have strength to tell her what he was trying to say. It was ironic when you think about it… the similarities between the Apollo's courageous flight and ours. It took our little boat eight hours to get from St. Pierre to Fortune that evening and the astronauts' trip to the moon took exactly eight days from the time of lift-off to splashdown. When they returned to earth, they left behind the simplest mark of man's first visit – footprints in the fine moon sand. And us… well, we left our teeth marks on the gunnels of that little French boat and the print of our hands and knees on Fortune soil when we finally landed.

Oh, we were a ghastly sight to behold when we staggered into the Customs Office. The two officers inside thought they were seeing ghosts when they saw our motley crew and I dare not repeat the expletives that one of them threw at the skipper for risking the lives in that storm. There was no mass shouts of jubilation like the astronauts got when they touched down on the moon's surface and the world heard the words they'd all been waiting for. "Houston, Tranquility Base here. The Eagle has landed."

Compared to the words of the crew on the Apollo, ours rang hollow somehow. "Quick… Where's the bathroom?"

Bruised, soaked to the skin and green from seasickness, we accepted the kind offer of a bystander to drive us to my sister's house in Grand Bank. Like the astronauts who brought back precious moon samples as proof of their visit, I still clutched what remained of my French Loaf. I'll never forget the shocked look on Helena's face as we filed into her house in the sad state we were in. "Where on earth did ye come from in this storm…?"

Without letting her finish, I hauled out the sodden French loaf from inside my jacket and shoved it into her hands. "You wouldn't believe it if I told you," I said. "I feel like we've been to the moon and back."

# Habit Forming

Have you ever sat in a room and listened to someone drum their fingers on a table, crack their knuckles, click their false teeth, or perhaps seen someone diddle one foot constantly? You may be too polite to admit it, but doesn't that rub your nerves right raw or make you feel like snocking them on the noggin? I'm sure we all know someone with annoying habits because every human being has some kind of odd ways or little quirks we aren't even aware of. Habits can be good and they can be bad, depending on which way you look at it. It could be something that you acquired as a child, a little gesture that you make, some word or expression that you use in everyday speech without even giving it a second thought. I can't begin to tell you how many times a week someone in passing will greet me with the same salutation. "Hi, how are you today?"

"I'm fine, thank you and how are you?"

"I'm fine, thanks."

We all know it's highly unlikely that a person is really "fine" all the time, so out of courtesy, we tend to say the same thing without thinking. It's a habit, you see. Oh, there's the odd one who will take it literally and launch into detail about what ails them, but unless you really want them to tell you how they are, it might be wise to rephrase that question once you know they're in the habit of answering truthfully.

I'd be willing to bet that if I asked each of you to tell me about a habit you've noticed about someone you know, you'd have no problem coming up with something. Some people do annoying things such as flicking the channel at a crucial moment in a story you're watching on TV, while others may slap you on the back when they talk to you or interrupt when you're trying to tell them something important. It may be a habit that amuses you, like the excitable way a friend waves her hands around when she talks, or how another makes a little gasping sound upon hearing exciting news, or it might simply be a comical expression on another's face when they are surprised. How about endearing little habits, like the way somebody clamps a hand over their mouth when they giggle or when you compliment someone and they shyly look away and shuffle one foot?

I think if we were to stop and take notice of the habits we've acquired over the years, we'd be surprised at the things we say and do. Take expressions and the way we speak, for instance. We all have our own little phrases and idioms, particularly in Newfoundland. One of my uncles always used the word wonderful to describe everything, whether he was referring to something good or bad. "That was some wonderful bad storm we had last night, wasn't it?"

Then again, he might use it in another context, but everyone knew what he meant. "That's some wonderful grand load of fish you brought in from the trap, me son!"

One of my sisters as well, habitually says the same word at least twice in every sentence. No matter if it is a question or a statement, she still adds the word "right." "When I woke up Sunday, I was feeling sick, right? I didn't even try to crawl out of bed, so I never got to mass this week, right?"

Oh, yes, old habits are hard to break, aren't they? I have one in particular that dates back 40 years, and while I found it soothing and relaxing, I nearly drove my mother foolish. "Lucy, you're getting right on me nerves rocking back and forth in that chair," she used to say to me. "You've been at it all morning, so stop it right now because you're making me stomach turn!"

I still rock every chance I get because that's my source of comfort when I'm feeling down or when I'm worried about something. I'm trying to wean myself from this habit when other people are around, but I still slip back to my old routine. I'm not even aware of it until someone brings it to my attention or I notice that the person's head is moving in sync with the rocking motion of my chair ... kinda like the little dog ornament my brother had in the back window of his old Chevy in the '60's.

If you stop and think about people's habits, I think you'll find that sometimes predicting what others will do in a situation may be to another's benefit. When we were youngsters, we knew when Mom was about to lose her patience with us whenever we'd hear her make a clicking sound with her tongue. "Tisk...tisk...tisk... if you two don't stop that bickering, you're gonna be sorry, I'm telling you..."

Then we'd take our scrapers and head for the door, especially if she had a tea towel in her hand. That was the other habit she had ... flicking a tea towel across your backside. It didn't hurt at all, but she had an awesome wrist flick, a knack she acquired from punching bread dough into submission every day of her life, and you knew better than to get her all riled up.

Through years of watching my parents and their friends play cards, I got to know the habits of the players and it was easy to predict who had trumps. When Mom didn't have any worthwhile cards, she'd lay them down and make that funny little clicking noise with her tongue, but if she had a few good ones, she'd hold them tightly against her chest. If my father had bad cards, he'd always say the exact same thing. "Well, b'ys, it's all in your hands now."

His reaction to a good hand was a dead giveaway, too, for he'd whistle softly and slam his fist on the table. "Okay, b'ys ... stop the talking now and let's get on with the game."

Indeed, all the little habits of each and every one of the players made watching the game from a distance much more interesting, for often the onlooker sees more than the actual players.

I'm sure you've noticed, as well, that the habits of others are often picked up by family members. Whenever my father was planning to go somewhere, he'd always get ready hours before he was supposed to go. He'd fold his hands behind his back and pace up and down the kitchen floor, pausing only now and then to glance at the clock. I've noticed that my brother Harve does exactly the same thing and, believe it or not, so does my son, Scott.

'Course my father had a few habits, too, as I recall. When we were growing up, he always used to look in on us before he went to bed at night and often in the winter, he'd come in to make sure the bedclothes were tucked in around our feet. As we got older, if we were awake, he'd pop his head inside the door and chat awhile about the weather or ask about school. My husband remembers only too well the first time we went to Lord's Cove after we were married. Daddy just couldn't remember Murray's name and called him "Buddy" for a whole week, but it seems he forgot that I had a husband as well. The very first night we got home, it was late and having had a long drive from St. John's, we went to bed shortly after we arrived. We had barely gotten into bed when the door opened and my father walked in and pulled up the window blind. "It's a pity to shut out that beautiful moon, Lucy... it's as bright as day outside," he said. "I think we'll have a good day fishing d'morrow by the looks of the moon..."

Murray bolted up in a sitting position and at that moment my father turned around and in the moonlight, I saw the stunned look on his face. "Ohh, the dear God... I forgot you had buddy here with you... I'm sorry about that, me son..." he muttered, and with his head down, he left abruptly.

Murray pulled the blanket up around his chin. "Is your father going to be checking up on us every night?"

"Oh, don't be silly ... he's not checking on us. It's just a habit he's had for years. He just forgot you were here, that's all."

I believe the little incident unnerved both Murray and my father, because neither ever mentioned it again. I did notice, however, that whenever one of them was going to bed, that they made a point of announcing it within earshot of each other.

I think sometimes we fall into the habit of doing little things that bring us comfort, you know, the same way a child carries a security blanket or sucks a thumb. I don't believe for a moment that they harm anybody and if it makes you feel good or brings you comfort, then what odds, right? There are times when I actually rely on some of my little odd routines to keep me sane, especially if I'm having a rough day. Take yesterday, for instance. The whole day was a series of bloopers as far as I'm concerned. For starters, I overslept and had to scravel out of bed to get to work, which meant that I had to leave without my wake-up cup of coffee. Then I made the mistake of taking a shortcut and ended up waiting 10 minutes for a train to pass and when I got to the jewellery store, I accidentally tripped the alarm and couldn't remember how to turn the darned thing off. At least the senior citizens who walk daily in the mall had a bit of excitement because they thought the store was being robbed and someone called the police before I got a chance to let security know it was a false alarm. And from that moment on, my whole day went so wacky that I can't even bear to tell you the rest.

When I got home that evening, I got into my old sweatsuit, got my cup of tea and sank into my rocking chair where I rocked until I nearly went cross-eyed. Oh, my, it felt some good! Now let me tell you, that's a habit I don't ever intend to break.

# Finding the Right Car

Lately I've been thinking about buying myself a car, but I'm not sure that's the right thing to do right now. I honestly don't know if I really want one, because I always have trouble finding the right car. We already have three vehicles at our house and since the four of us work and my hours are the most flexible, I'm the one who usually gets chauffeured everywhere.

I don't mind, really, because it's no secret that driving is not one of my passions. After all, we used to be a one-car family and my husband usually did the driving. We finally got a second car when our sons became teenagers and even then I hardly drove, for the boys took me everywhere just so they could have the car. Over the years, I've grown accustomed to not driving and I must admit that my absence behind the wheel has caused me a few problems. And when I said I'm having trouble finding the right car, I mean it...literally, because ME and CARS ...well, we just don't mix.

Allow me to explain. At the moment neither of the men in my house see fit to let me drive any of the cars. Now I'm not naïve enough to think that they're doing it out of the goodness of their hearts either. I could be wrong, but I suspect they just don't trust my driving skills because no matter how inconvenient it is for them, they'll get dressed and take me wherever I need to go. I consider myself a good, safe driver. I'm not one to brag, but I have never received a parking violation, let along a speeding ticket and I have it on good authority that the officers of the law appreciate my cautious driving. A nice policeman told me so in as many words a few years ago when he pulled me over. When I complained about all the reckless drivers who passed me and honked their horns, he appeared speechless for a moment and then, in a respectful gesture, he took off his hat. "You don't drive much, do you ma'am?" he said, wiping his brow.

"Heavens, no...it's been years since I ventured out on the highway," I said. "Can't you DO something about all those people who are driving like maniacs?"

"Ma'am, you were driving 50 km BELOW the speed limit," he said patiently. "If you're going to drive like this on the highway, then you'd better install a ramp on the back of your car."

However, on the rare occasion when I do get the car keys, I take the whole day to do errands, have lunch with a friend or shop. By the end of my day, I often forget which car I borrowed. Do you know how stunned I feel walking up and down the parking lot laden down with shopping bags, trying to recall if I drove the Buick, the Spirit or the Tempo? And when I finally recollect, I still wander around aimlessly looking for the car, because there could be 10 or 12 the same make, year and colour as the one I drove. Trust me when I say there's no way I can remember the licence numbers on THREE cars and often I forget to put my licence in my purse anyway. Naturally, I have to start looking for clues then, something familiar inside the car, because I dare not try to unlock a car door unless I'm sure it's the right one.

Even when I get picked up after work at night, I get into trouble. The lighting is not the greatest at our mall, so when I don't know who will be driving which car when I go outside, I have to try and figure out which of the half-dozen cars pulled up out front is mine. Don't you just hate it when you jump into a car on a rainy night, shake off your umbrella and then realize you're NOT in the right car? The only thing worse than trying to explain your mistake to a total stranger, is the humiliation of realizing that your husband is sitting in the car behind you flashing the headlights on and off.

I've also had the misfortune of locking my keys inside the car once or twice. The first time I had to call my husband to bring a second key and it galled me to have to do that, for I hate getting reminded of how forgetful I am. That's why, on the second occasion, I asked a young man in the parking lot to help and he tried to open the door with a coat hanger. We had no luck, but rather than call Murray, I waited until my son got home from work and he came to my aide. I swore him to secrecy and in turn, he solicited my services for laundry duty for two weeks.

My girlfriend also, hates to let her husband know about her car problems because he tends to be unsympathetic. She locked herself out of her car one winter night and, not wanting to give her better half the satisfaction of gloating, she called CAA ...only to remember AFTER they made up a new key at the cost of $75 that she had a spare one tucked away in her wallet.

Oh, sure, other people can make mistakes about cars as well as I can. Brenda, my hairdresser, can vouch for that. One day while my brother was visiting me, I borrowed his car to go get a much-needed hair cut. I parked beside a truck near the back entrance of the salon so I'd remember exactly where to find the car. Later when I went outside, I was a bit perturbed because I had apparently left the door unlocked, but everything seemed in order. However, when I put the key into the ignition, it wouldn't start. The steering wheel appeared to be stuck and I knew that there was a button underneath to unlock it, but no matter how many times I tried, nothing happened. Finally, I went back into the salon and Brenda came out to see if she could help. She tried to unlock the wheel, but to no avail. "This always works, Lucy, so I'm not sure what's wrong. My car is exactly the same as yours and all I have to do is press this button..."

She stopped mid-sentence. "My god, Lucy! This IS my car."

After we finished laughing, we realized that her car was

identical to my brother's ...even to the colour outside and inside. Apparently one of the other girls had borrowed Brenda's car to go to the drugstore and had parked it on the other side of the truck and I mistook it for mine. And that, of course, explained why the car was open and I was able to get inside.

I guess I've never had the urge to possess my own car. Of course, in my younger days I did, but after the first time when I blew my big chance to learn to drive, I somehow lost my desire. I think that's how my bad luck started. I was at college in St. John's when a friend bought his first new car... a Volkswagen Beetle. He was very proud of that little green Beetle and I wanted desperately to drive it. The very first time he took me for a drive on a Sunday afternoon, I begged him to let me try it out and after a lot of cajoling, he finally agreed. He found a dirt road near a pond and reluctantly he moved over to the passenger side and I got into the driver's seat. "I hope you at least know how to use the brakes and the gas pedal," he mumbled. "Are you sure you know how to drive a standard?"

'Course I had never driven a car before and had no idea what a standard or an automatic was. "Sure I know. My brother out home in the Cove got a car like yours...and it's bigger, too," I fibbed.

Things happened quickly and all I can remember is yanking the gear shift and jamming the gas pedal to the floor. My head jerked back as the little green Beetle leapt into motion and we sped downhill... backwards. I distinctly heard loud curses and colourful expletives in my ear as powerful hands grasped the steering wheel, kicked my foot aside and slammed on the brakes, just before the rear wheels of the car sank into the muddy water. He never did invite me out for a Sunday drive again.

In retrospect, perhaps that unfortunate experience accounted for the fact that I never did get a driver's licence until after my second son was born. Sometimes I think I never should have bothered at all, what with all the things that happen when I get behind the wheel. Either I get a flat tire, the car won't start or I run out of gas. And on the rare occasion when I have to go to a gas station, I'm a menace. I usually pull up on the wrong side of the pump, annoy the attendant by popping the trunk instead of the lid on the tank or, worse still, have him run after my car because I forgot to pay. I actually waited 10 minutes once to get gas and held up four cars behind me before I realized it was self-serve.

So, as you see, I think I'd be wiser to forget buying another car and stick to my regular chauffeur system after all. Even those new remote control gadgets that unlock the doors and turn on the ignition before you go outside couldn't help me. I just have this gut feeling that even if I misplaced my keys or couldn't recall at which end of the mall I parked, I'd still have trouble finding the right car. Lord help me, but with my bad luck and my memory, I'd probably forget that I even own a remote control.

# To See or Not to See

There was a time when I used to think that it was only old people who wore glasses, for I seldom saw anyone my age wearing them when I was a teenager. It was only when I started high school that I noticed I was having a problem with my eyes. Back before we had copy machines, everything had to be written on the blackboard in chalk. I didn't want the teacher to know I couldn't see well because I knew I'd get moved to the front of the class. And heaven knows, that's the last place anybody wanted to be, for at the beginning of the school year, there was usually a big scramble to get the best seats at the back of the classroom. Besides, if you had to sit up front, you missed out on all the fun and mischief that went on behind you when the teacher wasn't looking.

One day, however, when we were given a math test, the teacher saw me squinting my eyes when I was trying to make out the numbers she put on the board, and she asked if I was having a problem. Naturally, I denied it, but when I failed the math test, she sent a note home to my mother. She told her that I was having trouble reading what was on the blackboard or, more to the point, misreading it and suggested that I get my eyes tested when the eye doctor from St. John's came to the clinic in Lamaline. Mom said that she wasn't having anybody thinking I was stunned, so she lugged me off to see him despite my protests. I was appalled at the thought of having to wear glasses; and, more importantly, I was afraid I'd get teased and laughed at, so that was another test I was hoping not to fail – and I did.

Without even asking if I had a preference as to what style of frames I'd like, he pulled out a pair of glasses from a satchel and put them on me. "There you are, young lady," he said. "These will fit you just fine."

I thought they were the ugliest things I'd ever seen in my life. They were black with little rhinestones on the upper corner of the frames that curved to a peak in the shape of a cat's eye. Every time I tried to open my gob to tell Mom I hated the glasses, she shushed me into silence. There wasn't much to choose from anyway, for other than the ugly ones he shoved on my ears, there were only four pairs, two for men and two for women.

Fortunately, school was out for the summer by the time the glasses arrived in the mail. I bawled like a baby when I saw myself in the looking glass. I swore I'd never wear them, but Mom reminded me that she paid $25 for them, so I didn't have much choice.

I had a new teacher that September, and hoping Mr. Kitby wouldn't notice, I'd slip the glasses on and off just long enough to read the writing on the blackboard. However, when he caught me hiding my face in my hands so nobody could see my glasses, he insisted that I leave them on so I could see properly. A few of the boys snickered around me, and I squirmed in my seat as I felt my face go scarlet. Then, with his arms folded, he stepped back and looked at me with his head to one side. "Oh, my...they are very nice on you, Lucy," he smiled. "I think they make you very distinguished looking."

I think that was the kindest thing anybody ever said to me. Even though I suspect he was just trying to make me feel better because I was so uncomfortable, the fact that he said it in front of everybody boosted my confidence, so I held my head high and left them on. It took me awhile to adjust to wearing spectacles, but when I realized how much they improved my vision, I knew there were only two choices – to see or not to see.

I decided to wear them, but in the classroom only. I

encountered a couple of setbacks at the beginning when a few of the rhinestones fell out on one side of the frames and then, somehow, I snapped the nosepiece. I was none too happy when my father fixed them with a strip of white, sticky tape, and I was too embarrassed to wear them for a long time. I can't tell you how happy I was when the eye doc returned three months later and he was able to repair them properly for me.

Little did I know then that in the years to follow, eyeglasses would be considered fashionable and trendy. I've had at least 30 pairs of prescription glasses since that first pair I had in high school. I went from the small cat's eye glasses to large frames in different colours, some with tinted lenses in pink or blue, and others in different shapes and sizes that changed colour from indoors to outdoors. Whatever happened to be in style at the time, I wore them, whether they suited me or not. Sometimes when I look at old photos, I cringe when I see what I wore, for some of them were so large that they covered my whole face. Then the styles went back to the small lenses again. When I first got a pair of the round, wire-rimmed glasses like the ones John Lennon wore during the Beatles era, I thought I was the cat's meow.

People wore glasses, not just because they needed them, but because they were a status symbol and others thought that glasses gave them an intellectual appearance. I was mentioning this to a Newfoundlander I know here in Niagara, and he told me about him and his buddies when they first came to Toronto years ago. They actually got glasses because they though it would look cool when they went back home for a holiday.

"We were some cocky when we went home wearing our tight jeans, cowboy boots and tinted glasses," Rob said. "A couple of the boys even got all their teeth yanked out because they wanted to get a set of false teeth to go with the new glasses – figured it would make folks think they'd struck the big times in Toronto."

I suppose we all did foolish things or put on airs to try and impress others. I remember trying to imitate women in movies whenever I saw them taking off their glasses and pushing them on top of their hair. I would be so impressed when they'd take a deep breath, sit back and say something profound or poignant; so much so that I was tempted to try it myself, but I was afraid that if I opened my mouth to say something intelligent, it would come out the wrong way. Instead, I'd say it to myself in the mirror. "It really is true, you know, that a squid can swim forward and backwards without turning around."

That was 25 years ago, and I'm still waiting for the right moment to run that one by someone.

I remember an elderly lady in the Cove who wanted glasses badly, not because she couldn't see, but because one of her friends had just gotten a new pair. She kept insisting that her eyesight was terrible, even though the doctor told her she had perfect vision for a woman her age. One day when she was at our house, she was telling Mom that she really needed glasses because she couldn't see her hand in front of her sometimes. "My eyesight is wonderful bad, Lottie, and that's the God's troot," she said as she pointed toward the door of the back porch about 25 feet away. "You see that darning needle out there on the floor beside the step? Well, my eyes are so bad that I can barely see it from here!"

'Course there were always those who refused to wear glasses even though they needed to – like my father, for instance. He should've had glasses 20 years before he actually got them. In church sometimes when everybody stood during mass, he'd have to hold the prayerbook out in front of him to read the print. After awhile, his arms would be extended full length and Mrs. Bessie Lambe, God rest her soul, who sat in the pew in front of us, would clear her throat noisily when the book hit her in the back. Then Mom, of course, would be so annoyed that she'd give him a jab in the ribs.

For years now, I've been wearing bifocals, and as much as I'd like to have contact lenses, I can't tolerate them because my eyes are very sensitive. Last year I even considered having laser treatment, just so I can get rid of my glasses, but my doctor decided against it because I now have glaucoma. So I guess I don't have a choice in this one.

Mind you, I'm not complaining, but there are days when I thank God and Benjamin Franklin all in one breath – God for the gift of sight and Franklin for inventing the bifocal in 1784. Fact is, I do consider my glasses a blessing; but sometimes I also feel that they are a nuisance, especially when I stumble out of bed and stub my toe on something. I get really grumpy when I can't remember where I put them, for then I have to grope around to find them. I have two pairs of glasses, but if I lose one of them, I have to go searching for the second pair because I can't see well enough to find the ones I lost in the first place. It's just a vicious circle some days, for I'm always misplacing them. Without my glasses, I feel like all of my faculties are impaired. My son claims that every time I take them off, I tend to talk louder. "Geez, Mom, you're yelling again. Here, put your glasses on so you can hear," he'll say.

I find it very annoying as well when my spectacles get all steamed up when I go out in the rain, or when they get full of fingerprints. Sometimes I can't find anything in my purse to wipe them off with, so I have to wipe them off with anything I can find at hand. But I'm not the only one who has that problem. President George W. Bush does, too, so I'm in good company. During the presidential debates, I saw a clip of him on television with his glasses in hand in an obvious attempt to find something to clean them with. Finding nothing in his pocket, he looked around and, seeing one of his female aides talking to someone, he reached out and polished his glasses on the tail of her jacket.

I have to admit that there are times when I deliberately don't wear my glasses, especially when I'm at home. That way I can pretend that I don't see all the things that need doing around the house, and I can turn a blind eye to everything and anything if I see fit. Matter of fact, I'm seriously thinking about getting a third pair of spectacles – and judging by the stack of bills the postman just delivered, I think rose-coloured glasses may not be a bad idea. Having the choice to see or not to see is not the question for me anymore. Sometimes it is the answer.

# A Moving Experience

Moving into a different house is always very exciting and challenging. We've relocated so many times because of my husband's job that we pride ourselves on our efficiency, for everything has always gone smoothly. At least that's the way it was until our last move. Perhaps it was just bad luck or poor timing, but in any case, it was a moving experience I'll never forget.

It all started when we decided to sell our house and buy a newer one a few months ago. Nothing went right from day one. We saw a house we really liked in the same area where we lived, so we asked our agent to take an offer to the owners and he did. Well, he tried to, that is. Apparently, the house was being sold because of a marriage break-up between an elderly couple who, we found out, were engaged in a feud that would make your hair stand on end. I don't mean to sound unkind, but the Missus of the house was acting in a rather bizarre manner. Our agent discovered that she put the house up for sale without telling her ex-husband.

Needless to say, that put a dent in our plans, but once the lawyers worked things out between the estranged couple, the house officially went on the market. Because they weren't on speaking terms, they each enlisted their own real estate agent, so every time the ex-husband's sign went up, his feisty wife would kick up a ruckus and chase the salesman off the property with a broom.

I called them the Odd Couple because there was a continuous battle of the wits going on. No matter what price the husband put on the house, she would oppose it, so then he refused to sell.

I was very disappointed, but my husband was relieved.

"I had a bad feeling about this anyway," Murray said. "That house just wasn't meant for us, so let's forget about it. We'll find another one we like better, you'll see."

'Course, his reaction got my dander up and I said if I couldn't have that house, then I didn't want to move at all, so we decided against selling. Besides, we had already booked tickets to fly to Newfoundland in October and I didn't want anything to interfere with that.

Then, right out of the blue, our agent called to say that someone wanted to buy our house and that the other house was back on the market again. I was thrilled, but Murray wanted no part of it. I nagged and pleaded with him nonstop for two days until he finally gave in. Miraculously, the Odd Couple accepted our offer and we, in turn, sold our house. Everything happened so quickly that our heads were spinning. We only had five days to get packed, move house and get ready for our trip to Newfoundland.

We never got the chance to go back to look at the house again because the Missus was up to her tricks again and had the locks changed so her ex-hubby couldn't get in. Then she left Niagara Falls without signing the final documents and didn't tell her lawyer or anybody where she was going.

"What in the name of God did I get us into now, Murray?" I sniveled. "That woman must be right cracked going off and leaving us in a pickle like this!"

As usual, Murray stayed calm while the search began for the fugitive and eventually they tracked her down. When the moving van pulled into our new driveway with all our worldly possessions, we found her sitting on a lawn chair in the driveway as she waited for a taxi. She seemed so sweet and so "normal" when she apologized for the inconvenience that I felt sorry for her.

"There are a few things of my ex-husband's left in the house and he'll come to pick them up next week," she said.

"If he doesn't come, then you can keep whatever you want or throw it out for all I care."

Then, like the Queen Mother, she waved from the taxi as she drove away. The "few things" she had mentioned turned out to be every stick of furniture her estranged spouse owned, plus her personal belongings. Each room was full of furniture, the fridge had food in it and not one thing had been packed. Goodness, even the beds were left unmade and her slippers and housecoat were still in the bathroom along with her toiletries.

Honest to heaven, I almost had a heart attack. The movers were already unloading our stuff in the driveway because they had another pick-up that evening. Then it started to rain, so the only thing we could do was put everything we owned into the garage – all 29 years worth. Even the garage was partly full of their stuff, so the movers had to stack furniture and boxes from floor to ceiling. There wasn't even standing room in there when they finished.

And that was not the worst of it. Upon inspection, we discovered that the Jacuzzi tub was missing from the downstairs bathroom. The only thing left was the ceramic tile frame and a gaping hole in the wall exposing the plumbing. I could barely keep from bawling because that Jacuzzi room was a big selling point for us, but Missus had someone remove it as we later found out. Apparently she thought that her 75-year-old husband might be entertaining an entourage of young women in there when she wasn't home.

I suspect that's the reason she also ripped out the doorknob, the ceiling light and removed the shower head, but who knows what she was thinking? I was grateful that she didn't do any damage to the upstairs bathroom, because we needed at least one shower working. I had to go to work the next morning.

At least I remembered to bring a fit-out for work because, other than that, all I had in the car were two sweaters, a pair of jeans and a change of underwear.

Despite everything, I kept a stiff upper lip and plodded on, for my cats were not taking this move too well either. Yoko went berserk when we brought her in the house and she stripped a huge pile of paper off the kitchen wall before we could capture her. Poor Ono was so traumatized from the commotion that Yoko kicked up that she lost control of her bowels. I was afraid that she'd do her business on the furniture that wasn't ours, so armed with a roll of toilet paper and a box of kitty litter, I scravelled around cleaning up after her.

I was so stressed out by then that I ended up in the same condition as Ono, so Murray had to go to the drugstore to get me some Imodium. Next morning, I was still half-asleep when I crawled out of the sleeping bag I'd borrowed. When I stepped into the shower, I was rudely awakened by a cascade of ice cold water.

By now I had built up a grudge as big as a pork barrel against the Missus because she didn't tell us she had unplugged the hot water tank before she left. Nor did she mention that she never left the keys to the back door or the mailbox and that she had taken the remote control for the garage door with her. Murray wanted to cancel our trip because we had exactly two days before we were to fly home, but I dug my heels in. I just wanted to leave my troubles behind.

"No way am I cancelling now," I told Murray. "I don't care if I have to beg, steal or borrow clothes and lug it on the plane in a Carnation milk box, but I'm going home to Newfoundland no matter what!"

Our sons assured us that they'd take care of everything and get the furniture set up. Other than the thought of flying three weeks after the tragedy in New York, I tried to relax.

'Course, I didn't have to worry about packing, because everything I wanted to take was in the garage, even the dresser that held all of my undergarments. I darted to the mall as soon as the stores opened and bought a suitcase and some underwear. When I thought about the run of bad luck I'd been

having, I contemplated wearing all six pairs of my new undies –
just in case the airline lost the suitcase or if the plane went
down. It could happen, you know.

Anyway, I decided to put them in my shoulder bag and
nobody was happier than I was when we finally got to the
airport. Now that all the problems with the house were over, I
wasn't about to let anything spoil my trip home to
Newfoundland. And I didn't – not even when the security
scanner picked up a signal from my bag and they emptied the
contents on the counter. I was a little embarrassed when they
pulled out my knickers because the tags were still on them, but
they found what they were looking for. As soon as they
confiscated my nail clipper and my eyelash curler, I continued
walking with my head held high. After all, I was the proud
owner of a brand new house and I was going home to
Newfoundland. And to me, that's as good as it gets.

# Treasures in the Attic

Everybody should have an attic. It was one of the nicest things I remember about our old house when I was growing up in Lord's Cove. The attic was always my favourite place to play and even though my childhood home no longer exists, I still miss it.

I remember how excited my sisters and I would be when the time came to reopen the attic after a long winter. Every year when the warm May sunshine coaxed the steam from the freshly thawed earth, Mom would throw open the windows and doors to let in the fresh breeze. Before our old rooster could muster up a throaty cock-a-doodle-do, Mom would come upstairs and start whipping the feather mattresses and blankets off the beds, sometimes with us in them.

"What are ye all doing in bed on a beautiful morning like this?" she'd holler. "We've got to open up the attic and put all the winter stuff away, so get out of bed everybody!"

That was one chore my sisters and I never complained about, for we couldn't wait to get back in the attic again.

Not many people knew it was there. Our two-storey house had a peaked roof, so the attic ran the whole length of the house, with a small window under the eaves at both ends. There was ample space to play in at the highest point, but it gradually sloped, so you had to coopy down to look out the windows. The opening to the attic was in a large closet that was built in a semicircle around a brick chimney and you had to climb a ladder to get up there.

Our attic had a personality all its own. At one time, our house belonged to a merchant who had a shop in the back of the house and he used the attic for storage. There was nothing of value left there, but to us it was a special place where we could rummage through the nooks and crannies to see what treasures we could find. As I recall, there was a gramophone, a spinning wheel, old albums, slates that my oldest sister and brothers used in school, Christmas decorations, a rocking chair and an old suitcase full of knickknacks.

It was full of cobwebs, dust and spiders, but that just added to the atmosphere. I can still smell the musty scent of clothes that hung on hooks and bolts of old wallpaper that were piled in the corners.

However, it wasn't the things in the attic that intrigued me, but rather the way I felt when I was there. Over the years, it became my refuge – a place where I could have time to myself.

As a child, I loved playing dollhouse and hide-and-go-seek, and I would lie on the floor listening to the rain on the roof just inches above my head. The pungent scent of the felt after the sun dried up the rain always made me feel so contented that often I'd curl up in front of the window and watch the cobwebs glimmer in the sun.

Once when I fell asleep, I awoke to find a big spider walking across my face. I couldn't see my sisters, so I started screeching as I scravelled on hands and knees to get to the ladder. Before I knew what I was doing, I found myself down in the chimney room looking up at the hatch where my sisters were laughing their heads off.

"I'm telling Mom on ye and you're gonna get your ticky-tumps when I tells her!" I snivelled.

Later, when I realized that I had finally mastered the ladder without the help of my sisters, there was no stopping me from going up there alone.

When my sisters got too old to play in the attic, my friends Lorraine and Eileen would hang out with me. There we read comic books, played cards and Snakes and Ladders, and did a little play-acting. My father often let me borrow his battery-operated radio, so we listened to the music and learned the words of every song we heard. Sometimes we dressed up in the old clothes from the boxes and waltzed to the music, pretending that the mop or broom was a bewitching stranger.

Oh, yes, romance flourished in our attic – at least in our imaginations. We used to read romance novels whenever we could get our hands on them. We called them nurse novels, for usually they were stories about nurses and doctors falling in love.

We knew better than to let our mothers know about them, for they thought they were "dirty books." That's why we hid them behind the chimney, just like we did with Mom's old medicine book. I suspect she anticipated that my sisters and I would be snooping because we noticed that a few pages were conspicuously missing.

Years later, when I asked Mom about it, she confessed that she had torn out the anatomy pictures and the ones of a woman giving birth.

"I figured what you didn't know wouldn't hurt you and that's all I have to say about it," she said indignantly.

Still, the nurse novels made up for that. We'd sit with our backs against the chimney and read passages out loud, especially the endings where the doctor finally kisses the nurse. Then we'd swoon and giggle, for that was pretty risqué reading for us back then. It's no wonder that we all wanted to be nurses when we grew up.

The poor boys around home had no clue that up there in our attic, we were setting high expectations for them in the romance department. But it didn't matter, for they had their own suave style that could turn a girl's head.

As a teenager, I saw many changes, but the attic always stayed the same. In a way, that attic represents a coming of age for me, for even though I knew every item in it, I saw them differently as I grew older. The suitcases that once held knickknacks are reminders of sad goodbyes when my brothers and sisters began to leave home one by one. I missed them terribly.

The rocking chair was not just a piece of discarded furniture anymore, but rather a source of comfort. It was there I penned my first poem, wrote stories in my scribbler and cranked the old gramophone as it eked out a song on the only record we owned. The spinning wheel and the old slates from school spoke of days gone by and made me wonder what the future had in store for me. But it wasn't until I discovered my sister's journal on a shelf in the attic that I finally understood the importance of family. Marceline, the eldest child in our family, was 16 when I was born and she had gone away by the time I was six years old. Before I read her daily journal, I knew very little about her. I was the youngest of the family and never had the opportunity of knowing any of my four grandparents, but my sister's observations about them made me feel close to them. She recorded birth dates, the names of people who had lived and died in our community and the hardships that our own parents had to face in raising nine children.

Her last entry before she left home was about me. She made notes on when I took my first steps for her, how she'd rock me to sleep and take care of me as if I was her own child. By the time I'd finished reading it, I felt like I'd known her all my life. Now, whenever I picture her sitting in the attic in the same rocking chair where I sat years ago, it makes me smile. I wonder if she knew that with each word she wrote, she was leaving threads of the past – treasures in the attic for me to discover.

# A Good Argument

I daresay we've all had the experience of having a difference of opinion with someone and perhaps even letting it escalate into an argument. Who hasn't engaged in a little banter or had cross words with parents, siblings, spouses and friends? We wouldn't be human if we didn't. I'm sure we all recognize the telltale signs when an argument is about to start between two people. I call them fighting words, for you can see the glint in the eyes and hear the defiance in the tone of voice.

"Why do you always have to disagree with everything I say?"

"I'm not. You're the one who is always arguing with me!"

"Well, you started it!"

"No I didn't. You did!"

I think that a good argument fine-tunes the mind, for when we air our differences, it teaches us how to solve problems and to respect the opinion of others. However, I do believe that there are certain personality traits that make people take issue with everything. There's always someone who wants to prove that they are right and you're wrong, or who thinks that they're smarter than everyone else is. Whether it is for spite, revenge or pleasure, they just can't resist the temptation to challenge everything. In Newfoundland, the older folks used to call this verbal exchange "argin." They had their own expressions to describe people who liked to nitpick or start an argument. Often if someone started to argue over something he knew nothing about, they'd say he was a wind bag or that he was talking through his hat because he liked the sound of his own voice. "That bag of wind got more chaw than a sheep's head 'cause he's always argin about something so he can hear hisself talk."

For as long as I can remember, my parents always engaged in a little banter whenever they were having a game of cards. My father would say things to Mom just to get her goat and she usually fell into his trap. Whenever there was a Rook game and the men were losing, my dad would casually make a remark to my brother-in-law that Mom had reneged so they could win the game. 'Course Jim loves a good argument so he'd go right along with my father and play the devil's advocate. "Yeah, I think the women were cheating again... so it should be a misdeal!"

Well, those fighting words would get Mom's dander up.

"John, me son, you can arg till you're blue in the face if you wants, but I'm gonna prove you wrong!" she'd sputter.

What a ree-raw that would be when tempers flared and the women started arguing with the men! Mom would never back down, so she'd go through the last round of cards and account for every hand played. Then she'd slap the cards on the table. "Now, there's the cards I had, so put that in your pipe and smoke it, Mr. Know-it-all!"

My father knew when to bow out gracefully. "Well, Lottie, you can pull in yer horns now, me chile," he'd say as he winked at Jim. "Looks like you were right all along and I was wrong."

Actually, I think the purpose of the argument was to have fun, for once the game was over, they'd laugh about it. Oh yes, there are some couples who deliberately pick a fight with each other because they like making up. Others do it to keep the spark in their relationship and once they've said they're sorry, they forgive and forget. And there's always the odd spouse like 74-year-old Evelyn, who won't admit to her husband that she's wrong. I don't know how she does it, but she manages to make that dear man believe that everything is his fault. "I always have the last word," she laughs. "Never give in, my dear...that's the secret."

Sometimes couples can keep an argument going for days. They'll go to bed mad at each other and wake up still holding a grudge. If they want to push each other's button, the one sure way of doing it is to make innuendoes about the in-laws. "You're just like your mother... always wanting to get your own way!"

"Don't you dare drag MY mother into this! At least she doesn't barge in here without knocking like YOUR mother!"

We all know that scenario can lead to a lot of bad feelings. Thank goodness we don't have to challenge someone to a duel by striking the other across the face with a glove like back in the olden days.

Words and body language can convey anger and resentment just as well, for a scorned look, a cold shoulder or the silent treatment can be very effective weapons in perpetuating an argument.

Sometimes when folks argue, frustration and resentment can cause a rift in their friendship. And we all know that it's not easy for adults to get down off their high horses gracefully. Nobody wants to admit to being wrong. Now children, on the other hand, can forgive and forget easily. It's only when adults and parents get involved that things get more complicated. You remember argin with your friends when you were youngsters, don't you? You went off in a huff with your nose in the air and did a bit of name-calling. "I'm not playing with you no more, you brassy face...and just for that, I'm telling yer mudder that you stole coppers out of her pocket to buy bubblegum, so there!"

But the anger only lasted as long as it took to scarf down your dinner because you had made plans earlier to play a game of Kat and Kitten with that same friend you walked away from earlier. Oh, yes, adults could learn from those uninhibited little beings with the big hearts and the open minds.

I have to admit that sometimes I feel like blowing off steam. After all, I'm a female and I can always come up with something to argue about. First when we were married, Murray and I disagreed about who got to sleep on the right side of the bed. I suspect that he let me win that one because we were newlyweds. The next problem arose when I discovered that he was obsessed with sports...hockey, in particular. He was always glued to the television and it drove me crazy. I could stand in front of the TV wearing nothing but plastic wrap and he wouldn't even notice. "Hey...I'm watching hockey," he'd say. "Could you move just a little so I can see the screen...uhh, please...dear?"

To give him credit, he often watches a movie with me, but he falls asleep and I have to wrestle the remote control from him. That really annoyed me, but I kept my gob shut about it because he really was making an effort to stay awake. This one time, though, I rented a movie and he promised to watch it all the way through. Ten minutes into the movie he was snoring, so I woke him up. Naturally, he denied he was sleeping, so I gave him a second chance and again he fell asleep. I resisted the impulse to pull the hairs out of his moustache; instead I decided to prove a point. Quietly I uncurled his trigger finger from the remote and set his watch ahead one hour. Then I fast-forwarded the movie to the end and jabbed him in the ribs. "Murray, wake up!" I yelled in his ear.

He nearly fell off the couch. "What... what?? I wasn't sleeping," he said, trying to look alert.

"You promised you wouldn't sleep through the movie!" I accused.

"And I didn't...I was awake all along."

"You've been sleeping for over an hour...see, the movie is over already!"

Murray sat up quickly with a dazed look on his face, peered at the TV and then at his watch. Before he got chance to figure things out, I convinced him that he had slept through the whole thing...and he apologized. With my head in the air, I marched past him with that little black remote clutched in my fist. It was at that point that I realized why some people just can't resist having a good argument: it feels so good when you win, doesn't it?

# Live and Laugh

Someone once asked me what my most cherished memory about growing up in a large family back in Newfoundland. I didn't need to think about that one, for I already knew the answer. "We laughed a lot all through the years," I said. "No matter how bad things were, we never lost our sense of humour."

Even now as I think back, I can still picture my mother standing in the porch door calling out to my sisters and me. "Will you young rascals stop that tittering and laughing long enough to get the clothes off the line!" she'd say. "You're slower than cold molasses out there, so hurry up before the rain starts."

Goodness, how many times did she say that when she caught us laughing it up instead of doing our chores. Mom always tried to sound stern with us, but I suspect it was because she didn't want us to think she approved of our mischievous behaviour. I don't blame her for being cautious, not with nine of us and our friends traipsing through the house. Eventually, though, we'd catch her off guard and her stern countenance would soften despite her efforts to keep from laughing out loud. We knew by her shaking shoulders and the way she turned away to hide her silent smile that she saw the humour in our childish pranks.

Humour is a powerful tool, isn't it? It can lift your spirits, soften harsh words or hurt feelings or even be a buffer for pain. Every time you hear someone giggle or chuckle, or see them flash a cheerful smile, it tells you something about their personality. You can tell that they are friendly just by looking at their facial expressions. There's nothing more welcoming than a genuine smile – one that radiates from within and makes the eyes light up and sparkle.

A mere smile can tear down the barriers of race, colour or creed. It is universal and can be understood in any language. We've all seen it. You're sitting in a doctor's office or waiting for an elevator and someone makes eye contact with you. Without even thinking, you smile and before you know it, they smile back at you. Children do it all the time, for they are masters at spontaneous laughter. It is said that the average preschooler laughs or smiles at least 400 times a day, but by the time they reach 35, it happens only 15 times a day. If you watch children at play, you'll hear the unabashed, unbridled sound of laughter that is so sweet to the ears you find yourself chuckling along with them. If you've ever been in a nursery and seen new parents holding their first-born, you'll see the power of a little smile. The baby is only a few hours old and the parents are cooing and trying their darndest to make their little bundle of joy smile. The baby's face is a contortion of expressions and when the newborn grimaces from painful gas, one or the other parent will think it's a smile. "Look, he smiled at me! See...he did it again... honest to God he did!"

The sight of a baby's first smile is a milestone for parents, for in their eyes, it is a reflection of happiness that validates everything good they wish for their child. It creates an invisible bond that will always keep them connected. I know, because I experienced the same thing when my sons were infants. I remember hearing my first-born laugh out loud when I tickled his feet. I was more proud of that moment than I was when I saw the look of satisfaction on his face when he made his very first deposit in his potty.

Laughter is a wonderful outlet and it is released in many different forms – in a slow grin, a shy smile, a chuckle, a giggle or a rip-roaring belly laugh. I know my brother Raphael giggles a lot. He can never finish telling a joke or a funny story because he loses his breath from laughing and it takes ages for him to get to the punch line. But you can't help but laugh at his reaction. Once when he came home from Vancouver, we begged him to tell us some of his funny tales, so after supper he sat in the rocking chair and the rest of us piled onto the daybed in the kitchen. Mom was trying to sweep the floor around our feet and we were splitting our sides laughing at Raphael's stories. Finally, we were making so much noise that she lost her patience. "Raphael, will you stop filling their heads with yer foolishness, my son!" she said. "Stop it now, before I clouts you with the broom handle…"

Knowing full well that she could never resist his devilish grin, he made a grab for the broom and tried to pull her toward him. Thinking that she'd resist, he yanked hard and when she suddenly let go, the force knocked over the chair and he went head over heels on the floor. The rocking chair literally fell apart under his weight and he lay on top of the pile giggling so hard that it took three of us to get him up. 'Course Mom was upset, but she wouldn't dare give in and laugh in front of us. Later that night when she and my father were in the parlour, I heard her relating what happened. "Raphael can make the cats laugh sometimes," she chuckled. "No matter how hard I tries, I just can't stay mad at him."

Humour finds its way into every aspect of life, at weddings, birthdays, anniversaries, even at funerals. One of the nicest things anyone can say about a dearly departed is that they had a wonderful sense of humour. The ability to make someone laugh is an admirable quality. I tend to gravitate toward people who see things on the lighter side and I believe that being able to laugh at ourselves and at life in general builds character. Goodness, comedians are paid big bucks to amuse people…and we pay to see them.

As for myself, I enjoy watching reruns of Lucille Ball, Archie Bunker and Mr. Bean. Each night, I stay awake to watch my favourite shows, "Are You Being Served?" and "Keeping Up

Appearances." It doesn't matter that I've seen episodes more than a dozen times over because I still get a charge out of them.

You can find humour all around you if you listen and observe people in everyday life. It doesn't mean that you are laughing at them in an unkind way, but often something unexpected will tickle your funny bone. For instance, every time I get on an airplane, I always think about a dear lady from home when she flew for the first time. 'Course that was over 30 years ago when she was flying from St. John's to Toronto to visit her son. She was in her 80s then and was extremely nervous when she saw the size of the plane at the airport. She was afraid that it was too heavy, that it would just fall out of the sky, so it took a lot of persuasion to assure her it was safe. All went well until they were airborne, when the seat belt warning went off and a rather large man got up to go to the bathroom. Let me say here that the missus had a habit of "cussin'," as she called it. Her reaction was immediate as she blessed herself and screamed at the top of her lungs. "Oh, gentle Jezzus,…sit down, me son…sit down! You're gonna turn the plane bottom up!"

Oh, yes, whenever I visualize that scene, I can feel the laughter bubbling up inside me and I have to let it out. I think everybody needs to release tension sometimes and what better way to do it than to have a good belly laugh? While it may not be a cure for all that ails you, it can sure chase away the blues.

I highly recommend that everybody use their facial muscles to laugh at least once a day. If that's not possible, then smile at somebody and brighten their day. Remember, a smile softens, it brightens and it uplifts the mind and spirit. Laughter is infectious and it would do us all a world of good it we learned to laugh hard, laugh long and above all, to laugh often.

# A Different Perspective

I think we've all had to step back at certain times and ask ourselves that age-old question about life. Is the glass half-full or is it half-empty? The answer, of course, depends on the individual, for it's only natural that people see things differently. In our younger days when my sisters and I had a difference of opinion, we'd argue 'til the cows came home and my father always told us to stop and listen to what each other had to say. "There's two sides to every coin," he'd explain, "and all of ye got a right to your own opinion because one is just as important as d'other."

I can't honestly say that we always took his advice or that we stopped our bickering, but I think it did make us step back and see things through another's eyes. Sometimes that realization can be a valuable learning experience. At least that's how I felt recently when I watched a television program about people facing their fears.

I'm a cat lover, so when I saw felines being portrayed as sinister and threatening, it got my back up. One of the guests, a hefty truck driver, said he was afraid of cats and looked visibly shaken at the images of a cat stalking its prey. My initial reaction was one of ridicule. "For heaven sakes. A big lug like you afraid of a cuddly little cat!" I scoffed. "Grow up, buddy!" I yelled at the TV.

I didn't realize his fear was real until I saw the terror in his eyes as he watched footage of a cat pouncing on a bird. I felt ashamed for not seeing his point of view, for he had a bad, early childhood experience when a cat attacked him. Lord knows I knew what that felt like, for I had a similar reaction many years ago after I saw the movie "The Fly." The whole concept of a man going into a time machine was mind-boggling enough to me, let alone what happened when a fly got caught in the machine with the man. It didn't bother me when he returned with the head of a fly, but when the process was reversed and the fly came back with the human head, I almost fainted. The close-up of the fly on the wall showing the face and eyes of the man terrified me. For months afterwards I'd freak every time I saw the big, blue fish flies that hovered like vultures in the landwash when the men gutted their fish. I had nightmares about waking up in the darkness and hearing the anguished voice of the man in a fly's body crying out to me. "Help me...help me!"

I've always thought that children have a wonderful way of seeing things for what they are. Years ago my six-year-old niece stayed with my sister Leona and me in an apartment we shared with two other girls in St. John's. No matter what we cooked, Darlene wouldn't eat it and we literally pooled every copper we had to buy things we thought she'd like. After three days, we were down to eating cinnamon toast and drinking water. When one of the girls gave her some, Darlene loved it. We were so happy that she was finally eating that we kept feeding her toast whenever she asked for it. However, when she went home, she told her parents that the only thing we gave her to eat at our house was toast and water. I expect from her point of view, that's how she saw it.

I know my youngest son took a different perspective on a similar situation when he was only six years old. Someone once teased him about his flat nose and after that he was very sensitive about it. One morning I heard Tim tell his brother that he was growing a new nose and when Scott told him it was not possible, he got very upset. "I am so getting a new nose...you'll see!" Tim shouted.

When I went into the bathroom, he was looking at himself in

the mirror. The skin on the top of his nose was peeling from the sunburn he'd gotten several days earlier "See, Mom," he said as he pointed to the pink skin. "My new nose is growing up through the old one and it's a lot smaller, too!"

Sometimes two people can witness the same situation but their descriptions of it differ so much that you wonder if they'd really experienced the same thing. That's what happened when my sister Leona and I started talking about the Archbishop's visit to Lord's Cove back years ago when I was six and she was eight. Her recollection of that day was quite different from my own.

Leona recalled that the teachers had them practise how to courtesy properly and, as was customary, to kiss the Archbishop's holy ring. It rained on the morning of the big day but by afternoon it stopped and a thick fog rolled in. Every child in the Cove lined up along the roadside on Pump Cove Hill and waited several hours to greet Archbishop Skinner and receive his blessing. Leona remembered breaking out in hives because she was nervous that she might forget how to courtesy. Just as His Grace stepped out of the car, the sun broke through the fog and when Leona saw his outline against the sky with the sun shining around him, she thought she was seeing a miracle like the ones she'd heard about in the Bible. She was awestruck when he walked down the hill bedecked in his high hat and long vestments. "I thought he was really God and I was too frightened to look at him because I was afraid I'd go blind," she said. "After all that, I didn't even get to kiss his ring and I never knew if he blessed me or not."

As for me, I think I was too young to realize that I was in such godly company. I was standing behind Leona and didn't even notice that the Archbishop had arrived, for I was too busy hopping from one foot to the other because I was in dire need of a toilet. The teacher ignored my whimpering and made me stay in line, so when I looked up and saw His Grace standing beside me wearing a long dress and a funny hat, I started laughing because I thought he was dressed up to go jannying. "Oh, look...a mummer!" I said to Leona and giggled.

The teacher was giving me the evil eye so I knew I was in trouble, but I couldn't stop laughing. Then when the Archbishop extended his hand for me to kiss his ring, I got so confused that I did what I usually did whenever I got nervous; I yanked the tail of my dress up over my face! As soon as Archbishop Skinner walked past me, I bolted out of line and ran home – and not a moment too soon for the toilet, I might add. 'Course Leona went and blabbed on me to Mom and then she got all upset. "Glory be to God. The two of ye must've made a holy show of yourselves," she said. "The Archbishop must think I reared a couple of heathens!"

So much for my spiritual encounter.

Let's face it, if each of us took time to put ourselves in another's shoes and see things through their eyes, we might view the world in a different light and perhaps even accept what we don't understand. The other day when a friend of mine went to the hospital to visit a client on the psychiatric ward, she said she came away with something to think about. She had to ring the buzzer to get an attendant to unlock the door of the ward. When nobody came, she started knocking. As she waited, a patient shuffled up to the door and asked what she wanted. "I want to get inside," Joan said.

The man looked at her with a puzzled expression. "You want to get IN here?" he said incredulously. "Lady...I'm always trying to get OUT of here and if I was you, I'd turn around and run!"

Life's full of wonder when you have a different perspective on things, isn't it?

# Solid as a Rock

What is it that makes every native Newfoundlander who leaves the island long to come back home again? It is an age-old question asked of our people all the time. Although it is difficult to explain to outsiders, to those who have had to leave home to find work, the answer is obvious. We belong to Newfoundland... it's in our blood.

This may sound a little vague, but to Newfoundlanders, there is a big difference between being from a place and simply living somewhere. No matter how long we live off the island, we never call ourselves former Newfoundlanders. We always belong to Newfoundland... we are part of it just as surely as the sea surrounds our island, or the mighty Atlantic combers thunder upon our shores. No matter where in the world we go or how long we stay there, we seldom feel settled. There is always a longing in our hearts, a yearning in our souls that can never be appeased until we set foot on Newfoundland soil again. We'll use any excuse to go back; someone's birthday, an annual garden party, visiting friends, moose hunting, fishing or simply to get a whiff of the salty air. The sea forever beckons us home again. Each and every one of us has an innate sense of belonging and a deep awareness of our roots that is as strong and steadfast as the island itself.

The only way a non-Newfoundlander can understand how we feel about our island is to come for a visit and discover what and who we are. The reasons tourists want to return are as diverse as the many different dialects and cultures on our island. Nonetheless, two things will be implanted firmly in their minds: the lively people and the spectacular scenery. It is an experience a tourist will never forget because ours is one of the most colourful provinces in Canada.

The island of Newfoundland is often referred to as "the Rock," but don't let that fool you. The vision you conjure up may not resemble what you discover at all. Rocks... yes, we have lots of them in all sizes, shapes and colours. Some are the oldest in the world, left over from several ice ages. From an aerial view, this magnificent rock standing in the middle of the Atlantic may appear foreboding, primitive even. But there is a rough beauty in the towering cliffs and in the jagged 6,000-mile shoreline that wraps around almost every small settlement.

Amid the steep inclines and cliffs, you'll find brightly painted houses in small communities. There laundry flaps in the wind and children run and play freely in wide open spaces. In the larger towns and cities, there is a delightful mingling of the modern and the old. New houses are interspersed with beautifully preserved old houses and churches that have been around for decades. Once a tourist had climbed the wind-worn slopes of Signal Hill in St. John's where the historic Seven Year War ended and where Marconi received the first wireless telegraph, they'll get a sense of the history of our island. I know it made quite an impression on Duncan MacLeod, from Alberta. He dropped me a line to tell me about his visit to Newfoundland. I could find no better words than his. "Twice during my stay, I climbed Signal Hill, and twice I was rewarded with a 360 degree panorama which at once sent shivers down my spine. It made me want to cry. Standing there, I was suddenly aware that Eden, might in fact, have been a rock garden."

There is so much more beauty to be experienced; bubbling brooks, lily ponds, rolling hills, mountains, flatlands, and barrens are all resplendent with colourful wild flowers, berries and summer blossoms. The landscape is as varied as the climate, which allows you to experience all the seasons in one day. Ask any Newfoundlander. They'll tell you what to expect. "If you don't like the weather, wait 15 minutes... it'll change."

Weather conditions don't stop visitors from enjoying the many beauties of nature. To some the fog may seem dismal and cold. To those I ask, have you ever stood on a hillside watching the seagulls swooping and dipping from an azure sky and then see them disappear from your very eyes? No movie prop could ever recreate mystery and intrigue like the beautiful, elusive veil of fog that suddenly rolls over the land. Nothing is more invigorating than watching the power of the stormy sea as it sends spume into the air and waves thundering upon the shore. Then there is the luminous, salt-water moon hanging so low over the sea that a cat can be seen running across an open field. The night is so calm, that you can hear the sound of pebbles stirring with the ebb and flow of the tide.

Newfoundlanders don't even notice the weather, or the terrain, until tourists point it out. Campers and trailers parked along the roads and gravel pits are a common sight all summer long. One rainy day when friends of ours in Niagara Falls were visiting Newfoundland, they came upon two men who appeared to be stranded in a gravel pit. Their camper trailer was steeped in yellow clay and water. Thinking they were having trouble, my friend stopped and asked if they needed a tow truck. The men looked puzzled. "Now why would you want to do that?" one of them asked.

"Well it's obvious you're stuck. Why else would you be standing here in all this mud?"

The men exchanged knowing glances and smiled. "What part of the mainland are you folks from, eh?"

When the Newfoundlanders insisted that my friends stay for a mug-up, they happily accepted. During the conversation, the guys told my friends about an elderly couple from Alabama who stopped by their trailer the day before. They had been trouting in a nearby pond and they noticed that the couple had been sitting on lawn chairs by the side of the highway for over an hour. Thinking they needed help, the guys walked toward them and found them sitting with a picnic basket, binoculars and a video camera. "I wonder if you would be kind enough to tell us what time the moose would be crossing the highway?" the gentleman asked.

Apparently they had misinterpreted the sign that was posted for motorists driving at night. It read "Moose Crossing."

The hospitality in our province is superb, for the people are the heart and soul of Newfoundland. They are friendly, unpretentious people who are always eager to welcome visitors. We may seem a little shy at first but it is only because we want to be accepted the way we are. Newfoundlanders don't hold back at all. We are renowned for our bubbly nature and flamboyant way of entertaining with our storytelling, folk songs and dancing. Once you get to know us, you'll discover our trusting nature, the kind that sets us apart from all others. Where else but in Newfoundland can a tourist knock on somebody's door for directions and be invited to pull up a chair at the supper table?

I remember only too well how my father always invited people into our house whenever they stopped in Lord's Cove. I grew accustomed to the sight of Mom scrambling to tidy the kitchen when she saw my dad talking to somebody she didn't know. "Oh dear Lord, your father is lugging home somebody for supper again, Lucy" she would say. "Put the kettle on for tea and make sure the spare room is clean in case they wants to stay the night."

It didn't matter who they were, or where they came from, visitors always got the royal treatment around home. I remember one summer in particular when a couple from the United States stopped in Lord's Cove to buy a few fresh fish. My brother Fred was a fisherman so someone directed them to his house. From there his wife, Marie, sent them to the wharf where

Fred was sorting the day's catch. Not only did Fred give them free fish, but he took them for a ride in his dory and brought them home for supper. They entertained the couple all evening and when they prepared to drive to a motel in Grand Bank, Fred insisted that they stay the night because he thought it wasn't safe for them to drive in the dense fog. Matter of fact, they even gave the tourists their bed for the night. Before they went to sleep, Marie asked Fred how he knew these people. "Never saw them before in my life," Fred replied.

"Well then, who are they?" Marie asked. "I sent them to the wharf because they came asking for you."

Fred scratched his head. "I'll be darned if I know. I figured you must have known them. That's why I brought them home."

Marie sat up in bed. "You mean to tell me we have two strangers sleeping in our bed and we don't even know their names?"

Unperturbed, Fred pulled the blanket up over his shoulders. "Don't worry about it, Marie," he yawned, "We'll ask them who they are in the morning."

I've always believed the most wonderful asset that Newfoundlanders possess is our incredible sense of humour. We are not afraid to laugh at ourselves and our inadequacies. We are down-to-earth enough to know that you have to take life with its ups and downs. Our language and expressions are laced with a saucy wit that drips with irony on life in general. We have a unique way of expressing ourselves with quips that roll easily off the tongue. Don't make the mistake of thinking our quisms and vernacular reflect anything but what we are. We are simply preserving and cultivating the languages of our forefathers. Newfoundlanders never feel that we have to change, or even justify that fact, because we are proud of our heritage. However, on occasion we have to explain to visitors how we take liberties with the English language.

Once on a flight home to Newfoundland, I overhead a young man across the aisle patiently explaining his accent to another passenger. "You see sometimes we drops a letter on a word, then we picks it up again and sticks it on another word… whether it belongs there or not," he explained with a twinkle in his eye. "For instance, half a dozen apples might come out sounding like 'alf a dozen happles'. It don't matter how we say it… you still get six apples no matter how you slice them, right?"

I have great memories of growing up in a small community. Although most of us were not financially well off, we had something that was far more important. We had the support and guidance of everybody in the community, a network of family, friends and neighbours who depended on each other and who always had a kind word and a smile. Naturally, every family had their problems but they never faced life head on and accepted what they couldn't change. A trait, I suspect Newfoundlanders inherited from our ancestors. I think my father lived by that rule. "You can't keep trouble from knocking on your door," he would say, "but you don't have to invite it in and give it a comfortable chair to sit on."

Here in Newfoundland you'll discover an exceptional class of people descended from ancestors spanning four centuries. We are a hearty race who have struggled against hardship, poverty and the constant hazard of an untamed sea that has afforded a livelihood since John Cabot's arrival in 1497. Through it all, we have survived. As a result we have evolved into a fiercely proud people and like they mighty icebergs that inhabit the Atlantic Ocean, we have stood steadfast and strong. Newfoundland's first premier, Joey Smallwood, said it best when he described Newfoundlanders "…as proud as Lucifer and as cocky and independent as any little group of people in North America!"

These are the people who formed the backbone of Newfoundland over the centuries and no matter how hard times were, or what obstacles came their way, they endured and preserved. Perhaps that was the greatest gift our forefathers left to us. Many times I listened to my father and other fisherman as they came back from the fishing grounds with their boats empty. Day after day they would say the same words... words that gave them the courage to continue. "Tomorrow will be better, you'll see. The fish will come."

And sadly, when the time did come when the fishery closed down, we didn't give up hope that it will be as it once was. The sea will be teeming with cod and our boats will be laden with the day's catch. Like the mythical Phoenix, Newfoundland's spirit will once again rise from the ashes. We have seen good times and bad times. We have survived and will continue to do so. We will live through the spirit of our people, through our ancestors and through our children. Our beloved Newfoundland is and always will be, as solid as a rock.